THE KITCHENER ARMIES

The Kitchener Armies
The Story of a National Achievement

BY

VICTOR WALLACE GERMAINS

AUTHOR OF "THE 'MECHANIZATION' OF WAR"
"THE TRUTH ABOUT KITCHENER," ETC. ETC.

The Naval & Military Press Ltd

Published by

The Naval & Military Press Ltd
Unit 10 Ridgewood Industrial Park,
Uckfield, East Sussex,
TN22 5QE England

Tel: +44 (0) 1825 749494
Fax: +44 (0) 1825 765701

www.naval-military-press.com
www.military-genealogy.com
www.militarymaproom.com

In reprinting in facsimile from the original, any imperfections are inevitably reproduced and the quality may fall short of modern type and cartographic standards.

TO SUSAN

PREFACE

THIS story of the Kitchener Armies is an attempt to give a picture of the means by which those Armies were raised and the part they played in the war.

The amount of material gone through has been immense and, by way of focus, only cursory mention has been made of the Dardanelles. Reference to campaigns fought under special conditions, *i.e.* Syria, Mesopotamia, Salonika, etc., has been omitted.

It was on the West Front that the Kitchener Armies underwent their great trial of strength with the enemy, and performed their most valued services.

I must thank Colonel C. S. Collison, D.S.O., for some valuable notes on the training of the Kitchener Armies, and for his kind help in proof-reading.

I should like also particularly to thank the Librarian and attendants at the British Museum for their exceptional kindness.

If distinguished soldiers such as Robertson, Maurice, etc., are referred to briefly by their surnames, no discourtesy is intended. It is a tribute to their place in public esteem.

A list of some of the works consulted is appended.

THE AUTHOR.

WORKS SPECIALLY REFERRED TO IN THE TEXT

LORD GREY OF FALLODON : *Twenty-five Years.*
Sir GEORGE ARTHUR : *Life of Lord Kitchener.*
JOHN EWING : *History of the 9th (Scottish) Division.*
P. MIDDLETON BRUMWELL : *The Twelfth (Eastern) Division.*
G. H. F. NICHOLS : *The Eighteenth Division.*
Lieut.-Col. STEWART and JOHN BUCHAN : *The Fifteenth Division.*
Capt. V. E. INGLEFIELD : *The 20th (Light) Division.*
Lieut.-Col. H. R. SANDILANDS : *The Twenty-third Division.*
Lieut.-Col. G. S. HUTCHESON : *The Thirty-third Division.*
Lieut.-Col. J. SHAKESPEAR : *The Thirty-fourth Division.*
CYRIL FALLS : *The Thirty-sixth (Ulster) Division.*
Lieut.-Col. F. E. WHITTON : *The 40th Division.*
Brig. F. C. STANLEY : *History of the 89th Brigade.*
History of the Black Watch (Royal Highlanders) in the Great War, 1914-1918.
Col. H. C. WYLIE : *The Border Regiment, 1914-1918 ; The Green Howards in the Great War.*
History of the Cameronians (Scottish Rifles).
Lieut.-Col. H. F. N. JOURDAIN : *The Connaught Rangers.*
C. T. ATKINSON : *The Devonshire Regiment, 1914-1918 ; The Queen's Own Royal West Kent Regiment, 1914-1918.*
Capt. W. MILES : *The Durham Forces in the Field.*
War History of the 18th (S) Battalion Durham Light Infantry.
The 11th (S) Battalion Gordon Highlanders.
History of the King's Own Yorkshire Light Infantry.
History of the King's Shropshire Light Infantry, 1914-1918.
Histories of the Northumberland Fusiliers (Gen. Editor, Alfred Brewis).
Lieut.-Col. SHAKESPEAR : *A Record of the 17th and 32nd Battalions Northumberland Fusiliers (N.E.R. Pioneers).*

WORKS REFERRED TO IN THE TEXT

Lieut.-Col. WHITTON : *History of the Prince of Wales' Leinster Regiment (Royal Canadians)*.
REGINALD BERKELEY : *History of the Rifle Brigade, 1914–1918*.
H. C. O'NEILL : *The Royal Fusiliers*.
History of the Royal Fusiliers (U.P.S.), University and Public Schools Brigade.
F. W. WARD : *The 23rd (Service) Battalion Royal Fusiliers*.
Sir FRANK FOX : *The Royal Inniskilling Fusiliers in the World War*.
Capt. S. M'CANCE : *History of the Royal Munster Fusiliers*.
Major JOHN EWING : *The Royal Scots, 1914–1918*.
JOHN BUCHAN : *History of the Royal Scots Fusiliers*.
War-Diary of the 10th (Service) Battalion Royal Welsh Fusiliers.
R. F. TRUSCOTT : *A Short History of the 16th Battalion, The Sherwood Foresters (Chatsworth Rifles)*.
The 11th (Service) Battalion The Sherwood Foresters.
C. C. R. MURPHY : *History of the Suffolk Regiment, 1914–1927*.
R. A. SPARLING : *History of the 12th (Service) Battalion York and Lancaster Regiment*.
C. S. COLLISON : *The 11th Royal Warwicks in France*.
Capt. H. K. D. EVANS : *The 4th Queen's Own Hussars*.
Capt. F. J. SCOTT : *Records of the 7th Dragoon Guards*.
Sir H. MORTIMER RURAND : *The Thirteenth Hussars in the Great War*.
ROBERT H. MURRAY : *History of the 8th King's Royal Irish Hussars*
B. WILLIAMS : *Raising and Training the New Armies*.

My thanks are due to the various other regimental histories and records consulted.

V. W. G.

CONTENTS

I. The Old Army	1
II. The Call to Arms	25
III. The First New Army	38
IV. The Great Mustering	66
V. The Forging of the Giant's Sword—I	99
VI. The Forging of the Giant's Sword—II	132
VII. Loos and the Dardanelles	177
VIII. The Prelude to the Somme	195
IX. The Somme: Opening Phase	223
X. The Somme: Last Phases	270
XI. The Passing of the Kitchener Armies	294
Appendix: The British Empire in the War	303

The Kitchener Armies

I

THE OLD ARMY

WHEN, on August 4th, 1914, the British Empire declared war on Germany, the moral unpreparedness of our people exceeded their lack of physical preparation. We were the inheritors of a military tradition rich in glory, but it was a confused, if glittering, kaleidoscope of war in every quarter of the globe, in every age and against foemen of every race and creed. Broadly speaking, our wars of the eighteenth century had been wars of colonial and maritime expansion. The Navy had played the predominant part; the function of the Army had been to secure overseas bases for the fleet and to seize enemy colonies. If employed in Europe at all it was to serve only as a contingent to some allied army.

The Napoleonic Wars were fought fundamentally on this principle. The Peninsular campaigns were begun under the quite mistaken assumption that there existed powerful Spanish armies with whom our own forces could unite. Wellington was sent to the Low Countries in 1815 to march alongside not only Prussians but Austrians and Russians. It was Napoleon's offensive which precipitated events, and brought on the Battle of Waterloo. The idea of war on land, as a matter of concentrated national effort to strike an overwhelming and decisive blow in the decisive theatre of the war, had scarcely reached the national consciousness.

THE KITCHENER ARMIES

Such troops as were available were split up among a variety of what would now be termed "sideshows," *e.g.* the Walcheren Expedition and Graham's Expedition to Holland. The theory that Britain's real weapons in war were her ships and her money, and that the rôle of her Army was limited to seizing enemy colonies or acting as a small contingent to an allied army, continued to dominate our military preparations down to the very outbreak of hostilities in 1914.

The French Revolution produced conscription; the humiliating terms imposed by Napoleon on Prussia after Jena, and the limitation of her Army, led to the device of short service to evade this; Prussia, under the great organiser Von Roon, although a much smaller and poorer State, was able in 1866 to produce larger armies than Austria, her great and wealthy neighbour. Under leadership of Von Moltke she amazed the world by vanquishing her Austrian rival in seven short weeks, and four years later smote down France at Sedan. This succession of brilliant and dramatic achievements led to the drastic and far-reaching reorganisation of our Army, known as the Cardwellian system.

In 1870, the British Army was an eighteenth-century survival in a nineteenth-century world. Officers obtained their commissions by purchase—a system dating back to the mediæval "commissions of array";—men were enlisted for life; flogging was still a legal punishment; married sergeants slept in an ordinary barrack-room with nothing but a screen round their beds. Regiments—mostly single battalion regiments—were known by numbers going back to the dawn of our military history, and were scattered at haphazard all over the Empire.

The series of great reforms by Lord Cardwell began in 1870 with the passage of a Short Service

THE OLD ARMY

Act to build up an Army Reserve. The year following saw the Abolition of Purchase. The Peninsular War had shown that to maintain a battalion abroad at fighting strength it was necessary to have another battalion at home to furnish drafts. This was taken as the basis of the new organisation, battalions being linked in pairs, one abroad and one at home. The Army was territorialised, each pair of battalions being given a regimental district—usually a county. Militia and Volunteers for the first time were affiliated with the Regular Army. There were sixty-nine regimental districts, usually with two regular battalions, as many Militia battalions, and a varying number of Volunteer battalions—the Volunteers, it may be remarked, having come into being in 1859 as a result of an address delivered to Napoleon III by some of his colonels and an invasion scare due to this.

" Linking " broke up cherished regimental traditions. The Abolition of Purchase bore hardly upon officers who had paid more than the regulation price for their commissions. Cardwell had to face an opposition which was certainly fiercer and more vehement than anything aroused by any reforms subsequently; he did more to revolutionise the spirit of our Army than any other War Minister till the days of Kitchener.

The system introduced had its defects. The battalion at home was always a " squeezed lemon," its best men being drafted off abroad; short service meant a greatly increased demand for recruits; the British Army became dependent upon the " hungry hobbledehoy "; the number of " young soldiers " serving with battalions at home was unduly large. In 1911 a deserter charged in London was found to be only fifteen and remanded to the Children's Court. An excessive number of reservists was needed to

THE KITCHENER ARMIES

bring battalions to a war-footing, thus the Army Reserve was largely absorbed on mobilisation, leaving no surplus to replace losses or casualties in war. Perhaps the most serious defect was that the system left no " striking force " available to deal with a " little war " which did not warrant a general mobilisation. This was partially remedied by forming a special class of reservist who undertook to come up for service whenever called upon. With all its drawbacks the Cardwell system is one which has worked well in practice and has successfully stood the strain of two great wars.

The South African War, the greatest struggle fought by our modern Army before the Great War, acted as a searchlight upon the deficiencies and handicaps of our military organisation. The Cardwell system had territorialised the Army, linked battalions, created an Army Reserve. But it had not provided for the same steady all-the-year round training as in continental armies. Manœuvres were held on too small a scale and under conditions which were too unreal to afford training even in administrative work. In the battalions it was the *régime* of " Adjutant *cum* Sergeant-Major." A time-honoured story tells of the company-commander who, questioned by a general on manœuvres, " Captain W——, what are you here for? " turned to his N.C.O. and stuttered out, " C-c-colour-sergeant, what are we here for? "

The bitter lessons at the hands of the Boers were a valuable stimulant to military efficiency; the outburst of patriotism over Mafeking and Ladysmith popularised the Army; the soldier became " respectable," with results beneficial to recruiting. The effects of the South African War upon our general, social and foreign policy were far-reaching. For the first time it was realised that our small Regular Army was incapable of fighting a war of any magnitude to

THE OLD ARMY

a victorious end without help from newly raised non-regular forces. A Royal Commission under presidency of the Earl of Elgin reported, " No military system will be satisfactory which does not contain powers of expansion outside the limits of the regular forces of the Crown, whatever that limit may be." The Colonial Contingents opened up the vista of a truly Imperial Army, in which the forces of our great self-governing Dominions across the seas should play their part; the C.I.V., Volunteer Companies, and Imperial Yeomanry revealed the untapped stores of manhood which would be at the Empire's disposal in event of a really great emergency; the voice of execration raised against us from one end of Europe to the other illuminated the dangers of a policy of " splendid isolation." Great Britain, immersed in her own vast colonial and industrial expansion, had paid little heed to the changes which were transforming Europe into a huge armed camp. The signature of the Triple Alliance linking together Germany, Austria and Italy into a common policy had been followed by the Dual Alliance between France and Russia in 1892, since when these two great groups of States had watched one another with increasing distrust, and had armed upon an ever-increasing scale. Following the sensational overthrow of France in 1870, all other great Continental States had adopted the principle of the " nation in arms "; they passed the whole of their manhood through the ranks of their peace-time armies for periods varying from two to three years' service, and thus possessed the power to swell relatively small peace-armies by hosts of thoroughly trained reservists. Up to the time of the Kaiser's Kruger telegram of 1897, the sympathies of Great Britain had inclined rather to Germany and the Triple Alliance. France was traditionally The Enemy; in 1879 we had been on

THE KITCHENER ARMIES

the verge of war with Russia over Constantinople; our colonial policy had meant perpetual friction with both France and Russia in Africa and Asia. The Pendjeh and Fashoda incidents had brought us almost to blows. The ill-feeling between England and Germany stirred up by the Kaiser's tactlessness was deepened first by the German Navy Law of 1898, obviously an answer to the sharp language used by Lord Salisbury's Government, and then by the Navy Law of 1900, the menacing preamble to which ran to the effect that Germany must have a fleet so powerful that not even the strongest naval Power could attack her without putting to peril her own naval supremacy. The estrangement felt in British Court circles at the German Emperor's somewhat dictatorial attitude was echoed in the country as a whole when flamboyant utterances proclaimed to Germany, " Our Future lies upon the water," and " What my Grandfather did for the Army that will I do for the Navy." Great Britain, heretofore disposed to look upon Germany as a tacit ally and the Germans as a kindred race, felt herself menaced in that sea-supremacy upon which depended the very bread of her people, and confounded by an outburst of propaganda which presented her as an admixture of a modern Carthage and decadent Rome. Her love of sport was compared with the Roman love of gladiatorial contests; her professional Army was depicted as an assortment of mercenaries who thought only of their pay. The British merchant-classes were denounced as slothful, pleasure-seeking, and consumed with bitter envy of the thrifty industrious German tradesman. Such propaganda, usually emanating from bespectacled professors drunk with pseudo-historical analogies and innocent of any real knowledge of England or the English, did not fail to evoke counter-propaganda which proclaimed Ger-

THE OLD ARMY

many jealous of our wealth, lustful of our colonies, eagerly awaiting a favourable moment to fall upon us and extort an indemnity such as she had acquired from France. She would seize our overseas domains. The bitter anti-British sentiment in Germany, partly due to spite and jealousy, but partly due also to genuine indignation at what many Germans believed to be wanton aggression by a strong Power against a weak one, did not pass unheeded in Great Britain. Lord Salisbury's Government found itself confronted by what was traditionally the danger which British policy sought to avert—a union of *all* European Great Powers against us. The first impulse was to conciliate Germany. Baron von Eckhardstein and Mr Chamberlain worked together to promote the avowed adhesion of Great Britain to the Triple Alliance. The overture was repulsed by Germany. The logic of hard facts then forced this country to come to terms with France.

The Anglo-Japanese Alliance of 1901 and the *entente cordiale* of 1903 were successive stepping-stones along the path which led to Algeciras and Agadir. The collapse of Russia after her defeat by Japan, the menacing attitude of Germany towards France when she thought that country at her mercy, revealed the danger to Europe in general, and to Great Britain in particular, should Germany feel herself to be unchallenged mistress of the Continent. The effort of British diplomacy was now, and whole-heartedly, directed back into the traditional channel—that of upholding and maintaining the Balance of Power. Sir Henry Campbell-Bannerman, most amiable, inoffensive and peace-loving of men, felt himself forced, after Algeciras, to the extraordinarily grave measure of authorising " conversations " between the British and French General Staffs. British diplomacy reached out to Russia to settle outstanding

THE KITCHENER ARMIES

points of difference with that country. The Anglo-Russian Convention of 1907 saw the definite grouping of Triple Entente counterbalancing the Triple Alliance.

Meanwhile, the revelation of our military weaknesses in South Africa, the growing tension with Germany, had given rise to general uneasiness in England. The armed hosts of the Continent were separated only by a few hours' steam from our shores: what would happen, men asked, should our fleet be evaded or sustain a temporary disaster? A Royal Commission, presided over by the Duke of Norfolk, urged that a Home Defence Army should be formed based upon compulsory service. A committee, of which Lord Esher was chairman, made some unessential changes in army organisation. Lord Roberts, after ceasing to be Commander-in-Chief, had inaugurated a campaign for compulsory service; and although it would seem to have been rather the vision of Russia with her millions of men looming up against India, than fears as to the defence of the United Kingdom which was at the back of his campaign, the popular nervousness as to invasion gained him a very large measure of support. The spectacle of this great soldier who had devoted all his life to the service of his country, who had repeatedly faced death in her cause, whose career was as marked by brilliance of achievement and quality of intellect as by personal valour, and who mourned his only son killed on the field of honour, devoting the closing years of his life to warning his countrymen of the approach of danger, is not without its grand and tragic side. Nor was his campaign a vain and useless beating of the wind for the National Service League which he founded. It stimulated interest and thought upon matters of Imperial Defence and produced the atmosphere which later,

THE OLD ARMY

under stress of war and in dire need, helped the transition from voluntary to compulsory service. But to persuade a people saturated by eighteenth-century traditions of war, living in a land which for centuries had felt no foot of an invader, whose proudest boast was its freedom and who had established and proclaimed new ideals of civic rights and liberties, to submit to conscription with all its corollaries in the way of registration, police control and loss of personal freedom, was an enterprise which, in cold blood, no Government could seriously undertake. Nevertheless, the controversy aroused by Lord Roberts casts an instructive light upon the views which dominated our Government and the War Office in the days before the war. Apart from convinced anti-militarists, such as W. H. Massingham, the opposition to the proposed measure came mainly from the " Blue Water School." This followed the historical tradition of the British Army which was that the contribution of Great Britain in a war should be limited to her fleet and financial support rendered to her allies. Defence against invasion was primarily the function of the fleet, and attention was drawn to the offensive power of a naval blockade. The Army could act as a small contingent to a Continental army or could be engaged in colonial expeditions. It was customary to talk in somewhat vague terms as to the " mobility " of the British Army as compared with Continental Powers.

There is ample evidence to show that the views of the " Blue Water School " dominated at the War Office down to the very outbreak of the war. Nor did the National Service League propose to create a compulsorily enlisted regular army to operate overseas in time of war. Their proposals were limited to a conscript Militia for Home Defence. Certain alterations would, it was claimed, produce a

THE KITCHENER ARMIES

" striking force " of 270,000 " short-service regulars " enlisted voluntarily, but there was no conception of an army numbering millions of men to partake in an armed struggle in Europe. Nor was there even a hint that men should be raised by conscription for service overseas. Speaking of the expansion of the Regular Army under his proposed scheme, Lord Roberts says: " True it is that unless they (the conscript militiamen) volunteered they would not be available for service abroad."[1]

The agitation for compulsory service led to the publication, upon the intervention of the Secretary of State for War, Mr, subsequently Lord, Haldane, of *Compulsory Service* by Sir Ian Hamilton, which we may take as representing the " mind " of the reforms introduced some two years earlier into British Army. Passing by a great deal of special pleading on conscription, the doctrines proclaimed are those of the " Blue Water School." Stress is laid upon the " long range " of the British Army as compared with the " short range " of Continental armies. We have the customary hopes as to the mobility conferred by sea-power. . . . " Finally, they do not actually, personally know the General Staffs of foreign armies, or realise how hateful to those methodical minds is the idea of the shifting base and incalculable line of communications of a Power in command of the sea."[2] There is a reference to a Third Line to be based on " latent " conscription. This was to be a paper force similar to the " seemingly dead paper law of 1831 creating the Garde Nationale, which went within an ace of saving France in '70." It was to be compulsion applied at a carefully chosen psychological moment. " During perhaps two or three months of the South African War, conscription

[1] *Fallacies and Facts*, p. 160.
[2] *Compulsory Service*, p. 96.

THE OLD ARMY

would have been accepted, but I put it to you that the nation would never have swallowed the dose of physic during the preliminary or later phases of the campaign." But the formation of great new conscript armies for service overseas was not contemplated under *any* circumstances . . . " the Empire . . . fighting for bare life. Only drafts, and these only for short-range European purposes, could we reasonably demand from it." And on the following page, " If you wish to count your bayonets by the million, you must make up your mind to retrace the steps of Empire."

The reforms introduced by Lord Haldane illustrate the growing menace of the international situation: the need which was felt to furbish up our somewhat archaic military system. There had heretofore existed a scheme for a " striking force " of three army-corps, each of three divisions of two brigades, and two cavalry divisions each of two brigades. The grand total was eighteen infantry brigades and four brigades of cavalry. Under the Haldane scheme the " striking force " became an " Expeditionary Force "; the eighteen infantry brigades were redistributed into six " big " divisions, each of three brigades with the requisite complement of artillery, engineers and auxiliary services; the four cavalry brigades were grouped into a single division. The tactical theories which led to this grouping were a product of the Russo-Japanese War—the army-corps was revived at the very outset of the Great War. The most tangible advantage of the regrouping was that, accompanying it, was a " speeding up " of mobilisation which, due to the special circumstances of our Army, had been hitherto a much more cumbrous proceeding than with the Continental armies. This " speeding up " must be attributed primarily to the " conversations " with the French General Staff and

THE KITCHENER ARMIES

the desire to put our own Army immediately in line with that of our great French neighbour, should war be thrust upon us. The Militia—renamed Special Reserve—was joined on, " lock, stock and barrel " to the Regular Army—a measure originally proposed by Cardwell. It comprised seventy-four battalions, one to each pair of line-battalions, and twenty-eight battalions at slightly higher establishment, known as Extra-Special Reserves, supposed to be available for use on lines of communication, etc. They were never used for this purpose, however. The Volunteers, hitherto an inchoate assemblage of battalions varying very greatly in strength and establishment (some had twelve companies) and the Yeomanry, were now formed into the Territorial Force, fourteen divisions on the same establishments as those of the Regular Army. Before the war, however, the Territorial divisions were greatly under establishment. In 1914 there were 250,000 men instead of a nominal 320,000. The men were enlisted only for Home Defence and an inquiry in time of peace as to those willing to serve abroad in event of war disclosed 20,000 ready to undertake this obligation. The training of the men was limited to an hour's drill at odd times, and an annual training of eight to fifteen days. Lord Haldane's critics complained that the Territorials existed mainly on paper; that in the four years during which they undertook to serve, most of them failed to get as much genuine training as would be acquired by the average Regular recruit in four weeks; that the recruits to the Force were mostly lads and were not even required to submit to a medical examination; that they were armed with long Lee-Enfield rifles and converted 15-pounders which had been discarded by the Regular Army; that Territorial batteries were deficient in horses and harness; and that although the statutes of the Force provided that

THE OLD ARMY

it should be embodied for six months' training *after* war had been declared, no one could be sure that an invading army would be sufficiently obliging as to give us six months' notice before an attack. Such criticisms, although well founded at the time, did not take sufficiently into account the magnificent spirit which the Force subsequently displayed, the speed with which deficiencies in recruits and equipment were made good, the value of the machinery set up under conditions of discouragement and great practical difficulty. The Territorial Force subsequently undertook, cheerfully and effectively, duties which no one could have anticipated from them before the war and played a great and formidable part in the service of their country.

The establishment of the Imperial General Staff with arrangements for collaboration with the General Staffs of our great self-governing Dominions, the compilation of the War Book in which were traced out the various " moves " and measures necessary for the defence of a world-wide Empire at war, and which dealt with such factors as counter-espionage, the protection of our own cables and attack on the enemy's press and postal censorship, the treatment of aliens, protection of vital railways, junctions, etc., against surprise or treacherous attack, and a variety of other details, represented a great advance in the standard and scale of our military preparations. Begun in 1910, the War Book was continually revised and kept up to date. The draft Orders in Council needed to put all this machinery in motion accompanied the King wherever he went, even in profound peace, as well as being kept set up in type in the printer's office so that they could be circulated at a moment's notice.

The years from 1906 to 1914 saw a rolling cloud of hatred, suspicion and distrust settling down upon

THE KITCHENER ARMIES

the peoples of Europe. Successive crises cast the shadow of war on every chancery in Europe; every Government was at pains to burnish up its harness, sharpen spears and swords, and put its military house in order. The struggle waged openly in Press and Parliament and which meant Navy Laws and naval estimates, additions to armies and counter-additions to armies, propaganda for armaments and counter-propaganda for armaments, took the form behind the scenes of a secret but virulent struggle between intelligence officers of all countries, eager to pry out the future enemy's most secret plans and projects. This was a war, waged in the dark, which, as in the case of the Austrian Colonel Redl, at times took a form transcending the wildest fantasies of the cinema. Generally speaking, there has never been an age in which men thought more deeply on war; or the science of the chemist, the engineer, the metallurgist and the physicist were more eagerly pressed into the service of destruction; or the psychological and technical workings of new engines of combat had greater fascination for the thoughtful soldier or zealous naval officer; or in which Governments and peoples were more willing to make actual sacrifices in services and in money for the cause of military efficiency. But very few men, soldiers or civilians, were able correctly to estimate the form which the future struggle was to take. M. Bloch, whose predictions as to " trench warfare " have been so often quoted as evidence as to the " short-sightedness " of soldiers, thought that the mere *cost* of such a conflict would render it *impossible*. He failed to foresee the intervention of Great Britain, considered modern fortifications impregnable to any weapon save hunger, and that Russia could " last " a European struggle better than any other State—because she was self-supporting. The Boer War and Russo-Japanese War

THE OLD ARMY

alike upset M. Bloch's prediction as to the *impossibility* of war, and the actual course of the Great War by no means supported his general theories. The Swiss writer, Mayer, in some respects more successful than Bloch, shared his underestimate of England and the important part she was to play. This underestimate of England was, however, general on the Continent. Any intervention by her tiny professional Army was regarded more as a " gesture " than as a matter of serious military importance. Berchtold writes of Aehrenthal at the time of the " annexation crisis " of 1908, that this very able, well-informed and energetic if unscrupulous Austrian statesman regarded England as a " negligible quantity " on the continent of Europe, and Aehrenthal was in close touch with the military *coteries* around the Kaiser—even if he had his own private grudges against these. It is doubtful if the phrase " contemptible little army " was ever used by the German Emperor, but the phrase pretty accurately reflects the attitude of the Continental soldier. Even France regarded our help mainly as a matter of moral, financial and naval support. The Continental General Staffs saw their problem through a veil of their own traditions and interests. Germany, under influence of Von Schlieffen, had already planned her sweeping march through Belgium and dreamed of a new and greater Sedan: France pinned her hopes not alone upon her own exertions, but upon the hosts of Muscovy thundering down upon the German rear: Austria saw her problem as one of holding off Russian masses, guarding Germany's rear until, flushed with victory and leaving behind them a conquered France, the armies of the Kaiser could join those of the Emperor-king in a grand and concerted inroad into the Czar's dominions. Kitchener, writing from Cairo whilst the Agadir crisis was still rumbling,

THE KITCHENER ARMIES

thought that the impact of such mighty armies as the French and German, at so high a level of leadership, training and equipment, would be analogous to the collision of two express trains. It would mean " telescoping," " piling up," " loss of momentum." Trench warfare would ensue. It was " puerile " to suppose that " in a war between France and Germany the decisive battles would be fought in the first fortnight of the outbreak of hostilities, or that the presence of our six divisions in the field at the crucial point, and at the earliest possible moment, was the essential element of success." He went on to say that the war would be ended and victory achieved by the " last million " of men that Great Britain could throw into the struggle.[1] In other words, it was an eighteenth-century conception to believe that our little professional Army, admirable though it was, could decisively sway the balance between these huge Continental armies. But the keen enthusiastic staff-officers at the War Office, brought into close association with the French General Staff, eager to do the maximum possible to render British help prompt and effective, were, and inevitably, predisposed to see their problem through French spectacles.

" Y's " article in the *Fortnightly Review* on " The German Plan of Campaign against France," left little to be desired in force and clearness based upon the

[1] Kitchener was not the *only* soldier to reach this conclusion. The present writer recalls how when he reported to Sir Thomas Cunninghame, Bart., then a major in the Rifle Brigade and our military attaché in Vienna, that cool-headed, far-seeing soldier expressed very similar views. But in 1914 Kitchener was the only soldier with such convictions who was in a position to make these views effective, and who was prepared to take the responsibility of military preparations upon a titanic scale. Think of the outburst of ridicule which would have been his lot had his " three years' " prophecy been belied by a war ending, as was expected, in three months.

THE OLD ARMY

cool and scientific summing up of evidence.¹ Kitchener, always quick to appreciate genuine grasp in a military writer, thought the views there expressed to be well founded. But the General Staffs alike in France and England were hypnotised by the vision of the Russian masses pouring into Germany. Lord French in *1914* is candid on this point : " . . . in depending upon our Eastern Allies to the extent that we subsequently did, we showed as limited a prevision in the ' political ' as we did in the ' military ' outlook." The passage quoted follows one in which he writes: " At this time we never had the faintest idea of the actual political situation in Russia." The author is here dealing with the opening phases of the war. Yet the optimistic calculations based in those days on Russia would scarcely have been accepted in quite such an open-hearted fashion had there not existed a certain pre-war basis of assumption with regard to that country, in British Army circles, considered to be authoritative. Field-Marshal Sir John French had held in 1914 the responsible position of Chief of the Imperial General Staff. Sir Henry Wilson, who had served under him as Director of Military Operations, and who was in close and intimate relations with his military chiefs and prominent civilians such as Mr Winston Churchill, wrote on September 15th, 1914:

" K's ' shadow armies ' for shadow campaigns, at

¹ *Fortnightly Review*, September 1911. The writer correctly deduced the German plan to sweep through Belgium from a study of German railway developments on the German-Belgian frontier. He thought the best French " counter " to be not an inroad into Belgium but a concentration farther back behind the Franco-Belgian frontier. He correctly deduced further, that Germany would be on the defensive in Alsace-Lorraine. Kitchener entirely agreed with these views, and at once opposed the " forward " concentration of the B.E.F. near Mons.

THE KITCHENER ARMIES

unknown and distant dates prevent a lot of good officers, N.C.O.'s and men from coming out. It is a scandalous thing. Under no circumstances can these mobs being now raised, without officers and N.C.O.'s, without guns, rifles, or uniforms, without rifle-ranges or training grounds, without supply or transport services, without *moral* or tradition, knowledge or experience, under no circumstances could these mobs take the field for 2 years. Then what is the use of them? What we want, and *what we must have* is for our little force out here to be kept to full strength with the very best of everything. Nothing else is any good."

And two days later: " His (Lord Kitchener's) ridiculous and preposterous army of 25 Corps is the laughing-stock of every soldier in Europe. It took the Germans 40 years of incessant work to make an army of 25 Corps with the aid of conscription; it will take us to all eternity to do the same by voluntary effort." And October 4th comes a contemptuous reference to the Territorials: " . . . that splendid Territorial Army of ours, which Haldane and Johnnie Hamilton have for years said could put up a superb fight." [1]

It is easy to be wise after the event. Wilson, airing views which today seem ludicrous, was no worse than many other soldiers who have subsequently, and deservedly, acquired great reputations. M. Poincaré tells the story of a meeting between Foch and Kitchener:

" ' Do send us your new divisions as soon as possible.'

" ' You will have a million men in eighteen months ' is Kitchener's calm statement.

" ' Eighteen months,' murmurs Foch, half to

[1] *Wilson : Diaries*, Vol. I, pp. 178 and 187.

himself, ' I should prefer fewer men arriving a little sooner.' "[1]

In the days when, with limited resources, Lord Haldane and his military advisers were laboriously striving to polish up our rusting military harness, it was very generally assumed that a Continental struggle would see Great Britain in alliance with France and Russia, but that the Russian mobilisation would be slow,[2] and that Germany would feel justified in concentrating almost the whole of her armies in the effort to beat France to her knees before Russia got fairly into action. But the problem was regarded essentially as one of bolstering up France against a sudden overwhelming German onset. Let this onset once be stayed, let the Germans find themselves held up in France whilst the Muscovite millions came pouring into Germany, then, it was believed, the Teutonic invaders would be forced to call back troops to defend their own country and would be crushed ultimately between French and Russians as between hammer and anvil. The shock would be terrific, but it would be too terrific to last long; the decisive battles would be fought in the opening weeks of the war; everything depended upon rushing every available man to the decisive point for the decisive battle in the minimum possible time. Mr Winston Churchill, a leading politician and an influential Minister who was, moreover, in close association with Lord Haldane and the Imperial General Staff, writes:

" The fundamental uncertainty fluctuating from year to year . . . whether the Great War would ever

[1] *Memoirs of Raymond Poincaré.* Trs. by Sir George Arthur, Vol. III, p. 225.
[2] See Sir Henry Wilson's views quoted by Churchill, *The World Crisis*, Vol. I, p. 58.

THE KITCHENER ARMIES

come or not, had always been in strong contrast to the very definite and precise opinions of military men about what would happen if it did. Almost all professional opinion was agreed that the struggle would be short, and that the first weeks would be decisive."

An estimate prepared by the Imperial General Staff in 1911 credited Germany with 110 divisions, of which 20 would be left against Russia, leaving 90 to deal with France and Belgium. In reality Germany mobilised only 90 divisions—apart from Landwehr brigades—and left but *12* against Russia. The French were credited with a mobilised strength of 85 divisions, which with 6 British and 6 Belgian would mean, all told, 97 Allied divisions against an assumed 90 German. In reality, at the Marne, the Germans had 72 divisions and 10 cavalry divisions against 78 Allied divisions with 8 cavalry divisions. The French instead of 85 divisions mobilised only $60\frac{1}{2}$, to which were subsequently added 2 divisions from Algeria and some Territorial formations. The inaccuracies of the estimate alike with friend and foe illuminate the difficulty of gauging the war strength of a foreign army—even when that of an Ally.

On the basis taken, however, it seemed a reasonable assumption that the Western Allies would be able to hold up, and even to defeat a somewhat inferior German force—and then would come the Russian " steam-roller " sweeping down on Germany like a crimson avalanche of war.

Thus our pre-war preparations were based upon the fundamental misconception of a short, sharp war in which reserve armies would not and could not be utilised. To quote once more from Mr Winston Churchill, Lord Haldane " had concentrated all his efforts and his stinted resources . . . to place an

THE OLD ARMY

army of four to six divisions . . . on the left of the French line within twelve to fourteen days."

The matter of defence against invasion continued to excite study—and apprehension. The Admiralty whilst declaring, and rightly, that a large scale landing upon our shores was out of the question so long as we held command of the sea, steadily declined to give any guarantee that small enemy forces might not evade naval watchfulness. Even small forces, daringly handled, might do an immense amount of damage before being destroyed; and on October 22nd, 1908, a meeting of the Committee of Imperial Defence decided " that our army for home defence ought to be sufficient in numbers and organisation not only to repel small raids, but to compel an enemy who contemplates invasion to come with so substantial a force as will make it impossible for him to evade our fleets."[1] The strength—at the very outside limit—of a force which could be landed, was estimated at 70,000 men, and there followed the corollary that our Home Defence Army must at all times be strong enough to deal with an enemy landing on that scale. The fourteen Territorial divisions with the Regulars surplus to the Expeditionary Force would, it was believed, provide a Home Defence Army adequate for this need. Lord Haldane, speaking at the Imperial Conference of 1911, thus described the Territorial Force: " It is a citizen army which is retained at home for local defence, for resisting raids and anything that can slip past the navy, and which contains a section, now considerable, of those who are willing to go abroad for active service if occasion should require."

Sir Edward Grey [2] at the same Conference lucidly and concisely defined the motives which might force

[1] Asquith, *Genesis of the War*, p. 115.
[2] Afterwards Viscount Grey of Fallodon.

THE KITCHENER ARMIES

us to war: " . . . what really determines the foreign policy of this country is the question of sea-power. It is the naval question which underlies the whole of our European foreign policy. . . . If one Power or group of Powers attempted to make itself dominant in Europe, the weaker Powers assailed would appeal to us to help them. If while that process was going on we were appealed to for help and sat by and looked on and did nothing, then people ought to realise that the result would be one great combination in Europe, outside which we should be left without a friend . . . then the naval situation would be this, that if we meant to keep command of the sea we should have to estimate as a probable combination against us of fleets in Europe, not two Powers but five Powers."

Thus the Army was a weapon extending and consolidating that sea-supremacy which was as the breath of life to the British Empire and, in days to come, it was to secure British sea-power that millions of men from Great Britain herself and from her Dominions across the sea, fought in France and Flanders. So far as they could see ahead, Mr Asquith, Lord Haldane, Sir Edward Grey, and the naval and military officers associated with them, saw clearly enough. The trouble was that they failed to appreciate the titanic dimensions which the coming conflict was destined to assume, and this was an error shared in by practically every Government in Europe, by practically every soldier or statesman who actually sat in the seat of authority. Far away in distant Cairo, Kitchener had formed a different view. Here and there in the British Army and in other armies was to be found some comparatively unknown and insignificant soldier who agreed with this forecast. But economists and business men declared that Europe could not stand the economic strain of a prolonged struggle.

THE OLD ARMY

To sum up: the growing menace of the international situation had forced the British Government drastically to revise its military policy which, in 1914, was based upon the following principles:

A Great War, if it came, would be fought primarily to maintain our sea-supremacy.

The function of the Fleet would be to keep the seas open to our own shipping and close them to the fleets and commerce of the enemy.

The rôle of the Regular Army was to furnish at the earliest possible time and in the highest state of efficiency an Expeditionary Force to help our Allies.

The Special Reserve would provide drafts to replace losses from death or disease in the Expeditionary Force.

The Territorial Force was to give security against invasion and might furnish some additional drafts to the Regular Army.

The theory officially accepted was that the decisive battles in a Great War would be fought in the first few weeks of the opening of hostilities. The question of raising great new armies thus did not really arise, for such new armies, so it was believed, would not and could not be utilised. In pursuance of this theory, that of fullest possible strength at the earliest possible moment at the decisive point, the Regular officers and N.C.O.'s attached for training purposes to Territorial and Special Reserve units (in most cases the only men in such units possessed of specialised knowledge of military training), were recalled to their Regular units and sent to France; the Army schools of musketry, flying, cookery, etc., were all closed down and, perhaps most disastrous of all, the highly trained Regular staff-officers, intimately associated with the peace preparation of our Army for war, were all attached to the Expeditionary Force and their

THE KITCHENER ARMIES

places taken by retired officers, in many cases elderly or infirm or out of touch with modern requirements.

Then at the fifty-ninth second of the twelfth hour a new voice was heard, a new factor came into force radically transforming the entire military outlook. Kitchener was called to the War Office. And arising in their millions the civilian populace of Britain, answering the impulse of the greatest of British soldiers, set themselves to do what the staff-officers, wise in the lore of combat, proclaimed to be *impossible*; they set themselves to raise *new armies*. In doing this they upset the calculations and expectations of friend and foe alike; they achieved the greatest strategic surprise known to history. It is attempted in the following pages to give some idea as to how this miracle was wrought.

II

THE CALL TO ARMS

IT is doubtful if the younger generation, growing up in a world which has had its very soul scarred by the war and which has become accustomed to hearing this mentioned almost as a commonplace figure of speech, will ever realise the *unexpectedness* of the crisis when it burst upon us. Since the days of Agadir the thought of conflict with Germany had gloomed as a background to most far-seeing men and women, but to the great mass of our people, absorbed in their own interests, passions, hopes and fears, a great European struggle seemed a very, very distant peril. The tragedy of Serajevo stirred a throb of pity, a ripple of interest; but the average man or woman, if they had heard of Servia at all, regarded her as a very pugnacious little Balkan State and looked upon the whole pageantry of Balkan princedom, with its glow of resplendent uniforms and picturesquely dressed peasants, rather as stuff for a musical comedy. Even when Austria cast down her mailed gauntlet, those who had foreseen and who saw the danger were slow to believe their fears about to be actually realised. Other crises had occurred and had passed over; so would this one, it was said. As to the workaday, holiday-making, or pleasure-seeking throng, they shrugged their shoulders at the whole business. All *newspaper talk*, it was declared. The Press *must* have something to write about. Not until Russia had proclaimed her general mobilisation and Germany had warned her that unless this was countermanded she would accept the *casus belli*, did

THE KITCHENER ARMIES

it become clear even to soldiers that a Russo-German strife was in very truth inevitable and that Britain and France would be drawn in. The divisions in the Cabinet which, as we now know, existed as to what attitude England should take, faithfully represented the divided attitude of the country. Many people thought of a neutrality which would enable us if necessary to intervene all the more effectively when the combatants were exhausted, others were opposed to war in all and any form. Paul Cambon pressed with fierce vehemence for a clear and definite statement as to what policy England meant to take; Czar and President addressed themselves almost imploringly to Britain's King-Emperor. But Grey, faced by a divided Cabinet and a divided people, could not go farther than his famous " contingent " promise of British *naval* protection for Northern France—an impossible situation which would have meant strife in any case. Then came the German irruption into Belgium, settling all doubts and hesitations, enabling Government to speak to the country in language which every man and woman could understand. Britain's pledge had been given, her honour was at stake. The pleasure-seeking, work-seeking, indifferent multitudes, who thought little about Continental politics, and who cared still less, could answer the call of chivalry, could see the vision of a weak and helpless little State innocent of all aggression, trampled underfoot by a ruthless invader. The crowds gathered before No. 10 Downing Street broke into cheers as the fateful minutes rolled past without answer to England's ultimatum; they cheered the news of war, and all England cheered with them.

As early as August 3rd the cry had been raised, " Kitchener for the War Office." The country had confidence in the efficiency of the Fleet; it had not

THE CALL TO ARMS

equal confidence in the efficiency of the Army. Since Crimean days the War Office had a bad old tradition for muddling things, and the disasters of the early phases of the South African War yet lingered in public memory. Although Haldane had worked well with the soldiers, deservedly possessed their confidence, and had done excellent work under circumstances of great difficulty, he was not a very popular figure in the country. Pacifist elements had not much " use " for his Territorial scheme, or appreciation for his work in establishing the Imperial General Staff. Soldiers outside the War Office, on the other hand, if they believed at all in a national army, believed that this should be raised by conscription—and Haldane had proclaimed himself as " bolting and barring the door against conscription." One or two unfortunate phrases such as " my spiritual home is Germany " caused the cry to be raised that although Englishmen would not doubt his patriotism and whole-hearted devotion to his country, such doubts might be felt by our Allies. Kitchener, on the other hand, stood in the public eye as the embodiment of grim, relentless efficiency in war. And this it was felt was the thing most urgently needed. A legend had grown up about his name, a legend based not upon speeches but upon achievement, and the general feeling was that in a crisis of such unparalleled emergency, the Empire must have the *best* man available to control our military needs. On August 3rd the Military Correspondent of *The Times* voiced public opinion when he wrote: " Europe is in arms, and the greatest war of modern times is upon us. In these circumstances it must first be pointed out that the immediate nomination of a Secretary for War whose time is not fully occupied with other important affairs, is indispensable in the interests of defence. Lord Kitchener is at home, and his selection

THE KITCHENER ARMIES

for this onerous and important post would meet with warm public support. It is earnestly to be hoped that the Government will see their way to offer this appointment to Lord Kitchener, and that the Field-Marshal will accept it if only for the period of the war."

On the day following *The Times* declared in a leading article: " It is necessary that the affairs of the Army should be in the firm hands of a man in whom the public have confidence, and we do not know where we can find any head for the War Office who would more completely secure this confidence than Lord Kitchener." Other important journals echoed the cry.

It has been said that Mr Asquith's first thought was to restore Haldane to his old position at the War Office, but any suggestion that the Lord Chancellor, however gifted, should take over the supreme military direction of a world-wide Empire at war, was not without its ludicrous side. Some rather plain-spoken comments in the Press left no room for doubt as to the country's attitude, and on August 6th, Kitchener received his formal appointment—an appointment which meant less a change of personalities than an entire revolution in our military thought. In Mr Winston Churchill's words: " Lord Kitchener now came forward to the Cabinet, on almost the first occasion after he joined us, and in soldierly sentences proclaimed a series of inspiring and prophetic truths. ' Everyone expected that the war would be short; but wars took unexpected courses, and we must now prepare for a long struggle. Such a conflict could not be ended on the sea or by sea-power alone. It could be ended only by great battles on the Continent. In these the British Empire must bear its part on a scale proportionate to its magnitude and power. We must be prepared to put armies of

THE CALL TO ARMS

millions in the field, and to maintain them for several years. In no other way could we discharge our duty to our allies or the world.'"

The story of the New Armies is so intimately associated with the personality of the great soldier whose handiwork they were, that something may well be said here as to Kitchener himself. One who knew him intimately writes: " Kitchener was now 64 years old; his physical vigour was but little impaired by forty-five years of continuous work, his grasp of a situation was as firm as it was almost invariably correct, his keen blue eyes seemed to pierce the future and to give him that prevision which has been well described as almost uncanny. Much of his life had been spent in something like solitude, and if fierce energy had often marked his work he had yet accustomed himself to commune with his own thoughts and be still. Habit had led him to be a little backward in reposing trust in individuals, but those whom he trusted, whatever their walk in life, he trusted implicitly and almost unquestioningly. Selfless in his work and outlook, sensitiveness was an ingredient in his character, and if injuries were scarcely resented they were by no means unfelt." He was that rarest combination, the man of action who is at the same time a profound thinker, and his whole lifework might be regarded as an apprenticeship for the task which was to be his supreme achievement. As a young man, serving as a volunteer with Chanzy's army on the Loire in 1870, he had witnessed the collapse of the raw French conscript levies, and had learnt by first-hand experience that conscription minus trained officers, N.C.O.'s, or men, is no " Open Sesame " to victory. In the opening phases of the Sudanese campaigns, he had seen the same thing when Hicks Pasha's powerful but untrained force was cut to pieces by Mahdist volunteers armed with

THE KITCHENER ARMIES

clubs and spears. Later on, he had seen the unpromising material of the Egyptian Army moulded into excellent troops by good officers and N.C.O.'s, and as Sirdar had gained valuable experience in methodical preparation for war, administrative work, and executive command in the field. Later still, first as Chief of Staff to Lord Roberts in South Africa, then as Commander-in-Chief, he had commanded bodies of hastily raised and equipped volunteers such as the Yeomanry, C.I.V. Volunteer Companies, and South African and Dominion forces, whilst he had had pitted against him Boers who were purely volunteers, and without regularly trained officers or N.C.O.'s. He had seen the citizen soldier at his best and at his worst; had tested the havoc wrought by enemy bullets and shells on fine-spun theories.

His career subsequently to this had again brought opportunities of priceless value to the man who was to raise the New Armies. Sent to India to reorganise the army there, in face of what was believed to be the Russian menace, he had had to deal with the needs of an army of close on a quarter of a million troops held permanently almost on a war-footing. He had had to reorganise and redistribute this army and in so doing to tackle administrative and executive problems on a greater scale than had fallen to the lot of any other British officer. Controversy heaped around some of the measures he introduced: the war proved their value.

Thus, when on August 6th, 1914, he took over the War Office, this great soldier brought to the vast task which awaited him a store of knowledge, a wealth of practical experience far overshadowing that possessed by any other British soldier. Wilson, Robertson, Haig, Allenby, constituted a brilliant school of younger leaders: Byng and Rawlinson were to make their mark. But at the time none of these men could

THE CALL TO ARMS

have taken the place of Kitchener. Their knowledge of war was more theoretical than actual; their experience in the field had been limited to handling comparatively insignificant forces. Haig's Colesberg operations were a brilliant piece of work. But it was a brilliantly executed miniature.

On August 6th, 1914, Kitchener was a priceless asset to the British Empire, not alone on account of his quality of *flair* and the steadying effect upon public opinion of putting in supreme authority a man in whom the public had confidence, but because he was a soldier who was *more* than a soldier. His varied experience had brought him a broad knowledge of men and matters. Much of his experience in Cyprus, Palestine and Egypt had been gained in civilian capacities. He had toured the Empire on Imperial Defence, had acted as military adviser to the Australian and New Zealand Governments, and had appreciated the need for care and tact in dealing with these as well as the indubitable patriotism and good will of the peoples of our self-governing Dominions. Above all things he had had reality burnt into him. With the exception of Lord Roberts —then unhappily too old to serve—he was the *only* soldier in Europe who had actually, and successfully, commanded considerable armies in the field. This is training which no Staff College can give, nor any system of manœuvres. The Commander-in-Chief of an army in the field is forced to think for himself. If pitted against an enemy who is active, aggressive, reasonably well equipped, there rests upon his shoulders the heavy responsibility of victory or defeat; he cannot be academic in his views, for there is a daily round of problems to be solved; he faces a flesh and blood enemy eager to hit back. The gulf between war experience as Commander-in-Chief and the same experience as a subordinate is profound.

THE KITCHENER ARMIES

For the subordinate has nothing like the same responsibility on his shoulders, nor can he see things with the same breadth of vision.

Himself a highly educated man, Kitchener had none of the contempt for education sometimes shown by the " practical " soldier: when in India he had devoted care and thought to stimulating the intellectual life of the Army there, and had founded the Staff College at Quetta. But he was no slave to " schools," " cults " and " slogans." The " scientific " soldier too often saturates his mind with books, erects a vast and imposing edifice of theory, and lacks the essential element, practical experience, by which to test these theories. Peace-training for war has no lethal bullets or shells, manœuvres are held on too small a scale and under conditions which are too unreal to teach lessons, although to the thoughtful soldier they will always give valuable food for surmise. Thus, after a prolonged peace, the tendency with every army is to lend a too willing ear to attractive theories, to become academic in its outlook. Kitchener disliked and distrusted anything which savoured of a " school " of thought, and one of his rare manifestations of disapproval was heard in the case of a certain officer who seemed to him to be teaching unduly academic theories. For writers such as the late Lieut.-Col. G. F. R. Henderson, Maeckel, and John Codman Ropes, who showed adequate grasp of the practical side of their subject, he had warm esteem.

His extraordinary memory and unique grasp of the most insignificant as well as the largest problems of war, his mastery of administrative detail and capacity to work tirelessly himself as well as to rouse others to work as tirelessly in the common cause, the sheer impulse of self-confidence, resolution and energy which emanated from him, rendered him an

THE CALL TO ARMS

ideal leader for a civilian state at war. Great as was his foresight, he could not foresee *every* aspect of an unprecedented struggle; vast as was his energy he could not crowd into a few months the work which should have been distributed over as many years. Criticisms have been raised in many details.

His lack of knowledge of War Office routine may perhaps have been an advantage. Von Stein, the very able Prussian Minister of War, had also " never done any previous work at the Ministry of War " and was " only slightly acquainted with the organisation, the routine and the personnel." He considers that " as a newcomer I had the advantage of being able to approach the work independently and unhampered by precedent."[1] The War Office when Kitchener took it over was a very bad instrument. The men of outstanding personality, Wilson, Maurice, Robertson, etc., had gone off with the Expeditionary Force. Sir Charles Douglas, the Chief of the Imperial General Staff, an ailing man, soon found himself reduced to utter helplessness by an expansion upon a scale which exceeded his wildest dreams, and this bewilderment was shared by the generals around him. Until Robertson returned, the only people at the War Office, apart from Kitchener, possessed of genuine force of character and energy were Sir John Cowans, the Quartermaster-General, Major-General von Donop, the Master-General of Ordnance, and Sir Charles Callwell who, returning from retirement, had succeeded Wilson, his intimate friend, as Director of Military Operations.

" Jack " Cowans had many of the qualities of the successful business man, including a boisterous humour, a roguish eye, and a huge appetite for work. But he was concerned, and rightly concerned himself, only with supply duties, and had nothing to do

[1] *A War-Minister and his Work*, pp. 114 *et seq.*

THE KITCHENER ARMIES

with the general scheme for the New Armies. Major-General von Donop came in for much unjust criticism from men who could not realise that the production of munitions was a matter of laying down plant and accumulating skilled workmen, matters in which, owing to the small scale of our peace-time Army, we were gravely handicapped as compared with the Continental Powers. Callwell, shrewd, capable, gifted with a keen sense of humour, did not at first come much into contact with Kitchener.

The other heads of departments at Whitehall scarcely represented the British Army at its best, elderly gentlemen encrusted in an armour of red tape, toddling between the War Office and their clubs, overwhelmed by the tide of eager youths and ardent civilians clamouring to be of service to their country. Kitchener, later on, was harshly criticised for " usurping the functions of the Imperial General Staff," " attempting to centralise everything in his own hands," " interfering unduly with the work of departments." But in India where he worked with a well-selected team of subordinates—including men such as Haig—no similar complaints as to " fussiness " or " interference " were ever made against him. The Army considered him justified in his conflict with Curzon, and although some of his arrangements were criticised on military grounds, he was never accused of " over-centralisation." In 1914 he had often to interest himself in details because if *he* didn't, nobody else would. The departments concerned were not up to the mark.

The virtual abdication of its functions by the Imperial General Staff in the opening months of the war was due mainly to the personalities of the officers who occupied that very responsible post. A really strong man such as Robertson found no difficulty in working well with Kitchener. There is, moreover,

THE CALL TO ARMS

another side to this particular question. The French *Grand Quartier Général* and the German *Obertheeresleitung* all made very serious mistakes, and it is very unlikely that a British Imperial General Staff, even in full working order, would have avoided analogous errors. If, for instance, Kitchener could not always restrain his gifted and headstrong colleague at the Admiralty from doing those things which he ought not to have done, it seems very unlikely indeed that any conceivable C.I.G.S.—who would have lacked his prestige with the Cabinet—would have been more successful.

The concentration of power in Kitchener's hands had its advantages. Very important decisions were sometimes taken with a minimum of fuss and bother, as when white troops were taken from India and replaced by Territorials. Vast schemes of expansion were pushed forward long before the " General Staff Officer " element—alike in our own Army and in other armies—had grasped their necessity; and it is very possible that a stronger Imperial General Staff would have actively opposed Kitchener in this. On August 11th, after the War Minister had published his appeal for the First Hundred Thousand and had announced his plan for six new divisions, the Military Correspondent of *The Times* faithfully expressed the conventional military standpoint: " . . . it will take months to form such an Army and more months for it to become efficient . . . it will not be advisable in any way to diminish the value of our Reserve or Territorial formations for the benefit of a force which will take so long to create. The critical stage of the war is during the next few weeks, and we cannot afford to be caught swopping horses whilst crossing a stream." Many people talk about " General Staffs " or " Naval Staffs " as if these constitute an insurance against " error " in war. But these are all

THE KITCHENER ARMIES

human and fallible institutions, and the soldier or seaman of genius will always be worth more than the team of " able " men. For he is creative whilst the team is not. In 1914 an Imperial General Staff, sufficiently powerful to have rivalled the authority of the Secretary of State for War, would actually have introduced an element of indecision and vacillation when instant decision and whole-hearted resolve were the qualities most urgently needed. This would have been worth many victories to the German Armies.

In the task which awaited him, Kitchener's greatest asset was perhaps his power of appealing to the interest and sympathy of civilians, the knack which he undoubtedly possessed of getting civilians with him instead of against him. Broader in his outlook than the average soldier, much more accessible to civilian influences, the solid mass of civilian support behind him constituted his great mainstay; in fact it would be scarcely an overstatement to say that he got from civilians much more whole-hearted support than he got from many soldiers. He is an instance such as sometimes happens of the man of genius, doctor, engineer, or scientist, who, denounced by some of his own profession almost as a charlatan, finds truer appreciation from the broad masses of the public less concerned with professional jealousies or personal aspirations, and capable of taking a truer because more detached view. Kitchener's phrases, " The First Hundred Thousand," " The last million," " This is a young man's war," " New Armies," caught the public mind because they put into simple words conceptions which everyone could understand, and the truth of which smote even those without military training. He possessed in the highest degree the art of the crowd-leader; as a politician in peacetime he might have failed, but as the leader of a fierce and warlike crowd, surging to arms, high-

THE CALL TO ARMS

hearted with racial pride, whole-hearted in the pursuit of victory, he symbolised to an almost uncanny degree the strength and weaknesses of his own countrymen. He stood there as the embodiment of their genius for improvisation, their capacity alike in war and peace to govern themselves: he shared their contempt for mere cleverness when not allied with the capacity to dare or do, their distrust of the Ideal and gift for the rough and ready solution: he personified their stern and indomitable resolve, their steadfast courage, the grim resolution with which they could take punishment as well as deal heavy blows in answer. He personified their constancy in disaster, cool-headedness in peril, refusal to suffer themselves to be " rushed " by events. The methods by which he raised his New Armies were peculiarly *British* methods. No other country in the world would have set itself to raise these armies in quite the same fashion or have displayed so little foresight before the crisis was upon us or so much foresight when the emergency was to hand. No other people would have shown so little of the spirit of the scientific soldier or so much of the instinct of the born fighting man: no other nation would have left it to the very outbreak of the war to proclaim its alliances and to create an army: no other empire, having done this, would have squandered its blood and treasure so ruthlessly in support of its Allies, or have set itself to create an army with greater success. In a word, the story of the New Armies is the story of Britain's unreadiness for war and of her enormous energy when roused to battle.

III

THE FIRST NEW ARMY

ONE will fail to realise the spirit in which the New Armies were raised unless one bears in mind that the whole thing was an evolutionary process and that it was also a very individual process—perhaps the last example mankind will ever see of a really great soldier impressing his own particular personality on a world at war, living as an ideal and as an inspiration to victory to a whole nation in arms. Gone are the days when men went mad to the strains of " Tipperary," gone are the days when pamphlets and posters and placards announced, " Lord Kitchener wants YOU." But men answered the call, and they came not in thousands but in millions, and not from Britain alone but from the Greater Britains beyond the seas, and the memory of those days is a memory of deeds, and of a national readiness to suffer, to give and to dare. Time has dimmed the enthusiasm; sorrow has overclouded the glory of that great rising to arms. Yet the pride of achievement will always be with us; achievement such as is known to no other nation; which astonished even ourselves and which will go down to all history as perhaps the greatest epic of the war: the rising to arms of five million men, sundered by seas, oceans and continents, united only in a common patriotism and a common impulse to defend their country's cause.

The motives which led men to take up arms were many: patriotism, want of employment, ambition, personal courage, love of adventure, the sheer impulse of going with the crowd. But underlying all these

THE FIRST NEW ARMY

motives was the feeling that something big was at stake, that the triumph of Germany and of her Allies would mean something oppressive and reactionary to the world at large. The men who flocked to arms recked little of secret treaties or of diplomatic conventions behind the scenes: they reasoned subconsciously rather than consciously. Yet the mob, so-called by the unco-clever person, has an uncanny instinct for seeing into the heart of a problem. It has at times an almost feminine intuition, reaches its conclusions by no apparent chain of reasoning, by sheer instinct, and these instincts are more often right than wrong. The popular judgment upon men such as Mr Winston Churchill, Lord Haldane, Mr Lloyd George, Mr Baldwin or any other public personage, is a surprisingly shrewd judgment. Once formed, all the propaganda in the world will fail to shake it. Thus it was during the war. If at times lashed to a state of almost hysterical excitement by propaganda from press and platform, the public instinct was in general shrewd and sound, and it was this instinct which led men to join the Kitchener Armies, to pin their faith to a man whom few of them had ever seen, to venture their little all on the grim dice of war.

The professional soldier who studies this mighty outburst of patriotism is perhaps a little apt to be in the plight of the man who cannot see the wood for the trees. He sees mistakes—or what he thinks are mistakes—made in detail here and there; he calculates the tremendous cost of the process in blood and in money; and sadly reflects that had we been prepared in times of peace to expend even one-hundredth part of the energy put forth in war, we might have obtained the same results for but an infinitesimal fraction of the lives and treasure squandered. But in reasoning thus he forgets the

THE KITCHENER ARMIES

words of the very greatest of soldiers: " In war the moral is to the physical as three to one." Had our scale of peace preparations been actually greater, the enemy would have been aware of these efforts and made counter-efforts in answer. Had we openly proclaimed alliances the enemy would have known with certainty and beforehand all that we proposed to do. Many people assert that in that case there would have been no war. But this supposition is very debatable and the one thing which is certain is that our intervention would have been calculated beforehand. Preparations on our side on any large scale could not have been achieved in secrecy. The enemy by reason of his system of conscription could have replied to any increases in British military establishments which were a practicable proposition by counter-increases on a greater scale and at far less cost. It was the revolutionary nature of Kitchener's proposals, their unexpectedness, which constituted their greatest chance of decisive effect, and a country regimented, organised for war down to the last button, would never have shown the same fierce enthusiasm, the same spirit of going to war almost as if to a crusade, as was displayed by Great Britain and her Dominions in 1914. Every officer and man taking up arms in those great volunteer armies could feel that the Empire had exhausted every boundary of reasonable concession to avoid being plunged into war; he could feel that there had been nothing provocative in our policy, that we had maintained no armaments which could be twisted into a potential menace to Germany. Of the millions of civilians who left their homes and loved ones to face the hardships and dangers of the soldier's trade there were very few who had any motive of personal gain or personal ambition; they went mostly in the spirit of the man who says, "There's a very unpleasant

THE FIRST NEW ARMY

job to be done, but somebody's got to do it." There was about those Kitchener Armies a spirit of quiet, grim, fierce earnestness different to the spirit of the Old Army, alien to the spirit of the conscript armies of the Continent. They laughed and joked and grumbled and swore, but in their heart of hearts they all meant *business*. They brought to the career of arms the natural discipline of the football ground and the workshop; they tackled the soldier's job with the keen intelligence of the skilled artisan; the bulk of them were the type which is the very backbone of the country, decent self-respecting, industrious working-men, perhaps narrow in their views, at times Rabelaisian in their speech, not very accessible to a high-pitched idealism. But what they believed in they believed in heart and soul; no purely mechanical discipline could have locked them into the close comradeship which linked their ranks together, and, given the time necessary to gain cohesion and military training, these were troops cast in the mould of Cromwell's Ironsides, and no less terrible a foe.

The New Armies were the soul's awakening of an Empire at war, and constitute an almost unique blending of spirit between the leaders and the led. Speaking of his proposal to raise these armies, Kitchener declared in his speech to the House of Commons, May 31st, 1916: " Such an idea was contrary to the theories of all European soldiers. Armies, it had always been argued, could be expanded within limits, but could not be created in time of war. I felt, myself, that though there might be some justice in this view, I had to take the risk and embark on what may be regarded as a gigantic experiment. I relied upon the energy of this country to supply deficiencies of previous experience and preparation, and set to work to build a series of new armies, complete in all their branches." Note the

THE KITCHENER ARMIES

simplicity of the phrase, " I relied upon the energy of this country to supply deficiencies of previous experience and preparation." Kitchener was just as much prepared to trust civilians as they were to trust him. It is in this spirit of mutual trust that is to be found the real explanation of the success of what he rightly described as a " gigantic experiment." For the England of 1914 would not have swallowed conscription whether of men or of materials; she was out to smash Prussianism abroad, not to establish Prussianism within her own domains; before she would consent to any such measures she must first be convinced as to their dire and urgent need. But there was no way to convince her as to this but the bitter path of experience, and one could not wait to raise the new armies—until defeat had already been sustained. Thus it was necessary to start by exploiting the voluntary principle to the maximum degree; the country was not to be asked to sanction revolutionary and drastic measures until the necessity for such measures was patent to all, and it was obvious to all that the choice lay between such measures and the certainty of diaster. The voluntary system might be " wasteful " and " unscientific," but the real choice was between unscientifically laying the foundations of victory and of " scientifically " ensuring defeat.

One must stress again the evolutionary nature of the whole business. The Empire already possessed what was, as far as it went, a well-thought-out scheme of military organisation. There was the Expeditionary Force, highly trained Regulars, to go abroad and fight in France; there was the Special Reserve, semi-trained men, to provide a stream of drafts to replace the casualties of the Expeditionary Force; and there was the Territorial Force to beat off raids, provide for Home Defence, and perhaps to furnish a few extra drafts to the Regular Army. There the

THE FIRST NEW ARMY

thing ended. Every existing unit had its assigned function in the general scheme. Lord Grey tells the story of that first Cabinet meeting when Kitchener had proclaimed his intention of at once raising a million men, and had declared that even these would be but a first instalment: " As we walked away from the Cabinet a colleague asked me what I thought of this proposal. I replied that I believed the war would be over before a million new men could be trained and equipped, but that, if this expectation were wrong, the million men should of course be sent abroad to take part in the war. It was therefore clear that we should all agree to what Kitchener wanted."

This is a frank and honest statement which illuminates the atmosphere in which Kitchener had to work, the value of the instant decision made and the vital truth that nothing short of his great prestige would have induced Government actually to sanction proposals which most of his colleagues privately thought to be somewhat chimerical, and which were opposed tooth and nail by every official military expert. But Kitchener, a practical soldier dealing with a living problem amidst all the fog of war, faced with the fundamental uncertainty varying from day to day, from week to week and from month to month, of what the enemy might conceivably do next, could not start by tearing to pieces an existing organisation. As he himself subsequently expressed it: " . . . in the early days of the war the efficiency of the Home Garrison was a matter of vital importance, for a raid of a desperate nature, though obviously doomed to failure as an attempt at conquest, might certainly have paralysed our industrial powers which are now playing so decisive a part in the struggle. The necessity for keeping these Territorial Divisions intact and at their war-stations in day and night

THE KITCHENER ARMIES

readiness for an emergency is a point which I think it well to mention now, as it is one apt to be overlooked by those whose attention is riveted on the actual points of enemy contact."

There is no point upon which criticism has been raised more sharply than upon Kitchener's alleged failure to make the best use of the machinery set up by Lord Haldane in the way of the Territorial system and the County Associations. It has been suggested that he could have raised his New Armies more " scientifically " on this basis. It has even been suggested that owing to his long residence abroad he knew little of the Territorial Force and underrated and despised it. But Kitchener had commanded the troops assembled for the Coronation of King George V, a function at which all Territorial units were represented, and by picked men. His general attitude to the Volunteer movement was much more sympathetic than that of the average Regular officer, for he had commanded Volunteer units in South Africa and appreciated their value. Whilst Commander-in-Chief in India he had done much to support and to stimulate the Volunteer movement there. In Australia and in New Zealand he had advised upon and upheld an organisation very similar to that of Lord Haldane. His attitude to the Territorial Force was dictated purely by considerations of practical expediency. The organisation as it existed in August 1914 constituted a carefully planned framework around which to build up an army; but first of all it had been devised as a Home Service Army, and could not be transformed into a foreign service army by a mere stroke of the pen; and secondly, a Territorial unit cannot train itself and expand simultaneously. On August 2nd, 1914, the Military Correspondent of *The Times* wrote truthfully enough: " If war breaks out we may see

THE FIRST NEW ARMY

thousands of volunteers flocking to the Colours. But we need every man we can get for our general service army, and masses of untrained Volunteers in the Territorial Force will be rather an encumbrance than an aid." Due to no fault of their own, but to the conditions under which the Force lived in time of peace, the training of the Territorial units had been of a very exiguous character. The statutes of the Force recognised this and provided for a period of six months' embodiment of all Territorial units on mobilisation for the purpose of getting sufficient training to stand up to a highly organised foe. Thus, for Kitchener to have turned on to the Territorial units, sketchily trained officers, almost untrained men, all the vast streams of recruits who flocked to join the New Armies, would actually have reduced the Territorial Force to a state of chaos—without helping in the organisation of the New Armies. For the Territorial units were too weak to have absorbed this vast stream of men. It would have been the same thing as turning on a hose-pipe to water a delicate plant. One would have washed the whole thing away, roots and all. The fourteen Territorial divisions, if given the chance to absorb a limited number of recruits and complete their own training, might be expected quickly to become efficient. They could then take their place in the very front rank of the New Armies, if willing to undertake, as units, liability for foreign service; they could play, and did play, a part of enormous importance as a covering force to the New Armies, whilst these were mere agglomerations of ill-armed recruits; they answered their country's call in a most magnificent fashion, and provided a first reserve to the Expeditionary Force and an invaluable means of relieving half our Regular Army, and this, the best half, was scattered overseas in Gibraltar, Malta, Egypt and India. But

THE KITCHENER ARMIES

they could not have fulfilled any of these rôles successfully had Kitchener started by pulling them to pieces. As concerns the Territorial Associations, these actually played a part of far-reaching importance in raising the New Armies. The Fourth and Fifth New Armies were made up almost entirely of units raised under County auspices. But the real difficulty in basing a national military organisation on the County Associations lay in the fact that these bodies differed not alone in energy and efficiency, but in the wealth and populations of the regions they controlled. Had all the counties been uniform in area and importance no difficulty would have been experienced in working by counties, and the advantage would have been obvious. But one county, London, had a population of 4,521,685;[1] another, Rutland, had a population of 20,346; and between these two extremes came counties such as Yorkshire with a population of 3,979,964, and Northampton, with a population of 348,515. No matter what organisation was adopted it was necessary to break up the counties into military districts approximately equal in size—which, of course, was what Kitchener did.

Finally, one may perhaps venture to remark that many people in their resentment at unjust and ungenerous criticisms of Lord Haldane, seem to have fallen into the error of making equally unjust and ungenerous criticisms of Kitchener. Lord Haldane himself never had the faintest idea of using the Territorial Divisions for foreign service, or of using the County Associations as a means of raising armies of millions of men. It may be added that he was too honourable a man to have urged men to join the Territorial Force for Home Defence, with the idea of subsequently calling upon them to volunteer for

[1] Administrative county only, Census figures from 1911, the latest available in 1914.

THE FIRST NEW ARMY

foreign service under conditions in which it was practically impossible for them to refuse.

One must stress yet again the evolutionary nature of the process by which the New Armies were raised. Kitchener, when he came to the War Office on August 6th, 1914, had in his mind a clear and definite picture as to what he wanted—an army of seventy divisions. But he had not an equally clear and definite picture as to how to get what he wanted. To give again his own words:

" My immediate decision was that, in face of the magnitude of the war, this policy would not suffice. Whether our armies advanced, retired or held their ground, I was convinced that, not only had we got to feed the existing Expeditionary Force, and maintain an adequate garrison here and in India, but, further, we had to produce a new army sufficiently large to count in a European war. In fact, although I did not see it in detail, I must ask Gentlemen of the House of Commons to recognise that I had, rough-hewn in my mind, the idea of creating such a force as would enable us continuously to reinforce our troops in the field by fresh divisions, and thus assist our Allies at the time when they were beginning to feel the strain of the war with its attendant casualties. By this means we planned to work on the up-grade while our Allies' forces decreased, so that at the conclusive period of the war we should have the maximum trained army this country could produce."

Note those phrases " rough-hewn in my mind," " I did not see it in detail." There was no question of a cut and dried scheme, of working to fixed plans, rules or schedules. There was no material upon which cut and dried schemes, fixed plans or schedules could have been based. It was fundamentally a matter

THE KITCHENER ARMIES

of making the best possible use of an existing organisation, of snatching troops here, there, or wherever available to stem the enemy's onrush, of trying to raise the New Armies in a fashion which would not dislocate existing units or arrangements. These vast and intricate problems could not be solved in the calm of a professorial arm-chair; they must be solved amid the thunder and fury of a chain of mighty happenings. There was the rush of the German legions into France, the shock of the retreat from Mons, the epic story of the Marne and the grim death-grapple of First Ypres; there was the fighting front clamorous for men, the desperate call for help from our Allies, the ever-present fear that the enemy might attempt a raid upon our shores, an enterprise in which he had little to lose and much to win. The problem was thus continually to strike a balance between the urgent vital need of the present and the plans for future expansion: one must strive perpetually to pay Peter without robbing Paul. And as one traces the successive steps by which Kitchener solved this problem one can see in this process a certain element of sheer beauty, the hand of the master-artist moulding the raw manhood of the Empire into one grand harmonious design, building up his vast military edifice with swift, sure strokes, more as some master-potter moulds his clay upon the wheel of destiny, than in the spirit of the master-mechanic working with tools capable of mathematical precision. It is a story which will take its part in the artistry of war, an achievement, the marvel of which becomes the more marvellous the closer one studies it, and the successful accomplishment of which was the truly decisive element of the war. For without the New Armies there could have been no Somme; but for the Somme France would have been overwhelmed at Verdun; Germany would have

THE FIRST NEW ARMY

emerged victorious. Moreover, this story of the New Armies is without parallel in all history. Armies have been improvised successfully for defensive purposes. Without mentioning the Spanish Guerillas, Tyrolese Insurgents, or Boer Commandos, Washington successfully improvised the Continental Army in the War of the American Revolution, and the French Republic produced the armies of revolutionary France. But in all these cases it was a matter of fighting defensive wars under specially favourable conditions of terrain, such as forests, mountains, veldt, etc., whilst the newly raised forces had the stimulus and advantages of fighting to defend their own countries from invasions. The armies of the American Civil War, which form perhaps a closer parallel, were pitted against armies which were equally improvised and without regular training. But the New Armies differ from all these instances in that they were hastily improvised troops raised for the purpose of being transported across the seas; they were pitted not against equally improvised formations, but against the most highly trained and formidable regular troops in Europe; they had no advantage of terrain to compensate for lack of training; on the contrary they encountered this enemy upon his own chosen ground, behind fortifications planned with all the ingenuity of a highly organised military Empire fighting for its life—and vanquished him. They stood up to losses on a scale unparalleled in war and faced these losses with fighting spirit unquenched: they endured sufferings and privations, indescribable and almost inconceivable: and by the time the Battle of the Somme had drawn to its blood-stained close, the back of the enemy was broken, his *moral* was subdued; he chose rather to withdraw than to face the renewed ordeal of battle, and, until the unforeseen, the Russian collapse, pinned all his hopes of victory

THE KITCHENER ARMIES

not to battles on land but to the desperate issue of the unrestricted use of submarines. It was because they were Volunteer Armies that the New Armies emerged triumphant from this terrific ordeal. No conscript army could have triumphed over their difficulties of training, no conscript army could have been so successful *in training itself*. The individual earnestness of the men in the ranks was the element which truly made for victory. The men who fought and died on the fields of France in those tragic summer and autumn days of 1916 were the cream of Britain's manhood, the flower of her race. But if the price was high, no lesser price would have purchased victory: and the choice was between paying this price or defeat.

Old Army, New Army, Territorials, the names mattered little: it was Kitchener's *National* Army which fought the fight and won.

Thanks to the machinery set up by Lord Haldane and his military advisers the mobilisation of our Army functioned with unprecedented smoothness and speed, and provided six Regular Divisions and one Cavalry Division available for the Expeditionary Force. These troops were well trained and well equipped, but it was part of the peace conditions of our Army that the number of reservists needed for the transition from peace to war establishments was unduly large. Most battalions, after dropping " young " soldiers and recruits, could show a strength of only 22 officers and 456 men; the difference between this and the war establishment of 1020 of all ranks, was made up by men who had spent years in civil life, and who lacked the training in marching which renders the infantryman truly mobile. In the case of the first four divisions which were involved in battle before they had time really

THE FIRST NEW ARMY

to absorb their reservists, the results of this were very serious. It was due, no doubt, to the high proportion of reservists, and the actual shortage of Regular officers, that long before Kitchener came to the War Office there was planned, as one of the first " moves " of mobilisation, the separation between the regimental depôts and the Special Reserve—usually the third—battalions of regiments. These moved off to their war stations under the scheme laid down for Home Defence; and, under an order already mentioned, the Regular officers and N.C.O.'s " lent " not only to Special Reserves but also to Territorial units, as instructors, adjutants, etc., were sent to the depôts of their regiments. Kitchener was able to secure some of these subsequently to assist in forming the new armies, but most of them went to France either immediately or with drafts. The statement that instructors were taken away from Territorials and used for training new army units has been widely circulated and has caused a good deal of ill-feeling. It happened only in a very few cases and was due to arrangements made long before the war began.

The Special Reserve battalions mobilised at very high strength — on an average about 1500 men. But most of these were mere boys; the rest were the older classes of reservists or else partially trained men. Thus it is doubtful if any of these battalions could actually have produced 800 really efficient men, whilst the force lacked transport, staffs, mounted troops or field artillery. After the departure of the Expeditionary Force there would remain, of Regular troops, only 6 squadrons of Household Brigade Cavalry, 3 battalions of Guards, 2 line-battalions and 7 batteries of Horse Artillery, say a total of 7000 men. In view of the nervousness as to invasion, the somewhat chaotic condition of the Special Reserve, the

THE KITCHENER ARMIES

"feeding" duties devolving on this and the untrained state of the Territorials, it is scarcely surprising that Government, at the Council of War held on August 5th, 1914, decided to keep two Regular divisions—one-third of the Expeditionary Force—back as a security against raids. It was not until August 23rd that Kitchener could induce them to sanction the departure to France of the 4th Division, and the 6th Division transported from Ireland to the East Coast was kept there till September 9th.

Almost the first act of Kitchener as Secretary of State for War was to telegraph orders for each battalion of the Expeditionary Force to leave behind three officers and fifteen N.C.O.'s to form a nucleus for a fresh battalion, and for other units of the Expeditionary Force to leave behind proportionate *cadres*. It was an order which to the keen and enthusiastic officers and men, eager to be at the foe, came as a terrible blow, for everyone believed in a war which would soon be over. The officers left behind saw themselves relegated to an inglorious rôle in depôts, whilst their comrades fought in world-shaking battles: the N.C.O.'s shared their officers' feelings. The bitter complaints of the regimental officers were echoed by Field-Marshal Sir John French and his staff, who, filled with the doctrine "full strength at the decisive point," wanted every man upon whom they could lay hands, and grudged the retention of two full divisions in Britain as security against invasion. It was a time when nerves were strained almost to breaking point; and it is difficult from the calm of an office-chair to enter into the feelings of officers who saw their professional prospects ruined by what seemed to them an almost senseless act, or of generals who saw, as they thought, their prospects of victory jeopardised by wanton interference with the arrangements carefully made.

THE FIRST NEW ARMY

Yet the outburst of irritation over what was in reality, and as is now universally admitted, a wise and necessary measure, illuminates the extraordinary difficulty and complexity of the problem confronting Kitchener, the need not only for foresight but for calm strength and even ruthlessness on his part.

The working of this great soldier's mind during the early weeks of the struggle is, in fact, a fascinating study. It was a time when men's hearts were filled with the sense of dire emergency; their thoughts were bounded by the day and the morrow; few had thought to spare for the day after. The new Secretary of State for War, moreover, could not see his problems sharply defined in the light of our own after knowledge; to him they loomed mistily, seen through a distorting mirror of passions, hopes and fears, sheer *flair* and intuition must play their part in distinguishing the true from the false and in tempering confident aspirations by the cold logic of hard facts. And in this blurred confusion of the uncertain present and unborn future, with all its high lights of hope and black shadows of despair, we see Kitchener never at a loss, as sure of himself as he was capable of inspiring confidence in others, tracing out his schemes for the New Armies, converting, adapting, expanding, always with a fine sense of balance and a just sense of proportion, concerned always as far as possible to minimise the risks of a transition period, concerned always rather to build upon an existing framework than to start anything definitely brand new.

We have already seen that in the Cardwellian system, the last touches to which were put in 1881, the British Regular Army possessed a Territorial basis. There were sixty-nine regimental districts which, some of the regiments being four-battalion regiments, produced seventy-four pairs of Regular battalions, one of which was at home and one abroad. There

THE KITCHENER ARMIES

were in each district Special Reserve battalions and Territorial battalions affiliated with these.

But it has always been a special feature of the British Army that the regiment is an administrative, not a tactical unit. In other European armies and in the American Army, the regiment, usually three battalions, is kept together, the companies are numbered consecutively, they have such elements as the band, the colours and the officers' mess common to the whole regiment. Two such regiments form a brigade, and two brigades, with auxiliary arms and formations, a division. The British battalion, however, is an independent unit, with its own officers' mess, band and colours. The brigade is made up of four battalions, usually from quite different regiments, and three such brigades with auxiliary and ancillary services make up the division. The British organisation has the merit of flexibility. It is possible to graft an almost indefinite number of extra battalions on to existing regiments and thus to avoid forming new regiments lacking in traditions and *esprit de corps*.

Kitchener's policy was the very wise one of expanding and developing the existing organisation of the Regular Army. On August 7th Mr Asquith publicly announced in the House of Commons that the new War Minister had said " the Army needs men." He requested Parliament to sanction an increase of 500,000 men. On the same date Kitchener sent off a circular letter to the County Associations appealing for their help in raising the " First Hundred Thousand." Simultaneously newspapers and placards announced:

YOUR KING AND COUNTRY NEED YOU

A CALL TO ARMS

An addition of 100,000 men to His Majesty's Regular Army is immediately necessary in the present grave National Emergency. Lord Kitchener is confident

THE FIRST NEW ARMY

that this appeal will be at once responded to by all those who have the safety of our Empire at heart.

The phrase, " An addition . . . to His Majesty's Regular Army " is of far-reaching significance. What was really in view was an expansion of the existing Regular Army, not the establishment of something definitely and specifically new. The volunteers answering Kitchener's call were to be Regular soldiers enlisted for three years or the duration of the war; they were to be liable for service all over the world, or in any battalion or arm of the service in which men were needed. It was not to be a case of raising special corps with special privileges, nor was there to be risk of men becoming " time-expired " and marching off from battle just when they were needed—as had happened in the opening battles of the American Civil War.

This announcement and the appeal to the County Associations were drawn up on August 7th, one day after Kitchener's appointment: the outline for the organisation of the First New Army (K 1) was published only four days later. The existing military organisation of the United Kingdom provided for six " Commands," Irish, Scottish, Northern, Eastern, Western and Southern. Each of these " Commands " was to provide a Division complete in all arms and services, save that instead of a " Southern " Division there was to be a " Light " Division made by adding extra battalions to existing Light Infantry and Rifle Regiments. The system generally followed was to graft a new battalion on to every existing pair of line-battalions. In the case of some four-battalion regiments, such as the Rifle Brigade, however, three new service battalions were formed per regiment. The New Army battalions were to be numbered consecutively after other battalions of the same regiment; thus the Northumberland Fusiliers had

THE KITCHENER ARMIES

originally seven battalions, the 1st and 2nd, Regulars; the 3rd (Special Reserve); the 4th, 5th, 6th and 7th, Territorials; the 8th (Service) battalion was the first of the New Army battalions, which were all distinguished by the word (Service). By the end of August eight new battalions were forming for this regiment, all of whom proudly arrogated to themselves the fine traditions of the old " Fighting Fifth."

The Territorial basis adopted by Kitchener, his use of the County Associations are of particular interest, nor is there any real truth in his alleged reluctance to use the Territorials to the maximum possible degree. The Museum of the Royal United Service Institution displays a note written in pencil in his own hand to the Director-General of the Territorial Force under date of August 10th:

" Lord Kitchener desires to be informed as soon as possible which of the Territorial Battalions and other units

1. Volunteer for service abroad;
2. Partially volunteer; if so, how many of each category, officers by ranks,
3. Desire to form part of the Home Defence Force not leaving the country."

This was before any Territorial unit had volunteered for service overseas.[1]

The flood of recruits had begun to swell even before the call went forth for the First Hundred Thousand. Canada led the way by telegraphing an offer of 20,000 men. On August 3rd came a similar offer from Australia; offers of assistance and outbursts

[1] Save for the Northumberland Yeomanry, the Dorset Fortress Coy. R.E., the 6th East Surrey and 7th and 8th Middlesex, which had accepted the obligation for foreign service before the war. All told, 5 units and 17,621 men had accepted liability to serve abroad prior to 1914.

THE FIRST NEW ARMY

of loyalty poured in from all parts of the Empire. In the United Kingdom the boom in recruiting set in simultaneously with the order mobilising the Army. On Saturday, August 1st, the officer in charge of the principal recruiting office in London, Great Scotland Yard, attested only eight recruits; the two days succeeding were a Sunday and a Bank Holiday; the 4th of August saw a seething mass of men waiting to enlist and it took twenty minutes and twenty policemen to enable the astounded recruiting officer to force his way into his own office, after which he was kept at work without intermission attesting men. Men came from every class, from every creed, from every corner, and from every walk in life. Rich men, poor men, married men, single men, childless men, men with families, all joined in an outburst of enthusiasm which Kitchener's call roused to fever height. Lawyers, doctors, architects, engineers, artists, writers, clerks, navvies, bookmakers, book-keepers, tinkers, tailors, all felt the same impulse, all answered the call to arms. The peacetime flow of recruits for the Regular Army had comprised 30,000 men annually, less than 100 men per day, who were taken in by recruiting agencies in every important town all over the United Kingdom. It was not long before as many men were joining in a single day and recruiting staffs were quite inadequate to deal with these vast numbers. Prompt and energetic measures were taken. On August 7th divisional recruiting offices were opened in the London boroughs of Camberwell, Islington, Battersea, Fulham (Kensington Gardens). A day or so later new offices were opened at Woolwich, New Cross Road, Stratford, Lavender Hill and Peckham Road. Many men tramped for miles and slept under hedges for the chance to join up, others stood for hours waiting in queues. There was little cheering,

THE KITCHENER ARMIES

little excitement, but an undercurrent of deep earnestness. By the 9th most of the London Territorial battalions had recruited up to full strength. On the 11th recruits were reported as streaming in at 100 men per hour, 3000 daily (for U.K.) and 6000 men were recruited over the first week-end of the war.

Men were streaming in at a satisfactory pace, but Kitchener's first days at the War Office sufficed to disclose the bareness of the military cupboard in respect to those important matters of guns, rifles, equipment, uniforms, barrack accommodation, ranges, training-grounds and trained officers and N.C.O.'s without which no organiser can create an army. In the way of artillery equipment we possessed all told 2036 guns and howitzers, of which, however, one-third were obsolescent. The six divisions of the Expeditionary Force had a grand total of 484 guns, the 14 Territorial Divisions were armed with obsolete 15-pounder " converted " guns; their garrison and mounted batteries were similarly armed with material which was no longer first-class; other guns were distributed in coast defences and fortifications. The Territorial Infantry, armed in any case with the long Lee-Enfield, converted to charger-loading, an obsolescent weapon, was 160,000 short of the numbers needed even of these. The numbers of short Lee-Enfield rifles available sufficed just to arm existing Regular and Special Reserve units, with a very small reserve to replace wastage. The munitions supply for the Army in the field had been calculated on the basis of the Mowatt Report after the war in South Africa; the introduction of quick-firing ordnance had revolutionised since then the demands for shell; whilst instead of the war being, as had been anticipated by the War Office experts, a matter of at most four great battles each lasting three days, it im-

THE FIRST NEW ARMY

mediately developed into a struggle which beggared any comparison with South Africa.

The existing barrack accommodation provided at most for 160,000 troops. By clearing out married quarters at most some 100,000 further men could be accommodated.

Even in time of peace there was a grave shortage in officers for the Regular Army. Owing to lack of candidates young men had been accepted into cavalry regiments on probation and without any sort of military training. Military service had become unpopular with the class which had hitherto provided the bulk of the Regular officers. The number of candidates for commissions had actually become less than the number of vacancies, and instead of there being any really competitive examination for Sandhurst the authorities had to be glad to take any material which offered. The Special Reserve was upwards of 1000 officers short of its infantry establishment. The Territorial Force had a shortage of twice as many.

In that most important factor, the material of war, the failure to produce supplies on a scale adequate even for the small forces envisaged by the experts at the War Office in the days preceding August 4th, 1914, was the more serious in that facilities were lacking for their rapid manufacture. We were capable, for instance, of producing not more than 6000 rifles per month; and the rifle, although needed in greater numbers than any other weapon for an army, requires a longer time than any other before its manufacture can be begun, owing largely to the number of gauges of extreme accuracy needed in the process. Only two firms in the whole of Great Britain were capable of providing the web equipment; our resources for producing uniforms and the specially strong boots needed for soldiers were equally

THE KITCHENER ARMIES

limited; only one firm could produce Lewis guns. Messrs Vickers & Co. possessed the patent, and the only staff of trained personnel capable of producing machine-guns. In the matter of artillery *matériel* the cupboard was equally bare. The great armaments firms of Maxim, Elswick, Vickers, etc., were absorbed primarily by our naval needs; and Woolwich Arsenal, to which the Army looked for its guns and howitzers, had been reduced, for reasons of economy, to a mere skeleton.

" Did they remember, when they went headlong into a war like this," was the cry once wrung from Kitchener, " that they were without an army, and without any preparation to equip one? " And to French, reeling back after the disaster of Mons—a disaster incurred by neglecting his Chief's warning as to the formidable nature of the German march through Belgium, and the advisability of concentrating our small forces farther back—he wrote sadly and prophetically: " . . . pray do not increase my troubles by the thought that if the Division [the 6th Division kept back against raids] had been with you some of your men's lives might have been saved. Do remember that we shall have to go through much more fighting before we are out of the war, and that by prematurely putting all our eggs in one basket we might incur far greater losses. Believe me, had I been consulted on military matters during the last three years, I would have done everything in my power to prevent the present state of affairs in which this country finds itself."

Parallel with the need for men there lurked in Kitchener's mind the need for trained officers and N.C.O.'s, munitions, quarters, stores, equipment, guns, rifles, and machine-guns, and all these demands must be satisfied parallel with the need for increasing the forces in contact with the enemy, and feeding

THE FIRST NEW ARMY

their unceasing and urgent demands for men, guns and stores.

If we look into the system actually adopted by Kitchener we see that the general system followed was to provide for expansion by tapping, continually, *new* sources of supply whilst maintaining at high pressure every *existing* means of covering military requirements.

His first act was to detain 500 officers on leave from the Indian Army. These with the handful of officers " seized " from the Expeditionary Force were to act as instructors to his New Armies. He immediately gave orders for the manufacture of a grand total of 4648 guns and howitzers—nearly ten times the numbers provided for the original B.E.F. Orders were distributed for 3,860,000 rifles, apart from some 750,000 which were actually available. Unhappily the gun, rifle, and machine-gun are, as already stated, very technical arms to produce, and whereas with the great Continental armies it was a matter of expanding industrial establishments which already existed in a high state of efficiency and on a large scale, with the British Army it was a matter of starting from the very beginning by accumulating plant and skilled personnel. This proved a long process. To solve, for instance, the intricate problems involved in making fuses for shells it proved to be necessary to import highly trained watchmakers from Switzerland.

The War Office staff, being quite incapable of undertaking, with its own official machinery, an expansion upon so vast a scale, the sensible plan was followed of distributing the contracts as a whole to the great armaments firms and allowing these to sub-contract to smaller firms. This was the germ of the organisation subsequently set up by the Munitions Ministry, which, however, possessed

THE KITCHENER ARMIES

legislative powers and privileges denied to the War Office.

On August 14th Kitchener approved of plans for hutments to take 500,000 men, on the 17th he sanctioned the re-enlistment of ex-N.C.O.'s up to the age of fifty. A call for 2000 gentlemen to act as officers for the First Hundred Thousand had been published a few days earlier, and produced an eager rush for commissions.

On the 15th, the request to volunteer for foreign service was officially promulgated to the Territorial Force. This was a liability for which the pre-war constitution of the Force had made no provision; and it was hardly surprising that, at a time when the true magnitude of the struggle upon which we were embarked had not been realised by the country, and many men, held at home by family or business ties, believed that in any case the war would soon be over, and that by embracing this unforeseen liability they would seriously injure themselves without helping their country, the answer was not as immediate and gratifying as might have been desired. The historian of that fine corps The London Scottish writes with some sarcasm but with truth: " . . . Not all volunteered. It was a serious thing to ask of the men, especially in the circumstances of the time. For it must be remembered that they were being daily informed in official and unofficial reports that the huge French armies were winning victory after victory, that even the little Belgian Army was standing up splendidly against the invaders, that the Russian 'steam roller' was pushing on to Berlin, that Germany was already bankrupt, that her losses in the field were appalling, that the Germans were blunderers and cowards who 'could not shoot for nuts' and ran at the sight of a British bayonet. No wonder that many a man, who would have rushed

THE FIRST NEW ARMY

to help his country at any sacrifice if it were in danger, hesitated to involve himself in warfare however triumphant, for which his assistance, as he might well suppose, was not really needed."

Another keen Territorial officer writes: "Whilst at Derby the main subject of discussion was that of Imperial Service for Territorial units. So far as we were concerned a considerable number of officers and men had already volunteered. There were many others who had not actually done so, but there was no doubt as to what their answer would be. Of the remainder many were practically disqualified from serving abroad by reason of age, unfitness, family and business ties, and other reasons, and for them, in the light of the little we knew then, the decision was most difficult, and the need for it we hardly thought fair. The demand for volunteers was in the first instance put rather baldly, with little notice, and with apparently little realisation of the enormous difficulties under which so many were labouring, and it was not surprising that this appeal met with little response. A second earnest appeal, reinforced by the feeling that the honour, even the existence of the Battalion was in danger resulted in over 800 volunteering which was eminently satisfactory though it is impossible to avoid the feeling that many who volunteered did so against their better judgment. . . .

"All the other units in the Division having more or less similarly settled this vital question, training was started in earnest."[1]

This decision was taken between August 14th and 15th.

The rather unfair fashion in which the Territorials were treated in being asked to transfer "lock stock and barrel" to what really became a branch of the Regular Army has never been sufficiently realised.

[1] *The Sherwood Foresters in the Great War*, Vol. I, p. 18.

THE KITCHENER ARMIES

The present system of enlisting the Force avowedly for foreign service, if necessary, is a welcome guarantee that this sort of thing will never happen again. Kitchener himself was anxious that no unfair pressure should be exercised upon the men to cause them to volunteer. A press *communiqué* issued at this time under his auspices, and published among other papers by *The Times*, stressed the vital need of the Territorials for Home Defence and that the Territorial who volunteered for foreign service was not necessarily a finer fellow than the one who continued in his original job which was to beat off invasion. The Military Correspondent of *The Times* built upon this a proposal to form a new series of Territorial Divisions numbered from 15 onwards and made up of the men accepting liability for foreign service. Up to August 25th, sixty-nine Territorial battalions had volunteered as units for service abroad. Ten days earlier the principle had been laid down that to be recognised as a foreign service unit a Territorial battalion must show 75 per cent. of its members as willing to undertake this liability and must then recruit 25 per cent. extra to bring it to full war establishment. Some units such as the London Scottish, London Rifle Brigade, etc., fulfilled these conditions immediately. In some of the more thinly populated regions battalions were made up to strength by " swopping." Thus the 4th Royal Scots took two companies from the 6th, and the 7th Battalion of the same regiment took two companies from the 8th Highland Light Infantry.

To transform a Home Service Army into a Foreign Service Army something more is needed than a mere stroke of the pen; and it was a matter largely of " moulding " the Territorial Force, fitting it to take its part in a general national army on a scale undreamt of before the war began; but it was necessary to do

THE FIRST NEW ARMY

this in a fashion which would not render it incapable of fulfilling its original functions.

By August 16th, the organisation of the First "New Army" had so far advanced that it was possible to publish a *communiqué* announcing the numbers of the new divisions, originally 8th to 13th, their future distribution in training centres and the names of the commanders and staffs. The Light Division and 9th (Scottish) Division were to train at Aldershot, under Gen. Sir H. L. Smith-Dorrien, G.C.B., D.S.O., the 10th (Irish) Division under Gen. Sir Brian Mahon, C.B., D.S.O., was to assemble at Dublin and the Curragh, the 12th (Eastern) Division under Maj.-Gen. J. Spens, C.B., at Colchester, and the 13th (Western) Division under Gen. Sir A. Hunter, G.C.B., D.S.O., at Salisbury Plain. The training area and command of the 11th (Northern) Division was left temporarily undecided. Later on, Grantham was chosen.

Four days later there was published Army Order No. 324, August 21st, 1914, by which the First New Army came officially into existence. On August 23rd, there occurred the Battle of Mons, the first great clash of arms between British and Germans on the West Front. Almost on the same day the first important measure was taken to reinforce the troops in contact with the enemy, the 4th Division embarking for France.

IV

THE GREAT MUSTERING

THE First New Army, eighty battalions with their complement of artillery and auxiliary services, was formed upon small cadres drawn from existing units. Thus the 5th (Service) Battalion, The King's Shropshire Light Infantry, a typical battalion, started on August 6th with a nucleus of one captain, one lieutenant, and thirty of other ranks. In a few days' time this small cadre was expanded by a stream of recruits. Although men of education were not entirely lacking, the men joining up in the First New Army, generally speaking, were of the same class as the average run of Regular recruit; many of them were ex-soldiers and potential instructors and N.C.O.'s. The command of battalions was usually given to the Regular majors in command of depôts, who, being accustomed to train young soldiers for the Regular Army, were well qualified to transform the new battalions into efficient soldiers. By August 21st, most New Army battalions and units were at their training centres; the 5th Battalion The King's Shropshire Light Infantry was, for instance, at Blackdown Camp, Aldershot. The battalion formed, however, at that time a mere mob of unarmed men in civilian clothing, and a constant stream of new recruits was arriving from the regimental depôts.

On and immediately after August 21st, the official birthday of the New Armies, two far-reaching decisions were taken by Lord Kitchener. The 7th and 8th Middlesex, Territorial battalions which even in peace had volunteered as units for foreign service,

THE GREAT MUSTERING

and the 1st London Territorial Brigade which had accepted this obligation were warned for service overseas. Lord Derby's proposal to raise a " comrades " battalion from Liverpool was accepted on the understanding that the battalion should subsequently be taken over by the War Office, and should enjoy no special privileges of pay or service other than that the men should be kept together. This was the origin of the " Pals " battalions and units which " caught on " with such amazing success and which so greatly relieved the strain on the overburdened War Office.

One can trace in Kitchener's mind at this particular time four predominant considerations: first as quickly as possible to reinforce French, at that time in the opening and harassing phases of the retreat from Mons; secondly, as far as possible to decentralise, for the War Office, understaffed and almost without resources, could not provide for the numbers of men who were pouring in at an ever-increasing rate; thirdly, to combine what would otherwise have been sporadic efforts by local authorities, however energetic and patriotic, into a general and co-ordinated scheme of military expansion; fourthly, to leave no stone unturned to kindle the enthusiasm of the country, and to arouse the public consciousness as to the urgent and vital need for immediate and increasing efforts to attract men to the ranks and to provide for their requirements.

On August 25th the 11th (Service) Battalion of The King's Liverpool Regiment could announce that it was the first battalion of the New Army to reach its full establishment. In the same city Lord Derby's proposal to raise a " comrades " battalion aroused vociferous enthusiasm.

On that same 25th August, Kitchener gave his first speech in the House of Lords. He announced that

THE KITCHENER ARMIES

the First Hundred Thousand was practically complete but warned his hearers:

" I cannot at this stage say what will be the limits of the forces required, or what measures may eventually become necessary to supply and maintain them." On the same day the 10th " City " Battalion of the Royal Fusiliers was opened to enlistment from stockbrokers, clerks, warehousemen, and the like, and was completed to establishment the following day. Three days later there was published an appeal for the Second Hundred Thousand.

" The whole of the forces in South Africa have been sent home as quickly as possible. The garrisons of Hong Kong, with China, Singapore, Mauritius and Bermuda, will be relieved by native troops from India and corresponding British battalions will be withdrawn from India without waiting for relief.

" By these means I hope to get a Seventh Regular Division together here between September 12th and 15th and some time later an Eighth Division as well as a Cavalry Division. As soon as the first troops of the Seventh Division arrive I have little doubt but that the Sixth Division will join you. In the meantime your wastage shall be fully filled up." Thus wrote Kitchener to French on August 27th. But the urgency of the situation in France, French being in retreat before a powerful foe, needed even prompter measures.

Territorial battalions were placed under orders for Gibraltar and Malta so as to relieve the Regular troops there, and on August 31st, the Territorial battalions recognised as foreign service units such as the 7th and 8th Middlesex, London Scottish, London Rifle Brigade, Queen's Westminsters, etc., were authorised to form second battalions.

One sees thus even at this early stage the broad

THE GREAT MUSTERING

outlines of the Imperial concentration achieved by Kitchener and his general principle of taking nothing away without putting something in its place. Territorial units taken away from Home Defence, their original function, must be replaced by new Territorial units; Regular units taken away from garrison duties must be replaced by new units equally capable of undertaking such duties. It was to be a policy of minimising risks, of maintaining existing arrangements while providing for new emergencies.

Meanwhile the tide of national enthusiasm was rising. On September 2nd there was formed the Parliamentary Recruiting Committee, made up of leading men of all parties and to which the Labour Party gave official support on the day following. The Second Hundred Thousand was reached in a few days. Mr Asquith on September 5th could state that although Lord Kitchener had asked for 200,000 men, between 250,000 and 300,000 men had answered the call, of whom London had provided 42,000. Two days later he could add that out of 500,000 men authorised as an increase to the Regular Army, 439,000 had come forward, exclusive of enlistments into the Territorials. Parliament was asked to sanction an additional 500,000 men.

The recruiting figures for London indicate the growing sense of national peril:

August	26	1725
	27	1650
	28	1780
	29	1800
	30	1938
	31	1620
September	1	4200
	2	3600
	3	4028

THE KITCHENER ARMIES

Those fine Territorial battalions the 7th and 8th Middlesex embarked on September 3rd for Gibraltar, where they were destined to spend six impatient months. It was not without a sense of grievance that officers and men heard themselves condemned to a rôle which, if vital, seemed somewhat inglorious, and their sense of grievance deepened to exasperation when later they heard the London Scottish described incorrectly as the first Territorial unit to have the honour of service overseas, and read of this particular battalion as being actually in contact with the enemy. It seemed to the unfortunate officers and men as if they were being penalised for the very keenness and efficiency which had raised them to their high and honourable place among Territorial units. Every soldier will understand and sympathise with their feelings. In time of war it is difficult to conceive any duty more necessary but more distasteful than to be asked to take over garrison duty in a region distant from the clash of arms so as to relieve other troops for the purpose of battle. The real sacrifice made by Territorial units in undertaking this duty has not always received adequate appreciation.

On September 10th the East Lancashire Territorial Division, subsequently the 42nd, embarked for Egypt. This Division was destined later to play an heroic rôle in the Dardanelles campaign.

By the beginning of September recruits were streaming in at a speed which baffled all arrangements. Depôts calculated for at most 248 men were swarming with 1500, crowded like herrings in a box; the Rifle Brigade battalions of the 14th (Light) Division had reached a strength of 2500 men apiece. When on September 11th the Second New Army was sanctioned, the gigantic battalions of the 14th Division were drawn up at Aldershot. Company officers were told to fall out half their men to form new battalions.

THE GREAT MUSTERING

Within a few hours the material of the 20th Division was ready for officers and instructors. " At about 6 p.m. I was drilling with ' D ' Company of the Eighth Battalion," writes Capt. C. E. Jesser-Davis, who had come from Ceylon to join the regiment, " when I was sent to take command of ' C ' Company of the Eleventh Battalion. I found three hundred and twenty men and boys in every variety of civilian attire, mostly rather shabby (although one man was in possession of a white collar) waiting in the road with their newspaper parcels under their arms, and had to get them into the very limited accommodation allotted to me—one barrack-room and two or three bell tents."

The formation of three corps destined to play a considerable part in the war illustrates not only the feeling of self-sacrifice and enthusiasm which was seizing upon all classes, but the capacity of our people to organise themselves, a spirit of initiative and of willing co-operation without which the feat of raising the New Armies would have been impossible. *The Times* published the following letter under date of August 26th, 1914:

" SIR,

We attended the recent meeting at the Hotel Cecil to consider the formation of a corps of past public schools' men, and found that the organisers only required grey-haired, spare time veterans. We are between thirty and thirty-five, absolutely fit and game for active service. The meeting showed there must be hundreds of men in the same position as we are, who between the years of 1898 and 1903 were marksmen, and attended the Bisley musketry camps and Aldershot training camps with school or university corps. We have applied for commissions in the new Regulars, but find we

THE KITCHENER ARMIES

are too old. We have offered our services as musketry instructors, and are informed that we are too young, and that none under thirty-five are selected.

"After endless inquiries there seems to be only one way in which our services are acceptable, and that is by joining the ranks. Many advantages would result if we all joined the same regiment, and all public school men of similar age and qualifications are invited to attend a formal meeting on Thursday next, the 27th instant, at the address below, between 8 p.m. and 9 p.m., to discuss the formation of a 'Legion of Marksmen' with a view to offering its services *en bloc* to one of the new battalions now being formed.

"We should be obliged if you would insert this invitation in your columns.

"Yours,
"Eight Unattached."

"59A Brook Street,
 "Grosvenor Square,
  "W."

On inquiring at the address given it was found that six of the "Unattached" had already joined the 10th (City of London) Territorials, but that the manager of Claridge's Hotal had kindly placed a room at the disposal of those wishful to discuss a scheme. The meeting was adjourned thence. The first proposal was that men present, to the number of some hundreds, should follow the example of the six "Unattached" and join the same regiment in a body, but it was felt that some larger scheme was necessary to represent the Public School men as a class. Proposals were ventilated for a special corps with special privileges, but some of those present.

THE GREAT MUSTERING

knew that the War Office would not hear of any such thing and the idea was abandoned. Finally, Mr H. J. Boon put forward a scheme to raise 5000 men between the ages of twenty-one and thirty-five, possibly with age extensions to from thirty-eight to forty and for youths from eighteen to twenty-one, provided these could secure the consent of their parents.

Enlistment was to be open to all who had been to schools mentioned in the *Public Schools' Year Book*. It was hoped to raise the 5000 men within fourteen days. A Central Office was to be opened in London but enlistment was to be begun all over the country. When the corps had reached full strength it was proposed to request official sanction for the title " Princess Mary's Own."

A Committee was elected with Mr E. J. Stuart as secretary, and the first meeting was held August 28th. A letter stating the Committee's proposals was sent to the Under Secretary of State for War through Mr M'Kinnon Wood, and a meeting was to have taken place between Mr Boon and the Secretary of State on Monday evening at 6 p.m. Owing to Parliamentary duties, however, this proved impossible and Mr Boon was deputed to call at Lord Kitchener's private house. Here he saw Lord Kitchener's private secretary, Sir George Arthur, to whom he gave a copy of the letter already sent to the War Office. Sir George Arthur came back after a few minutes with a message from Kitchener, " Go ahead, and if you can raise 10,000 men I shall be all the better pleased."

A recruiting poster was drawn up the same night. A circular letter was drafted out and despatched to the Lord Mayors, Provosts and Mayors of fifty important towns. The first day, September 1st, of the inauguration of the recruiting campaign produced 300 applicants. On Wednesday 1200 men were

THE KITCHENER ARMIES

attested and medically examined. By September 12th, 5000 men had been enlisted and there was a waiting list of between 200 and 300 more. All the work of enlisting and attesting had to be done voluntarily and by amateurs: 25,000 forms had to be filled up, 10,000 index cards filed, many hundreds of letters had to be answered daily. Whilst the work was in full swing the Chief Recruiting Officer at Whitehall declared the whole proceeding to be invalid. The Corps, he said, was not officially sanctioned. Mr Boon hurried once more round to Kitchener's private house, Sir George Arthur listened to his plea for help, and after a few minutes brought a consoling message: "Lord Kitchener was tired out but the matter should have his first attention next morning." Next day, September 9th, the Corps received official sanction.

There was thus formed the University and Public Schools' Brigade (U.P.S.), the greatest value of which was perhaps as a reservoir for supplying officers. Its four battalions, the 18th, 19th, 20th, and 21st (Service) Battalions Royal Fusiliers—thanks to the valuable assistance of Lord Lurgan and the Hon. Arthur Stanley, C.B., M.V.O., M.P.—mobilised and went into training on September 18th at Woodcote Park.

Mr Boon, who had done so much to get the Corps going, at the time a bright young fellow of 52—with fifteen years of ranching in Texas to his credit—resigned the chairmanship and served as a private in the 18th Battalion. Then, fearful that he would not see service, "wangled" his age, joined the A.S.C. and reached ultimately the rank of Captain.

Almost simultaneously Lord Derby had been raising his "Pals" battalions at Liverpool. He broached the idea to Kitchener on August 24th. A meeting was held in Liverpool on August 28th, and

THE GREAT MUSTERING

2000 men offered themselves in thirty-six hours. Recruiting was formally opened on August 31st. Separate tables were arranged for the various trades as under:

Cotton Association.
General Brokers and Stock Exchange.
Provision Trade.
Seed, Oil and Cake Trade Association.
Sugar Trade.
Fruit Brokers and Wool Brokers.
Steamship Companies and Cunard and White Star Lines.
Timber Trade.
Law Society and Chartered Accountants.
Bank and Insurance.

Three battalions, the 17th, 18th, 19th (Service) King's Liverpool, were raised in a week, to which a fourth, the 20th Battalion, was added at the beginning of October, producing ultimately the 89th Brigade of the 30th Division.[1] The history of this Brigade is an instance—which can be paralleled by many others—of the fine results of voluntary effort, local patriotism, and a general spirit of enthusiasm. The War Office had promised seven officers but only five could be spared, two of whom were quite unsuitable. Thus, including Brig.-Gen. F. C. Stanley, Lord Derby's brother, then a Captain in the 3rd Coldstream Guards, only four Regular officers were available to organise what was at first a mob of 3000 civilians and ultimately increased to twice that number. But Brig.-Gen. Stanley was in himself a tower of strength;[2] the other officers

[1] There were also formed the 21st and 22nd Battalions as Reserves.

[2] Brig.-Gen. Stanley was fortunate in securing six N.C.O.'s from the Grenadier Guards who did yeoman service, and there were a few ex-Army officers.

worked whole-heartedly with him; whilst on the administrative side, the eager and enthusiastic support of the City of Liverpool was worth any amount of officialdom. The Brigade built its own camp at Knowsley Park and was comfortably settled in well-built huts whilst many other units were shivering under canvas or crowded into damp and insanitary quarters. Messing problems were solved with ease, and—thanks to the energy of Mrs Stanley—enough khaki cloth was secured to provide smart and well-fitting uniforms whilst most new army units were in unsightly blue serge—and lucky even to get that. The Brigade did not escape the general shortage of rifles and field service equipment—local efforts could not produce these—but it used the handful of D.P. weapons available to maximum effect, and established its own training school for officers which not only filled up its own commissioned ranks but provided officers for other units also. Altogether a very fine effort which reflects equal credit on Lord Derby, his gallant brother, and the City of Liverpool.

The raising of the 23rd (Sportsman's) Battalion of the Royal Fusiliers was a parallel effort on a smaller scale. That popular sportswoman, Mrs E. Cunliffe-Owen, later Mrs Cunliffe-Stamford, O.B.E., on chaffing some of her friends towards the end of August on not being in khaki, was challenged to raise a battalion of middle and upper-class men up to the age of forty-five. She promptly went with her friends to a post office and telegraphed to Lord Kitchener, " Will you accept complete battalion of upper and middle-class men, physically fit, able to shoot and to ride, up to the age of forty-five? "

The answer came promptly back, " Lord Kitchener gratefully accepts complete battalion."

Mrs Cunliffe-Owen got to work at once. The India Room at the Hotel Cecil was engaged as a

THE GREAT MUSTERING

recruiting depôt; the Officers' Association was persuaded to lend a dozen officers; the recruits were asked to fill in forms stating not alone their ages, nationality, etc., in the usual fashion, but also their qualifications in the way of riding, shooting or walking well; and Mrs Cunliffe-Owen, seated behind a screen, signed the papers herself. The 1st (Sportsman's) Battalion was raised in four weeks, and the superiority of women to men in the way of " getting a move on " was triumphantly vindicated when Mrs Cunliffe-Owen showed herself successful in hustling contractors into producing a fully equipped and model camp within nineteen days. This one woman without any elaborate organisation to help her, seeing into everything herself, even menus, was successful in producing two of the finest battalions in the British Army.

The Sportsman's Battalion was a unique collection of men. " In one hut at Hornchurch the first bed was occupied by the brother of a peer. The second by the man who drove his car. Both had enlisted at the same time at the Hotel Cecil, had passed the doctor the same time at St Paul's Churchyard. Other beds were occupied by a mechanical engineer, an old Blundell School boy, planters, a mine overseer from Scotland, a man in possession of a flying pilot's certificate secured in France, an old sea-dog who had rounded Cape Horn on no fewer than nine occasions, a man who had hunted seals, ' with more patches on his trousers than he could count,' as he described it himself, and so on.

" Every hut was practically the same and every hut was jealous of its reputation. Scrubbing day was on Saturdays as a rule, and it was then that the ' un-char-lady ' side of various men came out. They were handling brooms, scrubbing brushes, and squeegees for the first time in their lives; but they stuck

THE KITCHENER ARMIES

it, and, with practice making perfect, it was surprising to what a pitch of cleanliness things eventually got.

" Even church-parade has been dodged on a Sunday morning in order that three pals might unite in an effort to get the stoves blacked, the knives and forks polished, and a sheen put on the tea pails."

In the same battalion sleeping side by side were to be found a man who had gone up the Yukon, Frank Slavin the boxer, another who had been sealing round Alaska, trappers from Canadian woods, railway engineers from the Argentine, planters from Ceylon, big game hunters from Central Africa, others from China. With this as other high-class battalions the number of men taking commissions proved a serious drain on its strength, and the Commandant ultimately insisted that every man desiring a commission must procure two new recruits for the battalion. This saved the 23rd (Sportsman's) Royal Fusiliers from sinking into an Officers' Training Corps. When finally the battalion went to France it earned a fine fighting reputation. The following figures are of interest:

THE FIRST SPORTSMAN'S BATTALION
23rd (Sportsman's) Royal Fusiliers

	Officers.	Other Ranks.	Total.
Embarkation strength	31	1006	1037
Total drafts . .	188	3762	3950
Total effective strength	219	4768	4987

These figures, which only include men who genuinely served with the battalion, are an eloquent testimony as to the severity of the service seen. Roughly speaking, to keep it at a strength of 1000 men, 5000 were needed.

THE GREAT MUSTERING

A Second Sportsman's Battalion, raised after the First, formed the 24th Battalion Royal Fusiliers, and the 23rd and 24th Battalions formed part of the 99th Brigade of the 33rd Division.

This was the critical phase of the Marne fighting, perhaps one of the most critical periods in the whole war. The fashion in which Kitchener, overburdened with work and responsibility, was continually called upon to settle points which could quite well have been settled by subordinates will not fail to strike the observant reader. Civilians, bewildered and perplexed at the lack of understanding and sympathy shown by the War Office, were only too apt to regard Kitchener himself as a Court of Final Appeal in everything relating to military exigencies. Even soldiers, themselves outside the charmed circle of Whitehall, were apt to take the policy of appealing directly unto Cæsar—never with bad results if complaints were well founded or suggestions truly helpful. Lord Methuen, for instance, early in September struck by the bad conditions at the camp at Devizes, where the recruits were not only without arms or uniforms but without blankets, drinking cups, plates or dishes, wrote to Kitchener direct to draw his attention to the matter. The very next day one of Harrods' head men appeared on the scene with *carte blanche* to provide everything necessary for the men's comfort. In fairness to Regular officers in general it may be stressed that if there was lack of initiative and unreadiness to accept responsibility this existed mainly at Whitehall. Local regimental authorities showed no lack of willingness and self-reliance. The commander of the depôt of The King's Shropshire Light Infantry at Shrewsbury relates how he found himself without attestation forms for recruits, which had to be printed locally; five members of the Metropolitan Police, five of the

THE KITCHENER ARMIES

Shropshire Police, two warders from the Convict Prison and one Royal Marine were pressed into service as instructors, and did excellently. With the depôt crowded with about six times as many men as had been anticipated, the harassed commander found himself driven into ordering stores upon a great scale, and relates how a circular letter from Kitchener to the effect that O.C.'s would be held personally responsible for providing for the necessities of their men came as a welcome relief, for he might otherwise have been held liable for the financial outlay, which had been considerable.

By September 1st the recruiting wave had set in in earnest. On that day, a Tuesday, 30,000 men joined up. An appeal by Kitchener for soldiers' families evoked a generous answer. On the same day it was announced that the Ulster Volunteer Force was to furnish a division for the New Armies. Kitchener had seen Col. T. E. Hickman, Inspector-General of the Force, as far back as August 7th, and said that he wanted as many of the Force as he could get for France. This division became ultimately the 36th. The fifth week of the war, the total number of men joining up for New Armies and Territorials could not have been far short of 250,000 men.

The battalions and units of the First New Army were soon filled to overflowing. By September 3rd, for instance, the 8th (Service) Battalion, The Black Watch, at Albuera Barracks, Aldershot, was at full strength, but a draft of 200 men left Perth on September 6th and many more could be expected. Thus, on September 9th, sanction was given to form the surplus drafts into a new battalion, the 9th (Service) Black Watch. Practically all units being in like case, Army Order XII of September 11th, 1914, was issued creating the Second New Army by duplicating the units of the First. Kitchener, having now in view

THE GREAT MUSTERING

the formation of the 8th Division as a Regular Division by adding a brigade from India, the Light Division which had originally borne this number was renumbered as the 14th Division. The six divisions of the Second New Army were renumbered 15th to 20th.

Lord Derby's success in creating the " Pals " battalions in Liverpool had struck a note which resounded all over the country. Other cities and townships hastened to follow the lead set by Liverpool Thus, on September 1st, 1914, the late Duke of Norfolk and Sir George Franklin approached the War Office for permission to raise a battalion representing the City and University of Sheffield. The proposal being favourably received, a meeting was held the same day, an ex-Territorial Colonel who had seen service in South Africa was appointed Commandant, a Captain, also an ex-Territorial, was asked to act as temporary Adjutant, and in a few days the battalion was formed.

" You are a crowd, a good-looking crowd but a CROWD," said their Colonel lovingly, addressing them for the first time on parade. And he told them that their motto must be WORK. An eyewitness thus describes them:

" *Sans* uniform, formed up anyhow, the Sheffield Battalion looked a crowd. But they were an unusual crowd, one such as had not been seen in England before the Great War. Their ages ranged from 19 to 35. Standing there as privates were many men whom no other conceivable circumstances would have brought into the Army; five hundred pounds a year business men, stockbrokers, engineers, chemists, metallurgical experts, University and public school men, medical students, journalists, schoolmasters, craftsmen, shop assistants, secretaries and all sorts of clerks. . . . A well set-up strapping lot for the most part. They

THE KITCHENER ARMIES

represented one of which it might be hoped that the fire of military training would make well-tempered stuff."

In this crowd were to be found ex-N.C.O.'s, ex-Regular soldiers, ex-Volunteers and ex-Territorials, and some of these ex-soldiers who had been Guardsmen were heard to declare that men of the stamp of the Sheffield City Battalion learnt as much in three weeks as the average Regular recruit learnt in three months—perhaps a pardonable exaggeration. For three months the men lived in billets, coming to drill as if to their business places. Then they moved into a camp built at Redmires under supervision of the City Architect. On December 5th, 1914, they mustered 1131 of all ranks, and two extra companies, 500 men, were raised as a reserve.

The raising of the 17th (Service) Battalion Northumberland Fusiliers was another example of the private enterprise which so ably and enthusiastically seconded Kitchener's efforts. Over 2000 men from the North Eastern Railway had already joined the Army or Navy when the management decided to form a special battalion to enable N.E.R. men to serve together. A circular was drafted September 8th, calling all who wished to join to fill up and return the attached slip. The circular assured the men that provision should be made for wives, families and dependents, the Company undertook to keep the men's positions open for them, to pay contributions to Superannuation and Pension Funds, and to provide accommodation for the families of the men occupying the Company's houses. All this, it may be said, meant a considerable financial sacrifice which the Company shouldered gladly. Although the circular asked only for 1100 men, by return of post 3000 offered for service. Two letters may here be quoted in which men explained, not without a certain *naïveté*, their reasons for joining:

THE GREAT MUSTERING

"When the war broke out several of my chums who were Army Reserve men, were called upon to go to their respective regiments. One by one they went, and I felt 'Oh! I must go myself.' As I had a strong fancy for the Yeomanry, I took to riding a good bit at nights at home after my work hours. I tried to join them at Darlington, but could not get enlisted there, so went up to Newcastle, as I heard they were stationed in camp at Gosforth Park. However the day I went to Newcastle, the Yeomanry left and went to Castle Eden. At the same time it came to my notice that Sir Eric Geddes was raising a battalion of men drawn from the N.E.R. This was to give any pals the opportunity of joining the Army together. I thought this was very nice and got my chum, Harry Craggs, the only chum I had at home, to join with me. This was the 11th September, 1914. . . . How well I remember leaving home with a full box of clothes mother had so carefully put in for me, she being so particular as to my having plenty of underclothes to change in case of my getting wet some time. Many a time afterwards I have smiled to myself when out in France, wet through, with no change to put on, and no chance of getting any."

The second letter strikes a different note:

"A nation of shopkeepers, can they become a nation of soldiers?—and a nation of soldiers, Tom, John, Bill, Fred—and myself; what of myself?—a valuer, a soldier! What can I do? Why I cannot even load a rifle! Warned! Warned! but asleep—business and pleasure, work and play. Hard work, the foundation of a life's career, good and sound, but not a single idea, not the smallest means of holding and keeping my house, my work, my pleasure should any enemy come to take them away. Why!—

THE KITCHENER ARMIES

there should be hundreds, thousands like myself—fools. The hours wasted, the chances missed, without in the least cutting down work or pleasure, but the bill is presented and must be paid—and so cursing the missed chance I determined to enlist to-day."

Whether there were many who so earnestly regretted lost opportunities may be doubted. Nevertheless the battalion was sanctioned on September 11th. Recruiting began on September 14th, the minimum standard being: height, 5 feet 6 inches; chest measurement, $35\frac{1}{2}$ inches. Col. C. B. Preston, late of the Garrison Artillery, was placed in command, and the Company's medical inspector passed the men as fit or otherwise. Two large warehouses at the King George's Dock, Hull, were fitted up as barracks and the battalion was comfortably housed by October 1st. Both the Geddes brothers served with it; Professor Auckland Geddes arriving from M'Gill University, Canada, with four members of the Officers' Training Corps there, acted first as Company Commander and then as Second-in-Command and did yeoman service in training the younger officers. The battalion was fully armed and equipped within eighty days, almost a record for any New Army unit. One or two amusing instances are related of its training. The following dialogue is said to have been actually overheard: "No. 1330, you are warned for guard tonight, see that you turn out smart, and that your equipment and rifle are clean."

"Sorry, Sergeant, but I shan't be able to work late tonight—theatre you know, two seats. Sorry of course and all that but really——"

"There, there, my lad, stow it. You ain't wearing red tabs yet. Just you hand over those tickets; I'll look after the lady and tell her what a fine soldier you are, while you serve your King and Country."

Another who served in the battalion writes:

THE GREAT MUSTERING

"Rough as it was, however, we had many good times, which more than compensated for the hard training we had to endure. One had only to mention the name of Captain 'N' to raise a smile." This officer seems to have been rather over-particular regarding certain matters of military etiquette and highly critical of the minutiæ of a soldier's duty; so, when one evening as night was falling, he tried to get past "Big Geordie," who was on sentry at the Beach Huts, without giving the password, that canny warrior felt that the fates had delivered his critic into his hands, and gave his officer a bad few minutes, standing with his finger suggestively on the trigger, while Captain "N" shivered and expostulated, "It's me, can't you see it's me? Don't you know me?"

"Whae's me, anyway?" said Geordie, playing with his trigger.

"Don't be a silly ass, I've forgotten the password."

Finally Big Geordie relented and let him by, only to be severely "told off" for doing so.

And there is the story of the company which strayed on manœuvres. A staff-officer galloped up, equally vague as to his whereabouts. There was much discussion and flourishing of maps and it was then decided that the company must be under the B in Bardon.

A disgusted listener under cover of a furze bush was heard to remark: "Sounds as if we're under the Y in B——y well lost!"

The story of the 18th (Service) Battalion Durham Light Infantry is very similar. Early in September a committee was formed under chairmanship of the Earl of Durham which included Col. R. Burdon, M.P., Sir William Gray, and H. Pike Pease, Esq., and agreed to raise a battalion at their own cost from Durham, Darlington, the Hartlepools, Middles-

THE KITCHENER ARMIES

brough, Stockton, Sunderland, and Bishop Auckland. Lord Durham immediately placed Cocken Hall at the disposal of the battalion, which meant a saving of between £6000 and £7000 to the State, lists were opened for recruiting, September 24th, the minimum height being 5 feet 9 inches. Early in October the battalion reached full strength, and at the beginning of 1915 it mustered 1300 men. This was one of the few local units, the cost of raising which was borne entirely by private individuals, for when the battalion was taken over by the War Office, the committee declined to have the cost of raising it refunded as was done with other units. Col. Burdon and the committee were warmly thanked by Kitchener for their services. This battalion ultimately went abroad as part of the 93rd Brigade of the 31st Division.

The instances quoted are not isolated instances but were part of the general awakening of the public consciousness as to the magnitude of the struggle and the need for effort. The wave of enthusiasm had not yet reached its crest, but it was necessary temporarily to dam it, for the stream of recruits into the overburdened depôts had filled these to overflowing. On September 12th Mr Asquith announced the raising of the physical standard to 5 feet 6 inches. " Men will, of course, still be accepted if they are willing to be drafted into the reserve and to return to their homes until accommodation can be found for them. Men enrolled on these terms will receive three shillings per day while waiting to be called up." This apparently refers to the fact that many units had to be temporarily closed to enlistment even on the higher physical establishment. But it is hard to see why the measure of drafting men into the Reserve and calling them up when needed could not have been more generally adopted. The explanation is perhaps to be found in the prevalence at that

THE GREAT MUSTERING

time of the old " Regular " idea of reservists, as a partially paid force.

It had not yet been realised that the entire ablebodied manhood of the country constituted the real Army Reserve.

The recruiting returns for September had evidenced the impossibility of raising the New Armies on a rigidly Territorial basis. Whereas the depôts of the regiments from the thickly populated North and West were overflowing with recruits, to complete to strength the 6th (Service) Battalion of the Leinster Regiment (Royal Canadians) it was necessary to send a draft of 600 Bristol men. The flow of recruits from the Southern, Home, and Midland counties, whilst satisfactory enough, could not compete with the great industrial areas. The Durham Light Infantry, for instance, formed its 10th (Service) Battalion August 22nd, an 11th (Service) Battalion at the beginning of September, the 12th (Service) and 13th (Service) Battalions were raised September 16th, the 14th (Service) Battalion September 26th, and a 15th (Service) Battalion was completed to full strength by October 1st. The measures taken to form the 18th (Service) Battalion have already been described; thus, excluding battalions raised subsequently, Regular, Reserve and Territorial battalions, this one regiment raised in one month six battalions, all of which won distinguished reputations. The Suffolk Regiment, recruiting from a more thinly populated area, raised its 7th (Service) Battalion August 20th, its 8th (Service) and 9th (Service) Battalions early in September, its 11th (Service) Battalion September 25th.

Those fine Highland regiments, the Black Watch and Gordon Highlanders, recruiting from a large but sparsely peopled area which must already provide recruits for two Regular and one Special Reserve

THE KITCHENER ARMIES

Battalion, besides four Territorial battalions, could not provide more than three battalions each to the New Armies and it was doubtful if they would be able to maintain these.

"Besides the 3rd (Special Reserve) Battalion," writes the historian of the 11th Battalion Gordon Highlanders, "there were no less than four Territorial battalions of the Gordon Highlanders in Aberdeenshire at the outbreak of the war, namely the 4th, 5th, 6th, and 7th Battalions. The large demand for recruits made by these battalions on the county was so great that Lord Kitchener was doubtful from the outset whether any Gordon Battalions raised for his New Armies would succeed in maintaining their strength by subsequent drafts. He decided, however, to raise as many battalions as possible; time would show whether they could be maintained."

Thus when the Third New Army was constituted by Army Order 388 of September 13th, 1914, the Territorial basis taken originally in forming New Army Divisions was abandoned. The Divisions were numbered consecutively 21st to 26th, the sobriquets "Light," "Eastern," "Western," etc., were dropped. Instead of brigades being made up, in most cases, of four battalions from distinct regiments, it happened generally that two battalions of the same regiment served in a brigade side by side.

The fighting at Mons, Le Cateau, the Marne, and the Aisne was sorely taxing the Special Reserve battalions and Ordnance department to replace officers and men killed, wounded or "missing," guns, rifles and stores lost. The II Corps alone in the retreat from Mons and Battle of Le Cateau lost 7182 men and 38 guns; the loss of a man, moreover, usually meant the loss of his rifle. On September 5th the British Expeditionary Force was 20,000 men

THE GREAT MUSTERING

and 40 guns short of strength despite a stream of reinforcements.

If to replace men, guns and rifles was difficult, to replace officers was even more so. Thus we find Kitchener wiring to French on September 16th:

"We have sent you, since the war began, 593 officers to fill vacancies, and at rate demands are coming in from the front we shall soon be unable to supply well-trained officers. Units will then have to work with reduced numbers and staffs, which in some cases are apparently redundant and will have to be cut down. . . . I am trying to get well-trained officers everywhere, and hope to get a few more from India. Many of the officers sent home are only slightly wounded and sick and will rejoin their units in a short time. I hope to be able to continue to send drafts with a due proportion of officers, but it seems to me that, unless we stop all preparations of larger forces to continue the war, forces which are now being trained with the smallest number possible of Regular, Reserve, and dug-out officers . . . we shall be forced to take the steps I have indicated."

The interaction of the situation on the fighting front in France and the situation at home in the matter of raising, training and equipping new troops must always be kept in mind. There can be no doubt that Kitchener would have preferred to use the Regular units which made up the 7th and 8th Divisions, as a means of leavening and tempering his New Armies had he been free to do so. The tragedy was that the demand from the front for reinforcements was so great that Kitchener could not but cut down the number of trained officers and N.C.O.'s serving with new units to the irreducible minimum. The 7th Division, as matters were, was barely in

THE KITCHENER ARMIES

time to turn the scale in the bloody and desperate Ypres fighting. The 8th Division arrived just in time to relieve units in which brigades had shrunk to less than the strength of a battalion, which were worn out by days of terrific combat and which could never have withstood, unsupported, a renewed enemy attack.

The same reason, the urgency of the demand for reinforcements from the front, obliged Kitchener to take a measure, the necessity for which he always deplored, and to use a certain number of selected Territorial units as reinforcements for French's hard-pressed troops. These included high-class units, such as the London Scottish, the H.A.C. battalion, the London Rifle Brigade, etc., the ranks of which were filled by men of the stamp who normally take commissions. Kitchener was in any case opposed to any policy of breaking up the Territorial Divisions, and of using their units in an isolated and fragmentary fashion, and he always set his face very sternly against the well-meaning enthusiasts who urged him to send untrained troops, whether Territorials or New Army, to be butchered by thoroughly trained Germans. His reluctance to do this has aroused criticism and given rise to the legend that he underrated the Territorials, and despised them. Thus one critic writes: " The name itself [Territorial] was to him a stumbling block. In the war of 1870 he had been present at a battle on the Loire, probably Le Mans, in which the key of the position, confided to French Territorial troops, had been cast away, entailing the defeat of the whole army. He dwelt upon this incident to me on several occasions, and I know it had created fixed impressions in his mind. Vain to explain how entirely different were the characters of the troops forming the French and British Territorial forces—the former aged conscripts in their last period

THE GREAT MUSTERING

of service; the latter keen and ardent youths of strong military predilections. They were Territorials and that was the end of it."[1] The critic, however, is himself in error. The French Army of 1870 had no troops called Territorials. The troops who behaved badly at Le Mans were not " aged conscripts in their last period of service " but " keen and ardent youths of strong military predilections "; they were in fact the troops raised by the " seemingly dead-paper law," quoted by Sir Ian Hamilton as having come " within an ace of saving France in 1870." The writer is, in fact, confusing the French Army of 1870 with the same Army of 1914, raised, of course, on an entirely different system. Kitchener was quite right in declining to pitchfork British Territorials, at the time almost as untrained as the French Gardes Mobiles of 1870, into a decisive battle. Thus, when it was a case of providing troops in answer to French's desperate plea, he could not do other than take the only troops he had, which, by reason of their more advanced training or of the superior quality of the men in their ranks, might be trusted to give a good account of themselves before the enemy, and he must do this irrespective of his own desire to keep the Territorial Divisions intact or of considerations as to future policy. The London Scottish, the first Territorial battalion to serve in France, arrived there on September 16th. The story of this battalion illuminates the difficulty of working to plan and schedule in war, and perhaps, a certain narrowness in scope and outlook on the part of some very distinguished staff-officers in France. It had always been accepted that Territorial units would be given the opportunity of six months' intensive training before being pitted against a foe. The G.O.C. 2nd

---

[1] *World Crisis*, Vol. I, p. 236.

THE KITCHENER ARMIES

London Division, to which the battalion belonged, had thus carefully drawn up a scheme to train his men mapped out into stages, the first month being devoted purely to thorough grounding in squad drill, the handling of arms, etc. The London Scottish had just completed the first stages of this training when they embarked. Officers and men had had no opportunity to get training in field-work, reconnaissance duties, etc., other than the limited opportunities of their peace-training. It might have been expected that, having been despatched in answer to an urgent call, the battalion would have been sent up somewhere near the fighting line, or at least given an opportunity to fit itself for the ordeal of battle so soon to be thrust upon it. Instead of this it was sent to a base camp and employed on duties which could just as well have been performed by Chinese coolies, but which left the officers no chance to teach either themselves or their men. Then there developed the German offensive. " I am free to confess," writes French, " that on October 15th, 1914, the day on which I date the opening of the Battle of Ypres, I thought that the danger was past. I believed that the enemy had exhausted his strength on the Marne. . . . In my inmost heart, I did not expect I should have to fight a great defensive battle." The London Scottish, forgotten while things were going well, were called to mind so soon as matters were shaping badly. On October 31st they took part in the Battle of Messines, and then learnt for the first time that the rifles with which they had been hastily re-armed, Mark I Lee-Enfields converted to take Mark VII ammunition, could not really take this ammunition, the cartridges jammed in the magazines, and the rifles could only be used as single-loaders. One cannot well conceive a more terrible ordeal for young troops in their first battle

THE GREAT MUSTERING

than to discover that their weapons are almost useless. The fine temper of the battalion stood even this test, but the price paid in lives was terribly high. Much has been written about the Battle of Ypres, both fact and fiction. The one thing which does emerge, and that which brought us victory, was the splendid spirit of the regimental officers and men: like Inkerman and Albuera it was a Soldiers' Victory —won more in despite of bad leadership than as a result of any particular prescience shown by the Higher Command. But the Old Army was virtually annihilated. On November 12th the 1st Guards Brigade could muster only 5 officers and 468 men —out of a round 4000. The London Scottish could show only 280 officers and men out of 980.

The story of the experiences of the London Scottish has carried us somewhat ahead. By the middle of September it was clear that the wave of national enthusiasm roused by the New Armies was carrying the Territorials with it. At a time when every important city was raising " Pals " battalions and units, and the call to join Kitchener's Armies was thrilling through every village and hamlet, the Territorials could not and would not be content with what seemed, in the popular eye, the inferior rôle of Home Defence. Practically simultaneously with the Third New Army, a Fourth was authorised to be formed from the Special Reserve units which, having reached in many cases a strength exceeding 3000 men, were growing so large as to be unwieldy. Twenty-four New Army divisions were thus formed or forming apart from the local battalions and units springing up under private or county auspices. By September 21st, requests from Territorial units to be recognised as foreign service units had become so numerous that, under Army Order No. 399 of that

THE KITCHENER ARMIES

date, a general authority was issued to County Associations to form second-line Territorial units for every Territorial battalion or unit fulfilling the conditions laid down for a foreign service unit. The general idea underlying this circular was the welding of Territorials and New Armies into a single homogeneous national army. In view of the popular enthusiasm, no Territorial battalion, it was felt, would have difficulty in producing 60 per cent. of its war establishment ready to undertake foreign service. It could then recruit under practically the same conditions as a New Army unit. Home Service men could be drafted into the second-line battalions or units and play a valuable part, not only as security against invasion, but in helping to train and assimilate new recruits. The Force could thus be welded into the national army without dislocating it, or pulling it to pieces or rendering it temporarily unable to fulfil its original functions. This was a forecast fully sustained by facts. By the middle of 1915 there had ceased to be any real difference between Old Army, New Armies or Territorials.

In the last days of September 1914 Kitchener took further measures to complete the concentration of the Regular Army. Ten of the fifty-two Regular battalions had already left India by this time, six with the Indian Corps, and four to form a brigade completing the 8th Division. But there still remained in India what were probably some of the very best battalions of our Army, trained and seasoned Regulars at full war strength and without reservists. The War Minister rightly grudged the retention of these fine troops so far from France where they were so urgently needed. On September 30th, therefore, he asked the Wessex Division of Territorials to go to India as a unit and relieve white Regular troops there, explaining that this would enable him to form

THE GREAT MUSTERING

a new Regular Division for immediate service. Unwelcome as was the request to keen troops eager to distinguish themselves against the enemy, a high sense of duty led officers and men to accept the obligation. They were assured that their stay would be only temporary and that their services should count as war service. Kitchener's death prevented the latter promise from being passed into fulfilment, and the exigencies of the war in many cases kept these gallant troops eating their hearts out whilst their comrades were fighting.[1] The Division left for India on October 9th.

---

[1] Mr Winston Churchill's account of this episode in his *World Crisis*, Vol. I, p. 285, is both confused and inaccurate: " My military staff-officer, Major Ollivant, at this stage had a very good idea which provoked immediately far-reaching consequences. He advised me to ask Lord Kitchener for a dozen batteries from India to form the Artillery of the Royal Naval Division, letting India have Territorial batteries in exchange. I put this to Lord Kitchener the same afternoon. He seemed tremendously struck by the idea. . . . Forty-eight hours later, when I returned, I visited Lord Kitchener and asked him how matters were progressing. . . . ' Not only,' he said, ' am I going to take twelve batteries but thirty-one, and not only am I going to take batteries, I am going to take battalions. I am going to take thirty-nine battalions : I am going to send them Territorial divisions instead—three Territorial divisions. You must get the Transport ready at once.' This is very picturesque but it is not history. Kitchener started by sending out one Territorial Division, the Wessex, later 43rd. The Home Counties Division, later 44th, went nearly three weeks later, and the third Territorial Division (45th) was in reality a second-line division formed on cadres left behind by the Wessex in the amazingly short time of eight weeks. Thus a period of close on two months intervened between the despatch of the first and last Territorial Divisions to India. Incidentally Kitchener took not 39 battalions but 44. Earlier on in his book, moreover, Mr Churchill cites a memorandum published by him August 13th, 1911, and quoting Kitchener as then saying that if two native units were taken away for every white unit, white troops could be taken from

THE KITCHENER ARMIES

The Home Counties Territorial Division followed in the footsteps of the Wessex on October 29th, and a second Wessex Division went out on December 12th.

On August 4th the British Empire had declared war on Germany with the idea dominating the official breast that the struggle would be brief if terrific. Our participation would not extend beyond financial support to our Allies, the advantages to be gleaned from our sea-power, and our tiny Expeditionary Force, six divisions and one of cavalry would, it was believed, suffice to turn the scale in a European struggle. The rest of the nation could carry on with "business as usual." It was to be a limited liability war, a glorified South African campaign, something to give the civilian a pleasant titillation as he read the war news in his papers, a thrilling and epic drama at which well-dressed men and women could gaze in comfort from the stalls. Regular staff-officers smiled at the Territorials. They were something to reassure "old women of both sexes." The most venturesome suggested that *perhaps* the Territorials might provide Volunteer Companies for Regular battalions, or even a few selected units. Two months of Kitchener at the War Office had changed all that. The soul of the nation was afire; the tramp of men gathering for the fray rang through city, town and hamlet; the Territorials, transformed into a foreign service army, could look forward to writing their names on the pages of history in a fashion other than as a mere appanage of the Regular Army; with 24 New Army divisions, a total of 38 new divisions were already arming; two new Regular divisions

India and that six divisions could be set free in this manner. Thus it seems doubtful if the suggestion of the "military staff-officer," however estimable an individual, "cut much ice" one way or the other.

THE GREAT MUSTERING

had been formed, three more could be envisaged, troops from Canada, Australia and New Zealand were on the seas. It was a mighty outburst of patriotism, a wave of energy, courage and of general willingness to give, to work and to dare, which was still far from having reached its highest watermark. The men were there, the will was there, the means by which to mould these men into soldiers were still lacking. Yet the people of the Empire were destined to prove to all mankind that the nation, truly great in the arts of peace, can show itself no less great in the arts of war, for it brings to these arts the same spirit of creative energy which it brings to its social life in general. The man accustomed in times of peace to handle bodies of men in industry has learnt much of what is needed to handle them in war; it is no great step for the engineer to turn from handling machine tools to handle a gun—which is also a machine tool although of a different class. The mechanic can grasp without difficulty the principles of a rifle. Thus to transform the mobs of men assembling in their country's cause into trained and efficient soldiers was a matter of time and energy. Of energy there was no lack, but there was grievous lack of time. For the enemy's onrush must be stemmed, the overburdened Allies must be refreshed with the promise of speedy support. Time, in one respect our greatest friend, was in another our greatest enemy, for there was never any certainty as to what the foe might do next, and the drain of battle upon our fighting troops *must* be replaced. Kitchener's problem was simultaneously to provide for replacement and expansion, and both these problems were equally vital, for the collapse of our fighting front in France might spell a moral disaster ruinous to our cause. In those grim days he stood at the War Office, a grand and mighty figure, cool, confident,

THE KITCHENER ARMIES

purposeful, and the tide of British manhood rose up behind him, the voice of the nation cheered his iron resolve, seeing in him the embodiment of their own fighting spirit, absorbing strength from him and giving to him strength back again, the consciousness that the country trusted to him, as he trusted to the country.

V

THE FORGING OF THE GIANT'S SWORD—I

THE translation of a people unarmed and unprepared for war into those hosts of armed and disciplined men who brought low the pride of Germany will always be a study as fascinating to the soldier as it is inspiring to the civilian who puts his faith in democracy as the best form of government which mankind has yet evolved.

In turning to analyse the means by which were wrought that wonderful evolution, first from a tiny professional army, then to a vast volunteer army, and finally into a nation in arms, we may start by quoting two contrasting utterances by Kitchener himself:

" A National Force maintained at a high standard of efficiency can only be produced by the work of years. . . . If plans and essential preparations have been deferred until an emergency arises, it will then be found too late to act, because the strain of passing from peace to war will entirely absorb the energies of all engaged, even when every possible contingency has been foreseen."

" The thorough preparedness of Germany due to her strenuous efforts sustained at high pressure for some forty years, has issued in a military organisation as complex in character as it is perfect in machinery. Never before has any nation been so elaborately organised for imposing her will upon the other nations of the world; and her vast resources of

THE KITCHENER ARMIES

military strength are wielded by an autocracy which is peculiarly adapted for the conduct of war."

The first passage is taken from a memorandum upon the defence of Australia and is the considered counsel of a tried and trusted public servant to the Government which sought his advice, the second is taken from a speech to Parliament and in both is to be seen the thorough grasp by Kitchener of the enormous difficulties to be solved in creating his armies, and his equally just appreciation of the means and resources of the enemy. It was to be a matter of crowding into as many months the work which should have been distributed over as many years; it was to be a matter of expanding, improvising, and adapting whilst the strain of war was entirely absorbing the energies of all engaged; and it was to be a matter of creating, under these difficulties, an army capable of destroying the most perfectly organised and highly trained regular army in Europe. It was perhaps in this keen and vivid realisation of the difficulties to be solved and of the need for solving them, that there is to be found the secret of his extraordinary success.

By the beginning of October the general scheme for the New Armies had already been roughed out. The first three Armies—eighteen divisions with Army troops and auxiliary and ancillary services—were concentrated in the principal training areas in the United Kingdom; a Fourth New Army was in process of being evolved by posting recruits surplus to the needs of the first three Armies to the Special Reserve battalions. These were already much depleted by demands for drafts from the front, and as the fighting around Ypres at the end of October waxed fierce and deadly, the calls for drafts increased in urgency and frequency and reached at last such a pitch that men were being sent to the front with

THE FORGING OF THE GIANT'S SWORD

less than *six weeks'* training. Despite this, however, the flood of recruits was so high that the system introduced, which was that as soon as a Special Reserve battalion reached a strength of 2700 men, a new battalion should be drawn from it, worked well, and in November it was possible to form a new series of battalions which formed the original Fourth Army. But, partly because the training centres were already so crowded with divisions from the first three Armies that it would be impossible for long to concentrate these new divisions for training, partly because it was necessary to have reserve units behind the existing divisions to feed them with drafts, all these battalions and units drawn from Special Reserve units, and known as "K.4" were converted into Reserve units. A new Fourth Army and a Fifth Army were formed subsequently.

In October, Kitchener's main concern was to get afoot as many new units as possible. He had in his mind a clear and definite purpose which was to put in the field as soon as could be, and in the maximum state of efficiency, an army of 70 divisions with all their auxiliary services, supply and medical columns, and, moreover, to build up behind these the requisite organisation for feeding them with drafts and providing for a Home Defence garrison of 8 additional divisions. By the beginning of October, 18 New Army divisions had already been formed, and it was hoped to form 6 additional divisions for the original Fourth New Army. There were, besides, Mr Churchill's Royal Naval Division—soon to give a vivid and public manifestation of the justice of Kitchener's "fixed impressions" as to the unwisdom of using untrained troops against trained Germans—$12\frac{1}{2}$ Haldane Territorial Divisions, 2 of them earmarked for India; there were also 8 Regular divisions formed or forming. A grand total of $47\frac{1}{2}$ divisions, including the original Fourth New Army. This left

THE KITCHENER ARMIES

some 23 divisions still to be formed. Ultimately, as we have seen, the Fourth New Army was converted into draft-producing units, 12 additional New Army divisions were added with reserve units behind them, a Guards Division was formed by adding battalions to Guards regiments and forming the Welsh Guards, 3 new Regular Divisions, the 27th, 28th, and 29th were formed by taking white troops from India. Finally the tale of divisions was completed by filling up the cadres of the second-line Territorial divisions with recruits surplus to the New Armies, and thus forming a new series of what were in reality New Army divisions. It will be observed that Kitchener actually used Guards, Regulars, Territorials and New Armies with entire indifference; he wanted every unit he could lay hands upon and, to phrase it popularly, he didn't care a tinker's curse *what* a unit was so long as it could fit into his scheme, which was to produce a national, general service army, capable of going anywhere and of doing anything. Many people make the mistake of writing about New Armies and Territorials as if these were in some sense rival organisations. But the truth is that they were complementary organisations. Territorials and New Armies fought shoulder to shoulder; they served a common cause; if there was rivalry between them it was a healthy rivalry; if there was competition for recruits the Army as a whole benefited by such competition, for it meant increased efforts to bring men into the ranks; if there was competition for stores and equipment, the result was to open up new sources of supply which were very badly needed. The Territorials, putting out their contracts with local firms, or smaller firms, could cover their own requirements and thus relieve the overburdened War Office.

The complete total of 70 divisions was not, of course, raised at once.

THE FORGING OF THE GIANT'S SWORD

The War Office, under-staffed, overwhelmed with work, could not have undertaken to place on foot immediately so vast a number of men. Thus it was necessary to work on broad outlines, to adapt as much as possible and as quickly as possible from existing civilian resources, and very much had to be left to individual enterprise and energy. It is doubtful whether the annals of war can show any instance of more loyal, whole-souled and whole-hearted teamwork between civilians and soldiers than is to be found in the means and methods by which were raised the New Armies; in fact without this spirit of mutual help, self-help, sympathy and goodwill, the task of raising these armies would have been impossible.

Only part of the administrative burden was directly undertaken by the War Office—the first three Armies and first-line Territorials. As regards the masses of men gathering in cities and hamlets as their ancestors had gathered around the barons of old, burning with civic pride and county patriotism, eager that their cities, shires or boroughs should not be outdone in answering the common call, the system adopted was curiously reminiscent of the mediæval Commissions of Array. Sanction was given to some local authority or magnate to raise a body of men; they were given wide latitude in the appointment of officers; were to undertake all administrative burdens in connection with these new units; were to be responsible for their training and military efficiency until such time as the War Office should be prepared to take them over and to fit them into the general, national Army. In the early phases the part played by the War Office with such units was limited to what are known, in military parlance, as " directives," *i.e.* general directions were issued from time to time to fix a standard to which all units should work. But

THE KITCHENER ARMIES

little effort was made at meticulous supervision. It was a very elastic system, but one which worked well. In some cases the very wide powers given to the " raisers " were abused, local or family influences predominated in the appointment of officers. But as a general rule the standard of keenness and efficiency was high, the character and physique of the men was good, and it was from units raised in this manner that were built up the Fourth and Fifth New Armies.

The first three Armies started with the great advantage that their divisions were concentrated in a single area, and it was possible from the very first to follow a definite programme of training. But even with these Armies the difficulties to be overcome were very great and the call upon the patience, keenness and enthusiasm of the men was a very heavy one. In the case of the local units which were scattered over a wide area and usually without even as much as a single serving Regular officer per battalion, the difficulties of following from the very outset a well-conceived system of training, were wellnigh insuperable.

The first difficulty to be surmounted was the scarcity of senior Regular or ex-Regular officers truly capable of handling so large a formation as a division in the field. Due to the small size of our Army there were very few officers who had practical first-hand experience of what it meant even to handle a brigade, and of the comparatively few who possessed such experience many were too old or unsuitable for other reasons. The problem of finding capable divisional commanders was one which exercised Kitchener sorely, and he looked around with care for suitable selections. In some cases Regular brigadiers were taken from the Expeditionary Force, such as Brig.-Gen. Ivor Maxse, appointed to com-

THE FORGING OF THE GIANT'S SWORD

mand the 18th Division from the command of the 1st Guards Brigade in France; Maj.-Gen. R. H. Davies, C.B., a New Zealander, formerly in command of the 6th Brigade, to command the 20th Division; and Maj.-Gen. E. C. Ingouville-Williams, taken from the 16th Brigade to command the 34th Division. This was an excellent system, as the generals thus promoted were comparatively young, possessed of practical war experience, and were, moreover, men of outstanding ability. But, and particularly at the outset, it was difficult to follow such a system, as the original British Expeditionary Force possessed all told only 18 brigades, and the Army in France could not be deprived of all its best brigadiers.

A second source was to take retired generals who, from their personal character and previous experience, seemed likely to succeed. Thus, for the command of the 23rd Division there was appointed Col. (Hon. Maj.-Gen.) James Melville Babington, an officer with a varied and distinguished record alike in peace and war, and who had spent some time in command of the New Zealand Defence Force. The General was then in his 61st year, but this was among the most successful of all selections. The great difficulty was to find enough really well-qualified men to go round. Since 1909 the drill, tactics, and equipment, of the Army had been revolutionised; the " big " division as it existed in 1914 was a formation which the older generation of officer had never even seen; and even for the keen young brigadiers, suddenly to command close on 20,000 men after having commanded a brigade of 4000 men, represented a big stride forward. The appointments made for the first three Armies were, however, very successful ones.

The appointment of generals to command the new divisions, if a much more complex problem than is

THE KITCHENER ARMIES

popularly realised, was only the prologue to a long list of other obstacles both personal and administrative. Speaking in the House of Lords September 17th, 1914, Kitchener himself gave an outline alike of his future hopes and present perplexities:

" In the response to the call for recruits for the New Armies which it is considered necessary to raise, we have had a most remarkable demonstration of the energy and patriotism of the young men of this country. We propose to organise this splendid material into four new Armies and, although it takes time to train an Army, the zeal and goodwill displayed will greatly simplify our task.

" . . . No effort is being spared to meet the influx of soldiers, and the War Office will do its utmost to look after them and give them the efficient training necessary to enable them to join their comrades in the field. The Divisions of the first two Armies are now being collected at our Training Centres; the Third New Army is being formed on new camping grounds; the Fourth Army is being created by adding to the establishment of the Reserve battalions, from which the units will be detached and organised similarly to the other three Armies. . . .

" In addition to the four new Armies, a considerable number of what may be designated local battalions have been specially raised by the public-spirited initiative of cities, towns or individuals. Several more are in course of formation and I have received many offers of this character. . . .

" If some of those who have so readily come forward have suffered inconvenience they will not, I am sure, allow their ardour to be damped. They will reflect that the War Office has had in a day to deal with as many recruits as were usually forthcoming in twelve months. . . .

THE FORGING OF THE GIANT'S SWORD

" The creation of the New Armies referred to is fraught with considerable difficulties, one of which is the provision of regimental officers. I hope the problem of supplying officers may be solved by the large numbers coming forward to fill vacancies and by promotions from the non-commissioned officer ranks of the Regular forces. In a country which prides itself on its skill in and love of outdoor sports, we ought to be able to find sufficient young men who will train and qualify as officers under guidance of the nucleus of trained officers which we are able to provide from India and elsewhere. If any retired officer competent to train troops has not yet applied, or has not received an answer to a previous application, I hope that he will communicate with me at the War Office in writing.

" But our chief difficulty is one of *matériel* rather than *personnel*. It would not be in the public interest that I should refer in greater detail to this question, beyond saying that strenuous efforts are being made to cope with the unprecedented situation, and that—thanks to the public spirit of all grades in the various industries affected, to whom we have appealed to co-operate with us and who are devoting all their energy to the tasks—our requirements will, I feel sure, be met with all possible speed."

The story of the first three new Armies is a story of muddle which evolved into method; of a confused crowd of men who settled down into an army; of enthusiasm which, starting with a cruelly cold douche of lack of arms, lack of uniforms, lack of quarters, lack of officers, dirt, overcrowding, vermin, and terrible weather conditions—what officer or man who took part in the review of January 22nd, 1915, before Kitchener and M. Millerand, is ever likely to forget it?—continued to be enthusiasm, and gave a splendid

THE KITCHENER ARMIES

foretaste of the spirit which was to carry these troops over the winter in the trenches of 1915 and the ordeal of the Somme which ensued.

The general system with the first three Armies was to collect the men at the regimental depôts and then post them to the various battalions or units formed. An officer from the Cameron Highlanders writes:

" During this period we had great difficulties to contend with. We had to house and feed all recruits; they came in so fast that it was impossible for us to deal with them and despatch them to their units on the same day. It sometimes happened too that although we had practically cleared the barracks one evening there would be some 400 recruits on parade the following morning, these having come in during the night."

Another from the same regiment declares:

" The glamour of the kilt was irresistible. In Glasgow and the West of Scotland hundreds flocked to enlist in the famous regiment. The Glasgow Stock Exchange had, in an incredibly short time, raised a special company of its own, and, not to be outdone, the students of the University followed suit. Then for a few days every north-bound train carried its complement of recruits to the Cameron Depôt; soon the barracks were crowded out, and for a few nights men had to sleep where they could. Even the distillery at Inverness (already with an insect population of its own) was brought into use. Drills there were practically none, for it was impossible to handle the ever-increasing swarms of men. We were all civilians then and from the military point of view had nothing to recommend us save our enthusiasm."

The First New Army started with the advantage of

THE FORGING OF THE GIANT'S SWORD

a small number of Regular officers. Thus, the 8th (Service) Battalion Black Watch, raised by Lord Sempill of Fintray, Aberdeenshire, had the comparatively high number of seven Regular or ex-Regular officers, including the C.O. This battalion was part of the 9th Division.

The Second and Third New Armies were not so fortunate; thus the command of the 9th (Service) Battalion Black Watch, drawn as seen from drafts surplus to the 8th, was given to a retired major; there was a quartermaster, and Lord Sempill gave one of the three Regular officers attached to his own battalion to act as adjutant. There were two or three other Regular second-lieutenants, and a captain from the Reserve of Officers came forward to act first as company commander and then as second-in-command. There was a regimental sergeant-major, pensioned after 29 years' service, and two ex-colour-sergeants. The company officers were nearly all second-lieutenants and few had any previous military experience; there were a few old—and some very ancient—N.C.O.'s.

This was the unpromising start of one of the best battalions of the famous 15th (Scottish) Division. The Division was formed at Aldershot, September 15th, 1914; scarcely a battalion had more than four officers, including the C.O., adjutant and quartermaster. The 7th (Service) Battalion Royal Scots Fusiliers had *one* officer—just commissioned from having been quartermaster-sergeant in the Royal Garrison Artillery! This one officer was in charge of *900* men. The number of serving Regular officers with the Division worked out at less than one per battalion; in no brigade were there more than five Regular officers—including the staff. The senior regimental officers were retired Regulars, Militia officers or Territorials. But what officers there were,

were distinctly *good*. The Divisional Commander was Maj.-Gen. A. Wallace, C.B.; the brigade-commanders were Brig.-Gen. M. G. Wilkinson, M.V.O. (44th Brigade), Brig.-Gen. F. E. Wallerston (45th Brigade), Brig.-Gen. E. J. Cooper, C.B., D.S.O., M.V.O. (46th Brigade).

Accommodation at Aldershot was sorely strained. Barracks meant for one unit must hold two—and recruits continued to pour in. This overflow had to be put into tents, which soon became terribly overcrowded. The Headquarters of the 9th and 15th Divisions shared quarters with two brigade staffs in a building meant to house the staff of one brigade. Officers began to arrive, youngsters from the public schools, business men, medical students. Training was started in earnest and from the very outset the policy was adopted of giving lectures to officers and men after the day's work. There were a few ex-Regular N.C.O.'s, mostly pensioners, and where all were equally ignorant the problem of selecting N.C.O.'s from New Army men was serious. In some battalions there was adopted the expedient of choosing the most smartly dressed men—and most of those thus chosen proved to be excellent! The prevailing spirit was one of desperate keenness. One who shared their hardships writes:

" The discomfort was appalling. Crowded into quarters far too small for them, with one blanket or a piece of tweed apiece to cover them, without mattresses, or even the barest necessities of life, the men never grumbled; they knew that those in authority were doing their best, and were content. Luckily the weather was fine and no sickness broke out, but the first six weeks were anxious ones for the medical officers of the Division. In addition to overcrowding, the feeding of the men left much to be

THE FORGING OF THE GIANT'S SWORD

desired. But these and many other drawbacks, however, did not damp the enthusiasm of the new force. No praise can be too high for these young soldiers at this, the very commencement of their career. Every hardship was more than cheerfully borne. A jest carried things through on the blackest day. The predominant feeling was that they had a task to do and meant to do it."

There was practically no crime, and from the very beginning there prevailed strict order and discipline. Offences were due more to ignorance than to lack of goodwill. If at the outset men smoked perpetually on parade, even on Church Parade during service, and an attack practice was once completely stopped because the men fell out to eat blackberries, these were " teething troubles," inevitable in transforming a mob of civilians into soldiers. All ranks were ten hours a day on parade, including Sundays, and it was a common thing to find groups of young officers or N.C.O.'s studying their drill-books and teaching one another the rudiments of their new profession, long after they had been dismissed. The stamp of man joining up in the Second and Third New Armies was undoubtedly the finest type of British manhood. One company of one battalion (6th Cameron Highlanders) was made up entirely from the Glasgow University and High Schools—the Divisional historian rightly describes it as a shocking waste of good officer material.

On September 26th the Division was reviewed by Their Majesties the King and Queen, accompanied by Lord Kitchener and Sir A. Hunter. Even in their unarmed state and without uniforms the fine appearance of the men, the precision of their movements, despite their brief training, was very apparent. Owing to the shortage of clothing, the men were

THE KITCHENER ARMIES

asked to get good suits, greatcoats and boots from home. The princely sum of ten shillings was promised to every man presenting himself with these useful articles. For men to be excused parades owing to worn boots or general raggedness was in those days a common occurrence. The first consignment of uniform arrived at the end of September and was a weird and wonderful collection of relics of ancient days—scarlet tunics dating from 1893. Some suggested that Noah in a fit of inspiration had brought them with him in the Ark. These were to be worn with blue serge trousers; a few pairs of tartan trews were eagerly snapped up by the N.C.O.'s. One man was heard to remark that he had come down to be a Gordon Highlander, not a b—— postman.

Odds and ends of equipment dribbled along: early in October the first batch of D.P. rifles; shortly afterwards 100 modern rifles per battalion, which were each to form a " service " company for a sudden emergency. Then came a batch of the old buff leather equipment, waistbelts, scabbards and bayonets. Brodrick hats, dating from 1902, turned up and "a curious collection of civilian boots." Poor as the equipment was, there was keen competition to secure it. The quartermaster's motto ran, " Every man for himself." One battalion C.O. was heard proudly to declare that his quartermaster was the finest thief in the British Army.

Between November 16th and December the Division left its cramped quarters at Aldershot, the 44th Brigade moving into billets, and the 45th and 46th into hutments at Bramshott and Bordon.

The 15th Division has been taken as a typical division of the Second New Army. Fine as was the spirit of this division, however, it was not finer than the general spirit of the divisions of this Army; great as were the difficulties to be surmounted, those to be

THE FORGING OF THE GIANT'S SWORD

surmounted by the Third Army divisions were even greater, and those of the First Army divisions were scarcely less formidable. One of the battalion historians complains that " K. 2 " was " nobody's child." It was the younger brother to " K. 1," and considered its elder to be favoured in every respect. " K. 3 " might have referred in similar terms to " K. 2." In the general shortage of equipment the units first raised were first served. Take the 7th (Service) Battalion The King's Shropshire Light Infantry.[1] Formed at Shrewsbury, September 22nd, 1914, it had on October 1st a grand total of 3 officers with even a shadow of military training, 1 major and 2 lieutenants. There were 12 second-lieutenants, lads between 19 and 20, fresh from school. Its first issue of D.P. rifles occurred October 20th. The translation of this crowd into a battalion was not without its element of fun.

Dr Yeatman-Biggs, Bishop of Worcester, found a man breaking down one of his fences for firewood.

" You seem to be making yourself at home," he remarked.

" Yes, the old cock what owns this place won't know it again," came the cheerful answer.

And a man reprimanded for failing to salute the adjutant indignantly protested:

" Why, I 'ardly knows 'im."

The 8th (Service) Battalion East Surrey Regiment was formed on September 10th, 1914, by a lone Regular captain who, waiting at the Government siding at Purfleet, took into custody 1000 recruits who had arrived *sans* officers and *sans* N.C.O.'s " like a football crowd." Of these, 300 were men from Suffolk who really wanted to join a Suffolk regiment, about 200 from Norfolk wanted to join a Norfolk regiment, and there were even a few Welsh

[1] 25th Division, " K. 3."

THE KITCHENER ARMIES

miners. The captain managed to shepherd them somehow or other into the lines of tents waiting dark and silent on the grass, sorted them into squads of 24 men to a tent, warned them that if they went out and lost their tents it was no use coming to him and asking him which was *their* tent; and that it was equally useless to ask him which was 'Arry's or Bill's or Bert's tent. Then he left them to sweet slumber.

In this battalion, the Regular captain trying to lick it into shape being entirely strange to the men under him, selected N.C.O.'s by the simple device of parading the battalion and asking the men who thought they could control six to eight other men to step forward. After some hesitation several men offered themselves, and none of those who thus practically appointed themselves N.C.O.'s did badly —several won commissions.

The 8th East Surreys were part of the 55th Brigade of the 18th Division under the capable command of Gen. Sir Ivor Maxse. The Artillery was even worse off than the Infantry. By November no battery had more than two dozen horses to its 200 men, and for one battery to turn out in marching order meant borrowing horses from others; there was only one wooden gun per battery and it was possible to drill only once a week with a real 18-pounder. There were no dial sights, and wooden sights roughly marked in degrees had to be used for training. Yet this Division was ready to be embarked July 24th, 1915, after about nine months' training, and was soon regarded as in many respects a model Division. The forceful personality of its Divisional Commander and the keen spirit of the men are the real explanation.

The system adopted in forming the first three Armies, and the increasing scale of the difficulties to be overcome may perhaps be best illustrated by taking an average regiment of the line, the Border

THE FORGING OF THE GIANT'S SWORD

Regiment. This regiment recruited from the 34th Regimental District, and had its depôt at Carlisle. After mobilising the Regular Battalion for the Expeditionary Force, and the Special Reserve Battalion, which moved to its war station, there remained at the depôt 1 major (Reserve of Officers), 1 lieutenant (Special Reserve), 1 quartermaster; 1 major, 3 captains, all from the Reserve of Officers, joined the depôt subsequently. To form the 6th (Service) Battalion there were available 1 major, 3 captains (Reserve of Officers), 3 lieutenants and 3 second-lieutenants (Special Reserve). This battalion left at full strength to join the 11th Division " K. 1 " at Belton Park, Grantham. The 7th (Service) Battalion was formed September 7th on a cadre consisting of 1 captain and 1 N.C.O. and left on the 13th of the same month for Wool to join the 51st Brigade of the 17th Division, " K. 2." The 8th (Service) Battalion was a " Pals " unit and left on the 10th September for Codford, Salisbury Plain (75th Brigade, 25th Division, " K. 3 "). The 9th (Service) Battalion was formed and left on the 13th September for Lewes (66th Brigade, 22nd Division, " K. 3 ").

On one day the depôt of this one regiment sent off two full battalions besides a draft of 250 men to the Inniskilling Fusiliers.

An officer who commanded a battalion of the New Army with distinction writes:

" When the earliest units of the New Armies were raised, the commands of Battalions were given to the Regular Majors, who at the outbreak of war were commanding Infantry depôts at home; and a small number of junior Regular Officers was also sent to assist them. This arrangement worked well, as these Officers were accustomed to train young soldiers for

THE KITCHENER ARMIES

the Line Battalions, and fell readily enough into similar work with the New Armies. Moreover, generally speaking, they had now to deal with recruits of the type to which they were accustomed, for although the rank and file of the earliest contingents of volunteers included a fair sprinkling of the educated classes, the great mass was of the class from which the Army was recruited in peace time.[1]

" However the supply of serving Regular Officers was soon exhausted and the duty of commanding and training the new Battalions was then entrusted to a varied selection of men, but primarily to retired Regulars. Some of these were excellent, some were quite unfitted for their task. I can instance the case of a Battalion Commander, whose sole previous experience of war had consisted in 3 years' service (30 years previously) in the Submarine Miners! When I met him he had only just been found out, after mishandling his Battalion for something like 5 months!

" On the other hand the difficulties of these Officers were to some extent met by the fact that the ranks of the 2nd and 3rd New Armies were generally filled by a superior type of citizen; professional men and the like, who on the outbreak of war had either been unable to dispose of their practices and professions at once, or who, with families to consider and provide for, were unwilling to hazard all upon an adventure, which the majority of thinking people thought would be of very short duration.

" These citizens, both Officers and men, under proper tuition, quickly became excellent soldiers, and so appreciably lightened the task of their instructors.

[1] I speak with authority, as in the late August or early September of 1914, I was called upon to select about 1500 of newly joined recruits—men who had enlisted for service with the Expeditionary Force—for posting to the New Army.

THE FORGING OF THE GIANT'S SWORD

I can safely say that I have seldom seen finer bodies of men than many I saw under training with the 24th Division at Shoreham, in the Spring of 1915. They were of the best type of Englishmen—keen, solid, determined, and fit (if properly led and commanded) to go anywhere and do anything.

" What, in my judgement, was the principal fault in the training of many of these new Infantry units was an absence of any approved, systematic method of instruction. Such a method existed, of course, in the elementary training manuals, but many Officers knew little about these books and what they knew they were unable to properly apply. In my own case I had to prepare the daily training programmes for every company, commencing with Squad and Sectional training. And this, in spite of the fact that I had under me several Officers, including a Lieut.-Colonel, who had served in the Regular Army. In the result, the efficiency of a Battalion, in its early and critical days, was largely, if not entirely, in the hands of its Commander, who might or might not be conversant with the basic principles of recruit and company training. The Submarine Officer, before-mentioned, certainly knew ' damn all ' about either!

" One would naturally ask what the formations (whether Brigade or Division) were about to allow this state of things. The answer is that the Commanders of such formations were not always up to their work, or had not grasped the fact that they were supervising recruit, and not trained, battalions. In any case the answer does not exonerate the officials of the Army Council, who should have insisted upon every Officer, N.C.O., and man being trained in the properly progressive way from the very beginning."

It was, however, mainly with the Fourth and Fifth New Armies, 30th to 41st Divisions, that the elements

THE KITCHENER ARMIES

of inco-ordination in the early phases of training were most severely felt, these Divisions being made up of local units, the officers of which, if keen and enthusiastic, did not always possess the qualities needed for training men. With many of these units, officers such as the gallant and able author of these comments, were called in subsequently to polish up and to tauten up the general system of training. In the case of the first three Armies an Army Order, published soon after the declaration of war, laid down the general conditions of training. Courses of six months were provided for all arms, three months being for the recruit stage. Drastic " cuts " were made in the customary programmes of training, everything not absolutely necessary being eliminated. In the Regular Army, with no shortage in equipment, thoroughly trained officers and N.C.O.'s, to pass a soldier through every phase of training, needed about eleven months. When the late Col. Pollock declared it possible to produce a well-trained soldier within six months by methods of intensive training, most soldiers shook their heads. But to do this in the face of lack of instructors, lack of arms, barracks, uniforms, or equipment, was a wellnigh insuperable achievement, and the marvel will always be that so much was done under circumstances of such appalling difficulty.

Take a division of the Third New Army, the 23rd Division, study the Order of Battle of this Division, consider all that had to be done to transform it from a mere agglomeration of unarmed men into a highly trained and flexible organism. There were three brigades:

The 68th Brigade. Col. G. H. Ovens, C.B.

10th (Service) Northumberland Fusiliers.
11th (Service) Northumberland Fusiliers.
12th (Service) Durham Light Infantry.
13th (Service) Durham Light Infantry.

THE FORGING OF THE GIANT'S SWORD

The 69th Brigade. Brig.-Gen. F. S. Derham, C.B.
11th (Service) West Yorks.
8th (Service) Yorks.
9th (Service) Yorks.
10th Duke of Wellington's West Riding Regiment.

The 70th Brigade. Brig.-Gen. Sir D. A. Kinloch, Bart., C.B.
11th (Service) Sherwood Foresters.
8th (Service) York and Lancaster.
9th (Service) York and Lancaster.
8th (Service) King's Own Yorkshire Light Infantry.

Army Troops

8th (Service) The Leicestershire Regiment.
9th (Service) The Leicestershire Regiment.
9th (Service) South Staffordshire Regiment.

Of these, the 9th South Staffordshire was converted into a Pioneer Battalion and remained with the Division; the 8th and 9th Leicestershire were transferred to another division.

Thirteen battalions of unarmed and untrained men do not, of course, make up a division; there were needed, even on the 1914 establishment, twelve batteries of artillery, engineer and signal units, ammunition and supply columns, field-hospitals, etc., and staffs to control all these. It may be of interest to trace the steps by which all these were built up.

The Division concentrated September 16th, the 68th Brigade at Bullswater, the 69th and 70th Brigades at Frensham. It was a vast crowd of civilians, something like what is seen on a Bank Holiday, rather a jolly good-humoured crowd of big, strapping fellows whose underlying earnestness did not check a certain sense of fun. There were very few officers. The hard-worked War Office had made a mistake with the orders. Headquarters were temporarily fixed at the Pond Hotel. The Division went under canvas October 4th. Major H. J. Bartholomew, D.S.O., turned up as G.S.O. 2, but there were still only a handful of officers—even when all had received the right orders. There were no clerks; orders had to be passed from mouth to mouth. And now there sets in a process of rapid evolution. Men with experience of clerical work are collected from various units, typewriters are acquired, office-stationery appears. Two motor-cars become available, local companies of Boy Scouts do yeoman and willing service as orderlies. The principal difficulty is—cooks. As the Divisional historian plaintively remarks in any collection of Englishmen, one can find any trade under the sun save the man who can cook your dinner. The general summarily disposed of this difficulty by placing a contract with Messrs Lyons & Co. to feed his men while cooks were being trained; for the officers there were established brigade-messes under caterers. The men at first made a grotesque appearance on parade in odds and ends of semi-military, semi-civilian garb. Officers chaffingly remarked that this had its favourable side; it enabled them to distinguish one man from another. One company commander proudly displayed an individual resplendent in a bowler hat, khaki jacket, blue trousers, and smart brown boots. But most of the men had joined in their oldest civilian clothes, which were reduced to rags under stress of training. Gen. Babington obtained authority to spend £17,000 on clothing—which worked out at less than £1 per man—and promptly despatched two officers connected with the clothing trade to Yorkshire to purchase 20,000 sets of underwear and as many pairs of boots. It was not until the middle of October that an emergency blue uniform began to

THE FORGING OF THE GIANT'S SWORD

be available. The men were crowded 13 and 14 to a tent, and for a considerable time there were no tent-boards. Fortunately the weather was fine. A good-tempered, willing crowd, the men, of course, lacked the most elementary notions of military etiquette. The general, one of the few figures who then wore khaki, moved freely around the camp, talking to the men. One of them was subsequently told that he should have stood to attention, and was asked if he knew who the general was. The answer came: " I doan't rightly know who 'e be, but I reckon 'e be one o' t' Directors."

The First New Army had as many as six serving Regular officers per battalion, but the Second and Third New Armies had not more than one serving Regular officer per battalion to act as adjutant—and not always that. Other officers comprised:

Battalion C.O.'s and senior majors, mostly retired from the British or Indian services or ex-Militia officers—" dug-outs." The value of these officers varied very greatly. Mention has already been made of the revolutionary changes in the drill, tactics and equipment of the Army after 1909. Officers who had left the service before this—who were, of course, the vast majority—were out of touch with these new developments. Others again, the older generation, themselves trained in the *régime* of " Adjutant *cum* Sergeant-Major," had no idea of how to handle and train a mob of recruits. The very keenest element amongst retired Regular officers, unless crippled by financial reasons, already held commissions in Special Reserve, Territorial, or Yeomanry formations and could not always be spared from these. Such officers when available were the pick of the " dug-out " type, since they were well abreast of the latest developments. A very good class of retired officer was the type who disliked equally the routine of peace-time soldiering

THE KITCHENER ARMIES

and the social claims of service with auxiliary units, but who came back to the service at the very first call, drawn by mingled patriotism and a sense of adventure, and who, in a cool nonchalant fashion, was a master of those elements of soldiering which really matter. Some of the retired officers set to work with desperate keenness to make themselves efficient and to make others efficient also. Others were good average regimental officers, others again were either too old or else naturally incompetent. These, however, were only a small percentage, and as a class the retired Regular officers did fine work and deserved well of their country.

The ex-Militia or Volunteer officers had in many cases seen service in South Africa. The best type was a very good type with a rough and ready but sound grasp of the administrative work of a company, and a knack of handling men. Their chief defect was a disposition to set men to run before they had learnt to walk. They did not always grasp the importance of starting from the beginning, underrated the need for thorough and systematic *drilling*, failed to follow a well-thought-out and progressive system of training. But given a competent and up-to-date Regular officer to act as adjutant, these were defects which could be successfully countered.

Although one of Kitchener's earliest measures was to shorten the courses for Woolwich and Sandhurst, raise the age of entry to twenty-five, and to abolish all fees, thus quadrupling the annual output of officers, the casualties among Regular officers were so great that almost all these officers were absorbed in replacing them.

A certain number of commissions were given to Regular and ex-Regular warrant officers and N.C.O.'s. Many of these men did excellently and rose to the rank of captain; all did very useful work. Their chief

THE FORGING OF THE GIANT'S SWORD

defect as a class was lack of initiative and red-tapeishness.

Mention has already been made of Kitchener's efforts to attract young men of good quality to serve as officers. An officer who commanded a Special Reserve battalion at this time writes:

" Applicants for commissions were arriving at all hours and were accepted or rejected in a very short time. I only remember one acceptance which afterwards turned out badly. This was a gentleman of about my own age whom I accepted as a subaltern on the strength of a public school and other recommendations. However he proved to be a secret drinker, and when told he must give it up or go, chose the former alternative, with the result that he became so unwell that he had to be invalided out. The doctor told me that the sudden change to temperate habits had been too much for a constitution fed entirely on alcohol."

Douglas Story, the War Correspondent, joining this battalion, was made a captain straight away. Considerations as to seniority in fact were very generally disregarded in the desire to get the best man available, whoever and whatever he might be. No one who carefully studies the measures actually introduced during this period can fail to be struck by the very broad latitude given to commanding officers, and that the charges as to over-centralisation, as applying to the New Armies, often brought against the War Office, are singularly ill-founded. The officer already quoted goes on to state that the range and status of applicants for commissions increased rapidly. There were several lawyers among them, and the C.O. considered that his best " find " during those days was an actuary from Hong Kong whom he promptly put in the office to deal

THE KITCHENER ARMIES

with War Office memoranda needing abstruse calculations.

The bulk of the officers needed were found by granting temporary commissions to civilians who seemed suitable in age and other respects. The Public Schools and Universities supplied a large number, mostly excellent, and some of whom had received at least an outline training in the O.T.C. These did excellent work. Almost from the outset of the Volunteer Movement, most of the larger Public Schools and Universities had established Cadet Corps, Volunteer Companies, or Volunteer Battalions. One of Lord Haldane's happiest conceptions was to transform these into Officers' Training Corps. There were twenty-two units of the Senior Division (Universities and Inns of Court) and over one hundred Junior units (Public Schools). The standards and value of the training received fluctuated greatly. Some units were markedly good, others were poor. But they provided a number of men and boys who had at least an inkling of military training. Unfortunately the number even of these were far too few, and commissions had to be given to large numbers not alone of Public School and University men who had done no O.T.C. training, but to civilians in general who lacked even the rudiments of the professional knowledge required.

Among the best sources for junior officers for the New Armies were numbers of young men settled in the colonies or in foreign countries, and who flocked back to the Mother Country to offer their services.

The means adopted to supply officers for the technical and scientific corps such as the Royal Engineers, Army Service Corps, Royal Army Medical Corps, Army Ordnance Corps, Pioneer Battalions, and to a certain extent the Royal Artillery, vividly illustrate the general principle of team-work between

THE FORGING OF THE GIANT'S SWORD

soldiers and civilians which so powerfully contributed to the successful raising of the New Armies. The War Office and the heads of the civil professions worked hand in hand. Thus, officers for the Royal Engineers Field Companies were recommended by the President of the Institution of Civil Engineers, and by the Universities; Royal Engineers Railway Companies received their officers on nomination from the principal railway companies at home and abroad; the Tunnelling Companies of the same corps had their officers selected by the Mining Institutions of Great Britain. The Institutes of Chartered Accountants and of Civil Engineers were similarly asked to recommend candidates for the Army Service Corps alike for clerical work and for mechanical transport companies.

In this fashion the work of building up auxiliary and ancillary formations for the New Army divisions moved parallel with the formation of the Infantry units, but the difficulties to be solved with these highly technical services were even greater. Officers for Royal Engineers' units were sent for a seven weeks' course to Chatham; Artillery officers went for a similar course, first to one of the twelve reserve brigades established for training purposes, then for a month to Shoeburyness or Larkhill. But in so technical an arm as artillery the deficiencies in *matériel* were very serious. Dummy wooden guns could be made by enthusiastic officers to teach the elements of gun-drill; the 15th Division equipped itself with *wooden horses*, but the absence of dial-sights, range-finders, directors, without which a modern battery is almost helpless, was calculated to baffle the most ingenious.

Here is an outline of the evolution of the 23rd Divisional Artillery.

" We arrived," writes an officer, " to find the camp

deserted." A sergeant of the Army Ordnance Corps informed the wandering sheep that the Divisional Artillery was not being formed until Monday, November 9th. But a gentleman " in civvies " had been looking round the camp that day. This turned out to be Col. (later Brig.-Gen.) Elmslie, who was to command the Divisional Artillery. On Monday, November 9th, four more second-lieutenants were discovered meandering round, and whilst the Colonel was introducing himself, a sixth made his appearance. The Colonel called his officers into a marquee, gave them an outline as to what divisional artillery is supposed to be, and lo and behold the 23rd Divisional Artillery came officially into existence at Mytchett Camp, Aldershot; four brigades, each commanded by a second-lieutenant.[1]

The responsibility upon these young officers, however, was not unduly great, as there were no guns, no food and no men. Men began to arrive the following morning ; the camp was divided into four parts ; each man was given a blanket and a pudding-basin—the four brigades were *formed*. Training was at first a matter of squad drill and gun-pit digging, the appearance of the men with spade, pickaxe and the inevitable pudding-basin being a source of fun to the observers—if not to themselves. Some senior N.C.O.'s arrived to help in training but the equipment of the gunners continued to lag even behind that of the Infantry. The four brigades had between them *one* bandolier, proudly disported by the man on guard, who handed it over to the relieving sentry as a rare and precious heirloom.

Despite this, competition between brigade and brigade was keen, which the Colonel stimulated by

[1] 102nd Brigade, 2nd Lieut. Dawin ; 103rd Brigade, 2nd Lieut. Moss ; 104th Brigade, 2nd Lieut. Rusel ; 105th Brigade, 2nd Lieut. Hewit-Taylor.

THE FORGING OF THE GIANT'S SWORD

offering a flag to be given to the best all-round brigade at the end of each month. At the end of November there was great excitement, a party was to fetch guns. These turned out to be 27 old French 90 mm. But there were no horses and the guns must be man-handled. In December, by which time the 102nd and 103rd Brigades had moved to Ewshott, and the 104th and 105th to Lille Barracks, Aldershot, horses and equipment began to arrive, driving drill commenced in earnest, senior officers relieved second-lieutenants in command of brigades. By June 1915, 18-pounders and 4.5 in. howitzers, horses, harness, were streaming in, several Artillery officers arrived from a three weeks' tour in France, and the brigades came on in efficiency at a phenomenal pace. Even if the C.R.A. *did* inaugurate a lecture by inquiring blandly " if they realised that they couldn't *damned well shoot?* " it must be agreed that, " The training of the Artillery will always remain one of the most remarkable features of the war."

On September 29th, 1914, the Infantry of the 23rd Division had their first inspection by Their Majesties the King and Queen and H.R.H. The Princess Mary. Training began in earnest, greatly helped by the handful of ex-Regular N.C.O.'s. These were, of course, somewhat rusty, and if the New Army men got an impression of the Regular N.C.O. as a somewhat fatherly type, the age and loving-kindness of these patriarchs was responsible. In October, 100 Lee-Metford rifles were issued to each battalion for training purposes, and were passed round from squad to squad. In November, eight short Lee-Enfields arrived per battalion to be used for instruction. " Go think of it in silence and alone." Eight modern rifles for a thousand men. Parallel with these eight rifles there arrived 400 sets of old-fashioned equipment. Ancient water-bottles

THE KITCHENER ARMIES

and white haversacks did not appear till December to the accompaniment of " a horrible blue serge emergency uniform impossible to smarten up save by brass buttons." But despite all difficulties, training was carried on at high pressure—eight to ten hours a day, including Sundays. One of those who took part in this strenuous training writes: " Sometimes we did two hours' battalion drill before breakfast and *we liked it*." Owing to lack of equipment the early stage was devoted to squad drill, physical training, running, marching, night-work and entrenching. When it became apparent that owing to lack of equipment there was no chance of the Division going abroad till the following Spring, training was relaxed to the extent of Sunday being made a rest day.

December 1st and 2nd the Division went into barracks at Aldershot: the 68th and 69th Brigades to the North Camp, where they joined the field companies R.E., which were going through a terribly hard training; the 70th Brigade went to the Stanhope lines.

Trench warfare having set in in France, it was decided to add a Pioneer Battalion to each division. A census taken in each battalion as to the trades and occupations of the men showed the 9th South Staffordshire as having the highest proportion of suitable trades, and this battalion was thus converted into a Pioneer Battalion—with a welcome addition of twopence a day to the pay of the men.

On January 26th, 1915, divisional training began, and the 23rd Division moved in three columns to the Shorncliffe area, February 24th. Shortly before— and thanks to the wiliness of the Divisional Commander—they got the coveted khaki. Gen. Babington himself tells the story.

" The issue came about in this wise. I happened to be in the C.O.O.'s office and found him talking

THE FORGING OF THE GIANT'S SWORD

on the telephone to his Chief at the War Office. I said, ' Tell him to let us draw khaki.' The answer was, ' Impossible.' I then said, ' Tell him Lord K. is going to inspect us.' We got the khaki at once." Kitchener did, in fact, inspect two columns on the march, February 28th. One suspects that some little bird must have whispered this in advance to Gen. Babington.

In June 1915 the Division got its full issue of service rifles. Musketry was carried out at high pressure at Woolmer and Longmoor. Divisional and brigade staffs went to France for a week on one of those invaluable " Cook's Tours " to the fighting front which did so much to freshen up training at home.

At about this time the Divisional historian notes the case of an officer who, after having been on duty all night, fell asleep during a lecture, and was reprimanded by the lecturer. It is not without a touch of sardonic humour that the narrator recalls the horror this aroused. A long course of Army lectures, not always given in a very inspired fashion, caused them to be treated subsequently with less reverence.

About this time there also happened the episode of the half battalions which set out to practise that difficult operation, an encounter action. The scouts of each completely missed the other, and the antagonists finally blundered against one another, each in column of route. The battalion, the Pioneers, had been going through an intensive course of training in its own special branch, but the thing caused a roar of laughter. As the Divisional historian wisely remarks, such an incident is even more effective than war itself in showing the need for unceasing vigilance.

Mobilisation stores arrived at the end of July, including G.S. and limbered wagons, and hearts beat

THE KITCHENER ARMIES

high with hope as the prospect came nearer and nearer that the Division would join its comrades of the New Armies, who had already left for the front. A fever of impatience and a passion for efficiency to the *nth* degree seized on all ranks. The voice of guns was in the air, echoes from a distant past seemed to fire those young hearts, once again men murmured, " Fair sets the wind for France," those magic words, so oft repeated in those days yet never hackneyed, the spirit of the dead who yet lived and beckoned to others to follow in their footsteps.

On August 16th the Division had its last review before the King-Emperor and his Consort at Hankley Common. The Sovereigns had seen them earlier, not quite eleven months before, a mob of unarmed men, conspicuous only for their fine physique. Now they swept past, a highly disciplined, highly trained fighting force, afire with enthusiasm, aglow with *esprit de corps*, knitted together from a crowd of men into a single whole, as flexible as tempered steel, as hard and as keen, possessed of that corporate spirit which makes a division responsible to a single directing will, aflame with that pride in the Division which was so marked a feature alike with Old Army, New Army, and Territorials. There stretched behind them a dreary path illuminated but by the glowing torch of their own high courage and spirit of achievement, before them stretched a path more perilous still, an ordeal such as man has never faced before—and which it may be hoped he will never face again. They brought to this ordeal the same high temper which had carried them over the lesser but *nagging* ordeals of their early training—and if they died they did not die in vain.

Before we leave this Division to embark some ten days later upon the Great Adventure from which so

THE FORGING OF THE GIANT'S SWORD

sadly few were to return, one may perhaps quote a letter illustrating what was the real spirit of these men, decent, honest, God-fearing Englishmen:

"DEAR GENERAL BABINGTON,

"Now that the troops under your command have left Farnham, will you allow me, on behalf of the Committee which has run the Recreation Room in Farnham and also on behalf of the Farnham people to wish officers, N.C.O.'s and men God-speed and good luck? We very much appreciate the consistent excellent behaviour of the troops, and it has been a great pleasure to have had the opportunity to do something in a small way for their pleasure whilst at Farnham. Again I say, good luck to them all.

"Yours sincerely,
"(Sgd.) EDGAR KEMPSON."

The Mayor of Folkestone wrote in similar terms and referred specially to the "earnest yet cheerful" demeanour and "exemplary behaviour of the men."

VI

THE FORGING OF THE GIANT'S SWORD—II

THE 23rd Division has been taken as a typical division of the Third New Army. Its experiences were no different from those of the 21st, 22nd, 24th, 25th or 26th Divisions, nor did it surmount its difficulties with a finer spirit or march to battle with keener zest. The 20th (Light) Division, one of the group which comprised the 15th, 16th, 17th, 18th and 19th Divisions, had experiences only slightly dissimilar. Formed at Blackdown Camp, Aldershot, the original Order of Battle ran:

       59th Brigade. Brig.-Gen. G. Leslie

          10th King's Royal Rifle Corps.
          11th King's Royal Rifle Corps.
          10th Rifle Brigade.
          11th Rifle Brigade.

       60th Brigade. Col. A. E. W. Colville, C.B.

6th Oxfordshire and Buckingham Light Infantry.
6th King's Shropshire Light Infantry.
12th King's Royal Rifle Corps.
12th Rifle Brigade.

       61st Brigade. Col. O'D. C. Grattan, D.S.O.

11th Durham Light Infantry.
7th Prince Albert's (Somerset Light Infantry).
7th King's Own Yorkshire Light Infantry.
7th Duke of Cornwall's Light Infantry.

THE FORGING OF THE GIANT'S SWORD

Divisional Artillery. Brig.-Gen. John Hotham
- 90th Field Artillery Brigade.
- 91st Field Artillery Brigade.
- 92nd Field Artillery Brigade (Howitzers).
- 93rd Field Artillery Brigade.

Divisional Engineers
- 83rd Field Company R.E.
- 84th Field Company R.E.
- 96th Field Company R.E.

Signal Service
- 20th Div. Signal Company R.E.
- 20th Div. Train.

Medical Units
- 60th Field Ambulance.
- 61st Field Ambulance.
- 64th Field Ambulance.[1]

The Division started life with the 59th and 60th Brigades at Blackdown. The Artillery was nearby at Deepcut, the 61st Brigade was at Aldershot and went later to Woking. The R.E. units were at Chatham, the field ambulances at Aldershot, where they were training hard till June 1915.

No uniforms were available till November, when one suit of emergency blue was served out per man. A small batch of D.P. rifles arrived about the same time, and there were so few S.M.L.E. rifles that only one company could fire at a time. The Artillery had at first only enough harness for one six-horse team per brigade—of three batteries. Shortage of saddles was made good by private gifts. Each brigade had

---

[1] At the end of 1914, the 11th Durham Light Infantry, made up mainly of miners, were transformed into Pioneers and the 12th King's Liverpool Regiment took their place in the 61st Brigade.

THE KITCHENER ARMIES

only two 90 mm. guns and two 15-pounder guns. These had no sights, and wooden sights and wooden guns must be improvised to carry out battery drill. In February, one 18-pounder gun was issued to each battery. In the matter of retired Regular, Militia or Volunteer officers, and young Public School or 'Varsity men, or civilians of the stamp suitable for officers, this Division, in common with all the divisions of the First and Second New Armies, was somewhat better off than the Third Army. For by the time this Army was formed the supply from the Public Schools and Universities had run short, not only on account of the large number of new units already on foot, but because so many men of the " officer type " had enlisted direct into the ranks either of high-class Territorial units, or of " Pals " battalions. The alacrity with which men even of the very highest classes shouldered a rifle in the ranks had its awkward side, but it was a practical evidence of patriotism, the value of which can be scarcely overestimated. For the effect would hardly have been stimulating had every man of gentle birth or superior education shown eagerness to secure a safe or snug billet for himself whilst calling upon lesser men to do their duty to the country. The University professor who acted as a cook in his battalion was no doubt doing work which men without professorial degrees could have done much better. But he was at least giving a proof that he loved his country more than his own ease. Of the better-class men who joined up in this fashion moreover, most, ultimately, took commissions, and their training in the ranks, if rough, was a very sound and practical training for the work of handling men. There was in the 20th (Light) Division the usual shortage of trained officers and instructors. One or two experienced officers, however, were found for each battalion and there

THE FORGING OF THE GIANT'S SWORD

were a few re-enlisted N.C.O.'s. In February 1915 the Division went to camp at Whitley, which was a sea of mud with unfinished and leaky huts. Despite this the men continued keen and training became interesting. The issue of service dress begun at Blackdown Camp was completed; large numbers of horses, guns, and equipment became available for the Artillery. The Divisional Ammunition Column was made up with mules and formed under command of Lieut.-Col. J. R. Foster—then over sixty and who did well enough to retain his command all through the war. At the beginning of April the Division marched sixty-three miles in four days—not a bad performance for such young troops. There followed three months' hard work, including field-firing and night operations. The final touch before going overseas was the divisional training at Salisbury Plain. The Division embarked for France July 20th, 1915, after about ten months' training.

The famous review by Lord Kitchener and M. Millerand, January 22nd, 1915, cannot be omitted from any account of the early trials of the New Armies. It figures in every battalion and divisional history of the units taking part in it. One writes:

" Few who were present on that occasion are likely to forget it. Snow commenced to fall shortly after the battalion left Liss and continued until Frensham was reached, by which time everyone was wet through. After forming up, the Division waited in a biting wind for two hours before Lord Kitchener's party arrived. The inspection consisted of a hurried walk along a road, along each side of which the Division was drawn up. The whole ceremony lasted barely ten minutes, after which the half-frozen troops marched back to billets. The distance the 9th Battalion covered that day was twenty-eight miles,

THE KITCHENER ARMIES

the return journey through mud and slush being exceptionally trying, but only three men fell out."

Owing to the scarcity of rifles the men who proudly possessed them were put in front and Kitchener, who was not anxious that the bareness of our military cupboard should be fully disclosed, even to our Allies, diplomatically made the bad weather an excuse for cutting the review short. But the sharp-eyed French War Minister was not lightly to be deceived, and he was heard to remark that very few of the men had rifles.

In an order dated January 23rd, 1915, Gen. Sir A. Hunter, commanding Aldershot Training Centre, congratulated the troops and said: "They will understand that paramount considerations necessitated this demand on their personal exertions regardless of the weather conditions, which have been without parallel even in this wet winter." Adding: "The Secretary of State for War has desired that every officer and man on parade should be told of the satisfaction with which he noted the splendid bearing and appearance of all ranks and the pleasure with which he inspected so fine a body of troops."

Whilst during October 1914 the eighteen divisions of the first three New Armies were settling down to their arduous training, the war was in progress and national feeling was surging high. By October 11th the administrative work connected with the New Armies had progressed sufficiently for the "dam" on recruiting to be raised. The physical standard was reduced to 5 feet 5 inches. Some three weeks later this was again reduced to 5 feet 3 inches.[1] The terrific fighting around Ypres reached its climax and died down, leaving battalions and brigades mere shadows

[1] November 5th, 1914.

THE FORGING OF THE GIANT'S SWORD

of noble regiments—the men gaunt, hollow-cheeked spectres, dazed and bewildered and tried to uttermost limits of human endurance. The Indian Corps and 8th Division were now in line, but no one could say with certainty when and where the enemy would renew his onset. It was a matter of taking whatever troops could be spared to buttress up the shaky bulwark. Picked Territorials from all over Great Britain: the 9th Highland Light Infantry, 5th Cameron Highlanders, 13th County of London, The Queen's Westminsters, the Northampton Yeomanry, to mention only a few fine corps taken at random, went off to France until, by the beginning of 1915, no less than twenty-three Territorial battalions were sandwiched into Regular brigades, usually forming the fifth battalions of such brigades. But these Regular brigades were themselves no longer the splendidly trained units of August 1914. The losses in officers had been even greater than the losses in men.

"It was a fortunate matter for the country," writes an officer, "and a matter never really realised, that the two most important essentials for the soldier (after the first three months of the war) were courage and the ability to use his rifle. Had he been required to take the field with the knowledge of his profession and physical fitness necessary for open warfare, the situation would have been indeed serious."

The strain on the Special Reserve battalions to replace losses in the field was a very heavy one. The supply of trained or even partially trained officers and men was soon exhausted, whilst the necessity of providing a multiplicity of guards—mostly quite superfluous—cut heavily even into the limited opportunities available for training men about to be sent swiftly into battle. The type of elderly general in charge of Home Defence was more fussy than fear-

THE KITCHENER ARMIES

some—at least to an enemy. The officer from whom the above extract has been quoted relates how one of the type having read something about "Cossack Posts" in the *Training Manual* demanded why he had no "Cossack Posts" out—which meant that next day a line of posts had to be spread out confronting the "hostile" town of Maidstone. Of course, as soon as the general departed, the posts were withdrawn, but in the meantime the men had been taken from their training.

The surge of circumstance was such as badly to cut into any carefully designed and well-thought-out scheme of national military expansion: what had to be followed was a policy sufficiently elastic to provide for the unforeseen and unforeseeable. The most urgent need was to have a few good units on hand—for most of the Regular units at the front were mere simulacra, their ranks filled up with hastily or partially trained men, their officers in like case. Thus, as the Regular units dribbled in from India, they were collected into three new divisions, the 27th, 28th and 29th—the last soon to earn for itself an immortal name at Gallipoli. Theoretically it would have been better to have used these units to help in training the New Armies. In practice, these Divisions were authorised in November when the pressure on the fighting front was very great, whilst Kitchener, keenly conscious of the deficiencies of the New Armies in arms and equipment, was apprehensive at this time that the enemy might open a new offensive before the New Armies were ready. It was always his policy, during all this critical period, that "a bird in the hand is worth two in the bush." No soldier ever saw farther ahead or was more deeply conscious of future needs, no soldier was ever more reluctant to purchase the future at the cost of the present. His reluctance to break up good Regular units was

THE FORGING OF THE GIANT'S SWORD

inspired by the same policy which made him reluctant to break up the Territorial Divisions and which led him to adopt the simple standpoint, " first come, first served " with his own New Armies. Theoretically it seems incorrect to give a division of the First New Army six Regular officers per battalion, whereas divisions of the Second and Third New Armies had barely one Regular officer per battalion, or to give the First New Army battalions 400 service rifles apiece when the others had only 100 such rifles. Practically, however, it was a very sound policy, for, given any sudden emergency, one good division actually in being and to hand is worth any number of divisions which may be ready at some future date. Take that fine Division the 46th (South Midland). A Territorial Division, it could, upon mobilisation and after dismissing to second-line units men unwilling to serve abroad, produce an average of some 600 men per battalion who knew at least the rudiments of their job; moreover, it was in the position of being able to clothe the recruits needed to bring it to war establishment in khaki, and arm them with rifles; deficiencies in horses, harness, etc., could quickly be made good; its batteries were actually equipped with 15-pounder quick-firers, whilst New Army batteries were training with dummy wooden guns. But the arms and equipment which barely sufficed for the needs of the 46th Division, would have been ludicrously inadequate if divided evenly with the 18th and 23rd Divisions, its staff would have been similarly swamped. Thus Kitchener, instead of having one division fully armed and equipped, able to start immediately with a programme of intensive training, would merely have had three divisions, all in an equal state of poverty and disorganisation. What would have happened had the enemy made a raid on our shores? Or if he

THE KITCHENER ARMIES

had renewed his offensive in France? It is useless to look at these problems in the light of our afterknowledge, or from the standpoint of an office armchair. We must study them from the point of view of the man who had to solve them—and take the standpoint of a practical soldier. As matters were, the 46th Division was able to leave for France nearly three months before the first of the New Armies to do so, and was a welcome and powerful reinforcement to Sir John French's Army.

The period during which the first three New Armies were being trained and equipped for their grim and terrible ordeal might be compared to the rise of a fierce and tempestuous sea; it was an almost elemental process and one which passed the wit of even the most tried and experienced leader entirely to control and guide. It was a social cataclysm, a swell of passions, hatreds, energy, hope and despair, crosscurrents of human passions, swirling and eddying, to be caught in a series of great tidal waves sweeping aside old precedents, quenching established habits of thought, uniting all in a vast upheaval, a volcanic outpouring of explosives, men and metal, hurled at the enemy's lines. It was a process too vast to be controlled by books, rules and formulæ, the elements of which were in many respects incalculable; the wisest leader was he who knew how to tack and veer in the tempest, when to take and when to *give*.

Kitchener's cry at this time was perpetually for men, but if to train even keen and enthusiastic men amidst the paucity of trained and competent instructors, and with dummy guns and wooden rifles, was very difficult, to have trained *unwilling* men, under such conditions would have been a rank impossibility. In those great volunteer armies, and during the early stages, discipline was a matter, to a far greater extent than is popularly realised, of the

THE FORGING OF THE GIANT'S SWORD

natural self-respect of the men, and of their *willingness* to learn. The Regular captain who found himself in charge of a mob of 1000 recruits had no means actually available to *enforce* discipline. He could not have fought a thousand men with his bare hands, he could not have shot a thousand men with a revolver—he would have been *lynched* if he had tried. But with any Regular officer of average common sense, no need for *enforcing* discipline arose—at least no need opposed to that of the general instinct of the men themselves.

This instinct was against rowdyism, opposed to insubordination; it was not a matter of ramming discipline and training down men's throats, but of leading and instructing a crowd of eager and enthusiastic volunteers, desperately keen on learning their jobs. But a collection of surly, sullen, unwilling conscripts could not have been forced to submit to discipline—on a basis of one trained officer to a thousand men. They would not have shown the same patience under the hardships of the early training conditions as was shown by the volunteer soldiers of the New Armies; they would not have brought to the study of an unwelcome profession the same quick intelligence and the same eager zest. Thus, when one considers all the difficulties which had to be solved, and when one brings to these problems the mind and spirit of a practical soldier, one soon reaches the conclusion that conscription, whilst necessary in the later phases of the war—when there were available an adequate supply of trained officers and N.C.O.'s capable of *enforcing* discipline, no shortages in the matter of quarters, uniforms, arms and equipment—to hamper training, and machinery to check desertion—would have been, and from purely military grounds, a very disastrous measure if attempted earlier.

THE KITCHENER ARMIES

Failing conscription, the only means of getting men was to appeal to the country's patriotism; to educate public opinion as to the national peril. Thus, after the lowering of the physical standard there followed a recruiting campaign to attract men to the ranks, upon a scale which would have been inconceivable before the war. The three great parties pooled their resources in the way of propaganda, platform speakers, posters, etc.; every device which human ingenuity could suggest was employed to reach the public consciousness, to appeal to local and civic pride. Recruiting marches were held, convalescent officers and soldiers were asked to address meetings, the country was deluged with posters, some artistic, some dignified, some sentimental—for the British *are* a sentimental race. If Kitchener gave the inspiration, this side of the War Office organisation was primarily the work of civilians—and it was work splendidly done. There were issued some 54,000,000 posters, 8,000,000 letters were sent in a process of personal canvass, 12,000 meetings were held, 20,000 speeches were delivered from men who were either serving themselves or who were too old to serve their country. During the last months of 1914, 1,186,337 men joined up; and in the fourteen months from August 1914 to September 1915 there joined the Army 2,257,521 men. Even in the point of mere numbers these results could not have been bettered by conscription. For it was not until after this date that the problem of arming and equipping the men actually available was satisfactorily solved. Thus, even if we had had a million extra men we could not have used them, and the unwilling men would have been a burden upon those whose heart was in their cause.

During the last period of 1914 and first half of 1915 new units were continually formed, mostly " Pals "

THE FORGING OF THE GIANT'S SWORD

battalions, or units raised under local, civic or county ægis. The recruits enlisting directly into the New Armies were sent either to Special Reserve battalions or to the New Army battalions drawn from these—which were afterwards made Reserve units.

Towards the middle of 1915 these local units were collected into divisions and formed the Fourth and Fifth New Armies, but until the principal training areas had been left free by the departure of the first-line Territorials and divisions of the First, Second and Third New Armies overseas, these units and the second-line Territorials, did their training either in isolated camps or billeted over a large area, which meant that time was lost in concentrating the men. In the matter of food and quarters, however, they had not to experience the same discomforts and even sufferings as the first three Armies. Local authorities or committees looked after them well: schools, public baths, etc., wherever possible were made available for quarters; hutted camps were run up by local contractors. But all suffered from terrible disadvantages in the matter of lack of arms, equipment and of trained instructors; nor was it possible at first to exercise the same general supervision over their training as with the first-line Territorials and the first three Armies. Take an exceptionally good battalion, the 12th (Service) York and Lancaster Regiment:

October 22nd, the battalion received . . .	200 long rifles, D.P.
October 27th, another . .	200 long rifles, D.P.
October 31st, another . .	200 long rifles, D.P.
January 21st, 1915 . .	1000 long rifles, D.P.

All told 1600, of which 1000 must be returned between May 9th and June 10th. On June 21st, 500 of those given up were returned, leaving 1100

THE KITCHENER ARMIES

rifles, of which many were in bad condition, unfit to be fired. June 17th, 1915, 80 Short Lee-Enfields were issued for instructional purposes and served out to the N.C.O.'s. Not until November 30th, 1915, did the battalion receive its full complement of service rifles and equipment. It sailed for France as part of the 94th Brigade of the 31st Division, December 6th of the same year.

Lack of rifles, lack of guns, lack of uniforms, lack of equipment, lack of everything needed to make an army, these were the difficulties, nagging, heartbreaking, which exceeded even the lack of officers and men, the grim gaunt spectres which dogged the path of the New Armies at every turn, upsetting every calculation, imposing wearisome delays, forcing the harassed officer, striving to teach his men, into every resource known to hard-pressed ingenuity, the bitter and thankless harvest of the gospel of "Wait and See."

" I shall never have a good night's sleep," said Kitchener to a friend who said he was looking worn, " until I have two million rifles and their ammunition, and that cannot be yet."

Our pre-war preparations, as it turned out, were on a scale ludicrously inadequate even for the needs of our original tiny Expeditionary Force—and left nothing over either to make good losses in the field or to meet any demand for expansion.[1] In the first

---

[1] The reserve supply of shell and estimated manufacturing capacity, August 4th, 1914, were :

		Manufacturing output per month.
13-pdr. 1900 rounds per gun (30 guns) = 57,000		10,000
18-pdr. 1500 rounds per gun (324 guns) = 486,000		10,000
4.5 how. 1200 rounds per gun (1084 guns) = 129,600		10,000
60-pdr. 1000 rounds per gun (24 guns) = 24,000		100

On the assumption of a six months' war this meant 10 rounds

THE FORGING OF THE GIANT'S SWORD

six weeks of the war, for instance, 30,000 rifles were lost, 70,000 were needed to arm the Indian Corps when this landed at Marseilles; these rifles had to be taken from the limited supply available—which meant that the troops training at home could not be supplied. It was not until November 1914 that the first batch of service rifles became available for the First New Army, and then only in small numbers. In December 1914, out of 600,000 rifles needed for the New Armies only 400,000 could be supplied, of which 200,000 were D.P. rifles. Out of 400,000 rifles needed for the Territorials, only 240,000 could be issued. As the war settled down into trench warfare the demand from the front for Artillery, machine-guns, new weapons of every kind and munitions of every kind rose to a frenzied scream. In May 1915 there was produced in three days the amount of ammunition normally produced in a year, and by October 1915 production had swollen from 10,000 rounds of 18-pounder shells per month to the vast figure of 1,014,812, which does not include any deliveries from the Munitions Ministry—which did not produce a single round until shortly before the Battle of the Somme. The matter of munitions has been one of embittered controversy into which it would be profitless here to go. Suffice it to say that the shortage which actually occurred was part of a general shortage due to lack of foresight and preparation in peace, and which applied even to such harmless necessary items as the buttons of the soldier's coat.

One might best express it, perhaps, as that the requirements of our pre-war Army had been so small

per day per 18-pdr. Experience soon showed that 50 rounds per day were needed over periods of intensive fighting, and in the Ypres fighting, 80 rounds were sometimes fired per gun per day; individual batteries even fired 1200 rounds in 24 hours.

THE KITCHENER ARMIES

that Army supply had constituted a *luxury trade* and it was a luxury trade which suddenly and without warning had become a matter of mass production and of urgent vital need. In August 1914, for instance, the Birmingham Small Arms Company could produce only 135 rifles per week, and from lack of Government support had turned to the manufacture of motors, cycles, and sporting guns. The general confusion in the world markets due to the war and the rush to enlist by skilled workmen added to the difficulties. By January 1915—and although Kitchener on September 8th had warned such men that by staying at their factories they were helping their country's cause—10,000 skilled engineers had enlisted; out of 1,500,000 skilled and unskilled workers in the metal industries, 16 per cent. had joined up, and out of 920,000 men in the building trades, 178,000 had answered the call to arms. In 1915 out of 999,474 miners, 191,000 had volunteered. There was a lack of statistical material showing the distribution of the man-power available. On the Continent, even in Switzerland, a man or woman cannot change apartments from one side of the street to the other without filling in a registration form giving details as to age, religion, place of birth, occupation, etc. But such a system is alien to the spirit of British liberty, and was only unwillingly tolerated even during the war. The absence of any such system, however, rendered it impossible *scientifically* to distribute the man-power of the country between military and economic needs. The Trades Unions, moreover, had old-established and hard-won privileges, which they would consent to forego only under stress of most imperious national danger. The smouldering antagonism between Capital and Labour at times blazed out. The workmen accused the capitalists of profiteering. The use of one highly

THE FORGING OF THE GIANT'S SWORD

skilled man to supervise a row of machines tended by unskilled labour was prohibited by trade union rules; there were similar obstacles to the employment of women; whilst the high wages paid led to some unedifying scenes of drunkenness and " slacking." At the very outset of the war, Kitchener proclaimed the arrangements made for munitions as for guns, machine-guns and rifles, to be totally inadequate; he ordered that Government factories should at once be enlarged and set to work day and night shifts; contracts with private firms were distributed on a very large scale; at the end of September the War Minister imparted his uneasiness to the Cabinet and asked that £20,000,000 should be granted to the munitions factories to enable these to increase their plant and speed up their production. This was done, and a Cabinet Committee formed early in October with Kitchener himself as President, aided by Lord Moulton, Messrs Runciman, Lloyd George, Winston Churchill and M'Kenna, and Lord Lucas. Owing to labour troubles, however, the contractors were unable to deliver to time. Kitchener then asked for far-reaching legislative powers to check strikes and intemperance, and endeavoured to persuade the Trades Unions to consent to the temporary abrogation of their privileges. Government, however, was unwilling at the time to sanction the legislative powers requested—although they were granted to the Ministry of Munitions five months later.

The formation of the Ministry of Munitions may have been a necessary measure. The problem to be solved was big enough to merit a special department, and this department did its work well. But the foundations of its success were laid by others during the most difficult and trying period of the war; it " inherited," so to speak, the whole of the spade-work done previously; and to accord to the Munitions

THE KITCHENER ARMIES

Ministry a well-deserved meed of praise should not be twisted into ungenerous disparagement of the War Office which suffered from the general refusal to make pre-war preparations on an adequate scale.

Meantime, the expansion of the Army continued on a huge scale. The " Pals " system of recruiting was extraordinarily successful, producing a grand total of 172 battalions, 84 units of Artillery, and 48 of Engineers. The Tyneside rose enthusiastically to the call. October 23rd, 1914, one battalion was sanctioned; twenty-four hours later the raiser telegraphed for leave to form a second. On November 1st he requested authorisation for a third, and on November 18th for a fourth. All these battalions raised reserve units also, usually two reserve companies apiece. In October, the same year, the 15th and 16th (Service) Battalions Royal Scots were raised within thirteen days, each 1350 men strong. By December, the 17th (Service) Battalion had been raised—" Bantams "—recruited from little men between the heights of 5 feet and 5 feet 2 inches. This was a form of enlistment which also caught the public fancy and eventually the Infantry of a whole Division, the 35th, was formed from " Bantams."

Newcastle raised in all 10 " Pals " battalions, Manchester 8, Glasgow, Salford, Hull, 4 each; Lord Derby raised the Artillery for two divisions; Col. Meysey Thompson, and the Boroughs of Camberwell and Deptford, each raised the Artillery for one division; East and West Ham, Fulham, several other boroughs, Nottingham, the West Yorkshire Coal-Owners, and Col. Hammersley, all raised Artillery units of various types.

The first Welsh " Pals " battalion seems to have been raised September 3rd, 1914, and subsequently became the 13th (Service) Royal Welsh Fusiliers. On September 28th, a meeting at which Mr Lloyd

THE FORGING OF THE GIANT'S SWORD

George was present, decided to raise a Welsh Army Corps for the New Armies, but the number of Welsh miners serving in other units was so great that, Wales having already to maintain a Territorial Division, the 53rd, it was impossible to produce more than one Division, the 38th. Many " Pals " units were raised in the early part of 1915 and at the request of the War Office to complete the establishment of new divisions sanctioned. Thus the Chatsworth Rifles, 16th (Service) The Sherwood Foresters, were raised April 29th, 1915. They reached full strength by the end of May, and were authorised to form two reserve companies. The Battalion historian justly claims this as a fine performance, since it was at a time when the first flush of enthusiasm had died away. Most people will sympathise with his lament as to the difficulty of dividing 167 rifles among 250 men in a really just and equitable fashion. The Battalion joined the 117th Brigade of the 39th Division, July 19th, and left for France March 6th, 1916.

The story of the 33rd Divisional Artillery is another of those instances in which civic pride joined with patriotism and common sense to produce a magnificent unit in the teeth of heart-breaking difficulties.

It having been represented to Lord Kitchener that the teamsters, carters, etc., of Camberwell would form fine material for Artillery, sanction was given to the Mayor of this borough to permit Major Frederick Hall, M.P., to recruit the 156th Brigade R.F.A., January 14th, 1915. In March, there was authorised the 162nd Brigade R.F.A., which was completed to strength in May under command of Major Duncan. By June 1st, the 166th, 167th Brigades R.F.A., 126th Brigade (Howitzer) and Ammunition Column, had been formed from the population of

THE KITCHENER ARMIES

Camberwell and Dulwich—making the complete Artillery for the 33rd Division.

At first there were only dummy loaders and three 15-pounders available for training. By the end of July, four 18-pounders were received. Cold shoers were sent to Herold's Institute, Bermondsey, cooks to St John's Wood, artificers to Woolwich, every officer to a training course at Larkhill or Shoeburyness. Map-reading classes were given by Army Schoolmaster Wilmot; Lady Bathurst and the ladies of the district gave lessons in French and German.

At this time the men of the 156th Brigade and Ammunition Column lived at their homes, the 162nd Brigade in Gordon's Brewery, 166th Brigade in the Tramway Depôt, Peckham, and the 167th Brigade partly at home and partly in East Dulwich Baths.

Uniforms were served out shortly after May; batteries moved from London to Bulford in August; they were fully equipped with guns and left for France December 13th, 1916, after less than five months' intensive training as a thoroughly equipped unit.

The 34th Division might be quoted as a typical Division of the Fourth and Fifth New Armies. The units were almost entirely brand new, the men with little military training, the officers in like case. The Order of Battle in itself speaks volumes to a soldier:

Divisional Artillery.

152nd Brigade R.F.A.	Raised by the Mayor of Nottingham's Recruiting Committee.
160th Brigade R.F.A.	Raised early in 1915 by Alderman Stanefield Richardson, Mayor of Sunderland and Recruiting Committee. First C.O., Col. C. W. P. Parker, Royal Garrison Artillery, Territorial.

THE FORGING OF THE GIANT'S SWORD

Divisional Artillery—continued.

175th Brigade R.F.A.   Raised in Staffordshire by Col. Meysey Thompson.

176th Brigade R.F.A. (How.)   Raised in June 1915 by Committee in Leicester, presided over by the Duke of Rutland and Alderman J. North, Mayor of Leicester. First C.O., Col. L. E. Coker, R.F.A.

Divisional Ammunition Column.

Raised in Nottingham during the summer of 1915. Later moved to Codford. Personnel had little experience of horse-mastership. Lieut.-Col. C. A. Simpson takes command November 1915. " All ranks keen."

Royal Engineers.

207th Field Company
208th Field Company
209th Field Company
Signal Company
    All raised in Norwich by the Mayor (Gordon Munn, Esq.) and a Committee. Col. A. C. MacDonnell, R.E., in command. Later first C.R.E., 34th Division.

101*st Brigade.*

First assembled Ripon, June 1915. Brig. H. G. Felton, C.B., D.S.O., A.D.C.

15th Royal Scots   Raised September 1914, half in Edinburgh by the Lord Provost, half in Manchester by the Lord Mayor. First C.O., Sir R. Cranston, K.C.V.O., C.B.

16th Royal Scots   Raised in Edinburgh November 1914 by Sir George M'Crae and a Committee. Sir George M'Crae was the first C.O.

10th Lincolns   Raised in Grimsby September 1914 by the Mayor and a Committee. First C.O., Lieut.-Col. Hon. G. E. Heneage.

THE KITCHENER ARMIES

101st *Brigade*—continued.

11th Suffolks	Raised at Cambridge during September 1914 and following months by the Cambridgeshire and Isle of Ely Territorial Force Association. First C.O., Col. C. W. Somerset, M.V.O.

102nd *Brigade* (The Tyneside Scottish Brigade).

Brig. Trevor Ternan, C.M.G., D.S.O. Brigade concentrated in hutments at Alnwick end of March 1915. Brigade raised by Mr Johnstone Wallace (now Sir Johnstone Wallace, K.B.E.), Lord Mayor of Newcastle and a representative Committee of Scotsmen.

20th Northumberland Fusiliers (1st Tyneside Scottish)	First C.O., Lieut.-Col. Innes Hopkins, late Scottish Rifles.
21st Northumberland Fusiliers (2nd Tyneside Scottish)	First C.O., Col. V. M. Stockley, late Indian Cavalry.
22nd Northumberland Fusiliers (3rd Tyneside Scottish)	First C.O., Lieut.-Col. A. P. Elphinstone, late Indian Army.
23rd Northumberland Fusiliers (4th Tyneside Scottish)	First C.O., Capt. J. C. Campbell, Militia.

103rd *Brigade* (The Tyneside Irish Brigade).

Raised by a Committee of Irishmen presided over by Sir C. Parsons. Both Irish and Scottish Brigades were first financed by Col. Joseph Cowen, Stella Hall, Blagdon-on-Tyne.

24th Northumberland Fusiliers (1st Tyneside Irish)	First C.O., Col. V. M. Stockley, late Indian Cavalry.
25th Northumberland Fusiliers (2nd Tyneside Irish)	Lieut.-Col. H. M. Hatchell, D.S.O., late 18th Royal Irish Rifles.
26th Northumberland Fusiliers (3rd Tyneside Irish)	Lieut.-Col. Hussey Walsh, late 1st Cheshire Regiment.
27th Northumberland Fusiliers (4th Tyneside Irish)	Lieut.-Col. L. Grattan-Esmond, late Waterford R.F.A.

THE FORGING OF THE GIANT'S SWORD

Pioneer Battalion.

18th Northumberland Fusiliers — Raised by the Military Committee of the Newcastle and Gateshead Chamber of Commerce. First C.O., Major R. Temperley, T.D., late 6th Northumberland Fusiliers, Chairman of the Military Committee.

What a picture those dry printed names bring before us. Britain at war, setting herself to the unfamiliar business of raising an army in a fashion peculiarly her own, the Duke of Rutland shoulder to shoulder with the City Councillor, the Lord Mayor of Manchester and the Lord Provost of Edinburgh uniting to raise a battalion, Tyneside Irish and Scots and men from Lincoln and Suffolk. The " Military Committee of the Newcastle and Gateshead Chamber of Commerce," did anyone ever hear of such a title? Fancy the shout of laughter it would have raised before the war! Yet this Committee sprang into life at the very outset of hostilities with a meeting of business men at Milburn House, Newcastle, August 6th, 1914, which produced the Citizens' Training League, with Col. W. H. Ritson, V.D., Major R. Temperley, Major I. Leadbitter Knott, and Messrs W. J. Noble, J.P., and C. Cookson. The League began to train at the Grammar School, and from its loins were born the 16th, 17th, 18th and 19th (Service) Battalions, The Northumberland Fusiliers. A quaint performance, the fashion in which those New Army battalions were raised, yet with something fine in its quaintness. Those city aldermen and sharp-eyed business men who for once thought of something other than buying or selling or piling up property and stocks and shares, those hard-headed, dull, materialistic Englishmen who for once saw an

THE KITCHENER ARMIES

Ideal burning before their eyes, something which took them out of themselves, which caused them to plunge their hands into their pockets and more than that, to give their sons and to set themselves to drilling—and even in some cases to dye their hair and " wangle " their age and fight shoulder to shoulder with boys who might have been their sons. What mattered it if there were *some* who hung back and *some* who saw in their country's agony their own chance for gain? The spots on the sun's surface do not obscure the brilliance of his rays, and where so many were noble and so many were brave, why dwell on the pitiful handful who shirked and profiteered? And those retired officers, ex-Regulars, ex-Militiamen, ex-Territorials, what did it matter if all were rusty and some were fools? The fools were soon found out, the rusty ones furbished up; taken as a class, they did their part and worthily served their cause. Muddle and confusion and unpreparedness, and the clear white flame of patriotism shining through, transmuting chaos into order, uniting gentles and commons, nobles and burgesses, factory hands, agricultural labourers, miners, dwellers from town and dwellers from hamlets in a common bond of effort and suffering and danger. Oh, it is easy to mock and easy to jeer, easy to point out that this or that was wrong or could have been done better. But it is not easy to see how we could have won our cause had there been fewer men ready to die to defend it, fewer prosperous well-fed burgesses ready to dive their hands into their pockets and to give their money if they could give nothing else, fewer big-muscled, hard-handed, large-hearted men from fields and factories prepared voluntarily to take up arms, fewer gallant boys from schools and universities and counting-houses and business houses ready to set a personal example of all that patriotism means.

THE FORGING OF THE GIANT'S SWORD

Looking back on those days we may well take pride in our country, pride in the spirit which fashioned our New Armies; the spirit which brought us victory from the very jaws of defeat.

An officer of this Division writes:

". . . the ' Raisers ' were unhampered by any of the rules and regulations which control a government department, and as they conducted their own recruiting campaigns, in some cases in opposition to a rival body in the same town or area, they were anxious to do their recruits as well as possible, and every want was promptly supplied, without any thought as to how much was going to be recovered. In almost every case a great many business men were to be found amongst the ' Raisers,' and these formed sub-committees, each of which dealt with the details of that portion of the task with which its members were most conversant.

" The system worked well, in so far as the rapid raising and equipping of the force was concerned, and there is no doubt that these various local bodies saved the situation; without their aid the task could not have been completed, and they certainly deserve well of their country.

" Whether the country is justified in expecting individuals voluntarily and for no remuneration to undertake such difficult tasks and to incur such heavy liabilities, is doubtful.

" What these local bodies were out of pocket, after recovering all they could from Government, it is impossible to say. The amounts probably varied considerably. The net cost to one such body, which raised about five thousand five hundred men, worked out to just over £50,000, of which about one-tenth is represented by the amounts paid in connection with the raising, which were not recovered from

THE KITCHENER ARMIES

Government. Nearly four-fifths of the sum was expended on dependents and discharged men. . . . Once permission to recruit had been obtained from the War Office, which in some cases was not so simple, advertisements in the local press and a few posters brought together groups of men of all classes, who lined up in some by-road, under the supervision of some local celebrity with a certain amount of military training. If a young fellow had O.T.C. training, he was at once hailed out, invested with authority, and turned on to drill the remainder. Commissions in those days were easily got. Generally some elderly retired officer of the Regular, Militia, Territorial or Volunteer forces would be given command on the recommendations of the Mayor, Provost, or other head of the ' Raisers.' Before him would be paraded various aspirants for commissions, callow youths, young men, middle-aged men, nay, even old men. A few minutes' conversation, a few searching questions, and the applicant would withdraw. If he had met with approval, he would receive an order to join as soon as possible, with an intimation that his name had been submitted by the Mayor to the War Office for a commission as second-lieutenant in the ——. That was all. No competitive exams., no worrying delay. A casual system, no doubt, but how well it worked! There were, of course, cases in which the selections did not turn out satisfactory, but they were surprisingly few.

" As numbers increased, sections, platoons and companies were formed. Command of these was given without any regard for seniority. What was seniority worth when all were such recent recruits? Men with the necessary qualities of leaders and administrators were picked, and pushed on from rank to rank with a celerity which shocked some of the old *régime*.

THE FORGING OF THE GIANT'S SWORD

" Clothing and equipment, being in the hands of the ' Raisers,' came along fairly quickly, although khaki was not obtainable for some time. Arms, however, were scarce; the Infantry did not receive their final issue of rifles till very shortly before embarking. . . .

" In spite of all difficulties, however, training went on vigorously; the keenness of all ranks was wonderful. *Esprit de corps* was quickly evolved; platoon rivalled platoon; section rivalled section. The progress of other units was closely watched. Officers were sent off on courses of all sorts, and returned full of knowledge. Wounded officers appeared; not yet fit for active service, but fit to teach us. How eagerly we listened to them! So it went on and rapidly the recruits of the autumn grew into soldiers, and by the summer of 1915 there were murmurings at the delay in despatching us overseas."

The soldier glancing through the Order of Battle will note that although most of the battalions were formed in September, October, or November 1914, they were not concentrated in brigades until March and June 1915. Until this occurred battalions must train as best they could, hampered by the usual shortages in the way of arms, equipment and instructors, and scattered in billets. During 1915 an average number of one million men were being trained in the United Kingdom, apart from the armies fighting on the different fronts. Besides the New Armies and First and Second-Line Territorials, on November 24th, 1914, a general authorisation was issued to the County Associations to raise Third-Line Territorial units wherever possible.[1] Of this vast

[1] It was hoped by this means to relieve the Second-Line Territorial units from the necessity of furnishing drafts and thus to enable them to become efficient for Home Defence or for Foreign Service. This expectation was only partially realised.

THE KITCHENER ARMIES

number of men, 800,000 had to be billeted on private houses. The original provision for hutments to take 500,000 men was increased to nearly a million, besides remount establishments, aeroplane sheds, hospital huts and rifle ranges. But great difficulties were experienced in obtaining timber, etc., labour, and an adequate inspection staff. Water had to be laid on to the camps, gas or electric light, drainage and sanitation provided. Roads had to be repaired and sometimes new ones built capable of taking heavily-loaded wagons. Within a year, despite all difficulties, hutments had been built for 750,000 men, but it was not until the Spring of 1916 that the problem of quarters was completely solved.

Rifle ranges were thrown up with great rapidity; thus the 17th Northumberland Fusiliers (Pioneers) built on Bardon Moor near Leyburn, Wensleydale, a great range with 56 duplicate targets, a trench in front 4 to 5 yards wide, and a huge embankment behind with some 12,000 tons of earth. To do this, a light tramway had to be laid down. The task was completed in sixteen working days.

It was shortly after the concentration of its three brigades in camps, two at Alnwick and one at Ripon, that the 34th Division as such came into existence. The story of its birth is worth relating as an instance of the hurry and confusion of those days. About June 15th or 16th, 1915, a Staff-Officer was discovered wandering around the streets of Ripon plaintively inquiring of all and sundry, "*Where is the* 34*th Division?*" The Staff-Officer was one Major R. F. Lock, R.A., who flourished an official document proclaiming him to be D.A.A. and Q.M.G. of the 34th Division of the Fourth Army. After mental cogitation, he wended his weary way to the Headquarters of the Fourth Army, where, after bleating awhile, he received the surprising information

THE FORGING OF THE GIANT'S SWORD

concerning the 34th Division that he was IT. At all events nothing else was known about it. Lock, after recovering from the shock, displayed that courage and initiative which has made the British officer what he is, and promptly took two houses, assembled clerks, and proudly emblazoned the device, Headquarters, 34*th Division*. Some officers of " G " arrived a few days later, and about another week later Maj.-Gen. E. C. Ingouville-Williams, C.B., D.S.O., arrived from France where he had commanded the 16th Brigade.

" The 34th Division was lucky in its first Commander. A thorough soldier, as much at home on the ' Q ' as on the ' G ' side. He knew what his men were entitled to, and he saw that they got it. Absolutely fearless, and apparently never tired, all ranks trusted and loved him, and there were few dry eyes among the crowd of mourners when he was laid to rest in Warley cemetery on July 23rd, 1916 " ; killed in action, he was succeeded by Maj.-Gen. C. L. Nicholson, C.M.G., who had also succeeded him in command of the 16th Brigade.

The 101st Brigade was now concentrated at Fountains Abbey; the Divisional Troops were at Kirkby Malzeard, six miles distant; the 102nd and 103rd Brigades were close at hand. Divisional training could begin. But there were the usual deficiencies. The 176th Brigade R.F.A. did not receive its first howitzers till August 13th, 1915; the full complement did not arrive till November 24th. The Brigade had only three days' gun practice before it embarked; two battery commanders took command less than ten days prior to embarkation. Due to the scattered fashion in which battalions had done their training, several senior officers from the British Expeditionary Force had to be imported, and at the end of September the Division was concentrated at

THE KITCHENER ARMIES

Sutton Veney for intensive training. It embarked for France, January 7th, 1916. Some of its units raised in September 1914 had thus 16 months' training. Given adequate instructors and equipment, they would have been ready in half the time.

Ere we leave this Division to go overseas, one adventure of the worthy Lock should have an enduring record. Before the Division had gone to Sutton Veney, news came that 300 mules were arriving for the Divisional train. Lock was told by the station-master that they would arrive in twenty minutes and must be unloaded at once. He rose gallantly to the occasion, collared the G.S.O. 3 and six Military Police; the mules were unloaded, and just when the entire station-yard was a mass of kicking, squealing mules, *another* train arrived with *another* 300 mules. Lock had kindly unloaded the 31st Division's mules for them.

The process of raising new Divisions went on all through 1914 and continued until late in 1915. The 40th Division, raised in December 1914, was re-numbered 33rd Division, and a new 40th Division was created April 1915.[1] In January 1915 another series was formed. The Staff of the 59th (North Midland) Division received a curt War Office telegram, *Are you prepared to receive troops?* The answer was in the affirmative, and in ten days 10,000 men were switched into this Division—then the 2nd North Midland Territorials—in the organisation of which that youthful veteran, Brig.-Gen. Hugh M'Call, 72 years old, did yeoman service. Eleven other divisions were built up in similar fashion early in 1915, which, however, suffered from

---

[1] The change in numbers was due to the transformation of the original Fourth New Army into reserve units and the formation of a new Fourth Army.

THE FORGING OF THE GIANT'S SWORD

shortages in officers, equipment, etc., to even greater degree than the New Armies.

The first group of divisions to go to the assistance of Sir John French's Army were First-Line Territorials, the 46th, February 24th, 1915; the 47th, March 9th; the 49th, 50th, and 51st, April 14th, 16th and 30th. All told five, to which must be added the 55th and 56th, formed from Territorial battalions serving in France, attached to Regular brigades, since November and December 1914. There were thus the equivalent of seven Territorial divisions which actually constituted the first reserve for our field Army. The first New Army Division to go to the front was the 9th (Scottish) Division, May 9th, 1915, followed by the 12th (Eastern) Division, May 29th. Three New Army Divisions, the 13th, 11th and 10th, went off to the Dardanelles June 13th, July 1st, and July 7th, in the order mentioned, and the last three First-Line Territorial Divisions went to the same destination at almost parallel dates: the 52nd, 53rd and 54th, May 18th, July 14th, July 23rd. Thereafter came a steady flow of New Army Divisions to France. The 14th (Light) Division, June 18th, completed the tale of the First New Army. In July came six more Divisions,[1] the 15th (Scottish), 17th (Northern), 19th (Western), 18th (Eastern), 20th (Light) and 37th.[2] In August came two,[3] the 23rd and 24th, followed in September by another batch of five,[4] the 22nd, 21st, 26th, and 25th. This made up the total for the first three Armies save one, the 16th (Irish) Division, which, although a Second Army formation, owing to special difficulties did not get to the front until December 17th, 1915. The other

[1] July 7th, 12th, 16th, 20th, 24th and 28th in order named.
[2] The 37th was a Fifth Army Division.
[3] August 15th and 30th.
[4] September 4th, 9th, 19th, 25th respectively.

THE KITCHENER ARMIES

divisions, 18 in all, went to the front in periods varying from ten months to a year after embodiment. A truly amazing performance when one thinks of all the difficulties to be surmounted. Our little Expeditionary Force of 6 divisions had expanded to 9 divisions within two months—Indian Corps and 7th Division; to the equivalent of 12 divisions in another two months—8th Division and Territorials; to 18 [1] by the end of April 1915; to 20 by the end of May; (21, including the magnificent Canadian Division;) to 29 at the end of July; and to 37 [2] by the end of September. These figures, wonderful though they be, do not fully illuminate the vast expansion. Four Territorial divisions, three New Army divisions, the Royal Naval Division, the Australian and New Zealand Division, and the 29th Division were engaged in the Dardanelles; [3] Townshend was fighting at Kut-el-Amara; a campaign was in progress in East Africa. A total exceeding 47 divisions were in actual contact with the enemy; 24 more divisions were being trained in England.

In October 1914 the Canadian Division had arrived in England—a grand total of 30,000 men. One glance at these fine troops convinced Kitchener that he wanted as many more as he could possibly get, and he telegraphed at once to the Canadian Government suggesting a second division to be formed from the men—some 10,000—superfluous to the first. To this the Canadian Government cordially agreed, and the 2nd Canadian Division was organised in May 1915, to be followed by a third at the end of the year. The Australian and New Zealand Division

---

[1] Including the 28th (Regular) Division arrived, in France January 15th, 1915.

[2] Including the 27th (Regular) Division, arrived in France September 19th, 1915.

[3] Apart from dismounted Yeomanry.

THE FORGING OF THE GIANT'S SWORD

was formed in January 1915, and the 2nd Australian Division in August of the same year.

The drain upon the Special Reserve battalions to furnish drafts must never be forgotten in considering the vast expansion of those days. The 3rd Battalion, The Queen's Own Royal West Kent Regiment, for instance, sent out 2450 N.C.O.'s and men—the equivalent of $2\frac{1}{2}$ battalions at full war strength —during the first twelve months of the war. The 3rd Battalion, The Border Regiment, sent out 44 officers and 2336 N.C.O.'s and men.

From November 1914 to June 1915 an average of 125,000 men joined the Army and Territorial units per month; between August 1914 and May 31st, 1915, 20,000 temporary commissions were issued for the Regular Army; by the end of 1914 scarcely any students were left in the larger Universities capable of bearing arms; all had joined the forces.

During this time, it must be remembered, the Navy was also in the throes of a vast expansion and had, justifiably, a prior call upon the industrial resources of the country. There were under construction:

Battleships and Battle Cruisers .	7
Light Cruisers . . .	12
Destroyers of the largest class .	65
Overseas Submarines . .	40
Coastal Submarines . . .	22
Monitors:	
Heavy	18
Medium	14
Light	5
Sloops	107
Motor Launches . . .	680
Ex-lighters with internal combustion engines . . .	240

All these, which exclude the " light " battle cruisers

THE KITCHENER ARMIES

Courageous, Furious and *Glorious,* were due to complete at the end of 1915. There was in process the building of aircraft in vast numbers, the arming of merchant ships, the building of hutments for a million men, which meant demands upon highly skilled labour and raw materials in the way of sanitation, electric lighting, telephones, etc. The Army needed millions of uniforms, but the supply of khaki cloth was limited, and blue serge taken from post office and police stocks had to be worked up into emergency uniforms. The articles listed in Ordnance stores as needed by the soldier include some 30,000, ranging from boot-brushes to button-sticks, from razors to high explosives. The average civilian firm could not supply these needs, and had first to extend or adapt their plant and to acquire raw materials of special quality.

Looking at the thing temperately and dispassionately it is hard to see how the results achieved, which were truly wonderful results, could have been improved upon. War is a time of great nervous strain, and the anxieties of the day led to much criticism from men who were impatient to see results and had no idea of the vast practical difficulties to be surmounted. But not all British merchants were profiteers, not all politicians were prepared to sacrifice their country for their own personal gain, not all retired generals were wooden-headed martinets, not all labour men were conscienceless agitators, not all public officials were soulless bureaucrats. Had there been any such spirit of general moral rottenness, Great Britain must have lost the war. Seen in its true perspective, this rising to arms of an unarmed people has its lofty and inspiring side; it is not lacking in an element of sheer grandeur, it is a story without parallel in history, and which will ring through the vaults of Time.

THE FORGING OF THE GIANT'S SWORD

On August 17th, 1914, Kitchener had directed that six centres should be formed at the Headquarters of "Commands," at which newly joined officers could get a month's training. One month is at best a very short time in which to acquire the art of handling men in battle, but in 1914 even this shadow of a military education had to be cut out, as it would have meant leaving the battalions with hardly any subalterns. The first three Armies had thus to train their own officers, and from the very beginning. It was a rough and ready business. The young officer began by being drilled like a recruit, he attended lectures given by senior officers, and he started straight away by teaching and commanding men. For a youngster fresh from school to find himself teaching recruits things which he had himself learnt only the preceding evening was the rule rather than the exception. But if to try to teach others is no bad way in which to teach oneself, the system followed, crude though it was, was not without its advantages. The youngster of the right stamp brought to his task a sheer *vim* which would have been lacking in peace-training; the men were as keen as he was himself, and in those early days it was no uncommon thing to find officers and men joining in a friendly discussion as to the exact meaning of some abstruse diagrams in the text-books. This lack of lucidly written and graphically expressed text-books, be it remarked, was a serious handicap in the earlier phases—although it was subsequently remedied. The Americans, when they came to raise their armies, profited by our errors in this respect and produced some really excellent little books of the *Hundred Points Concerning the Rifle* type. The progressive training of the battalion—and of the young officer—was a matter mainly of the divisional and brigade staffs, and the Regular adjutant. The work done by

THE KITCHENER ARMIES

this handful of Regular officers was wonderful. It has been sometimes suggested that the New Armies never saw the Old; it had vanished from wounds or death before they arrived in France. But in the Regular adjutants of their battalions—if lucky enough to possess one—the New Armies had before them a living embodiment of the spirit of the Old. There were, of course, exceptions, but in general the only degrees of value were *good*, *very good*, or *excellent*; for these officers to devote two hours in the morning personally to drilling the battalion before breakfast, the rest of the day generally to controlling training, and the evening to teaching a class of young officers and N.C.O.'s, was no uncommon thing. In most cases the voice of the adjutant rapping out his commands on parade was the earliest introduction of the raw young subaltern into the art of commanding men; their influence can scarcely be exaggerated. Most of them worked like niggers, striving to lick their battalions into shape; they brought to their job a spirit of sound, healthy sportsmanship and a high standard of professional knowledge; they were the very soul of the first three Armies. Next to the example and guiding hand of the adjutant, the lectures by senior officers were of greatest value. Here again it was a matter not only of precept. " Good morning, young gentlemen," said Gen. Maxse briskly on one occasion, "and good morning to *you*, young gentleman," to one who was keeping his hands in his pockets.

Wounded or convalescent officers from the front were used in training with great success and were able to speak from practical experience. The system of " Cook's Tours " to the front, adopted about the middle of 1915, was also a valuable and helpful measure which enabled senior officers to brush up their knowledge and to keep themselves abreast of the latest requirements.

THE FORGING OF THE GIANT'S SWORD

Classes in special subjects, musketry, machine-guns, etc., were held by energetic seniors; ex-Regular officers also played a powerful part—even if the very pronunciation of " platoon " was a stumbling-block to some of them, and it came out variously as " pathoon," " pontoon," and even " spittoon."

Later on training grew more systematised. Early in 1915 the system of one month's training for newly joined officers was revived and extended. The rush for commissions had now set in; most battalions were overstaffed with officers; thus there were formed Young Officers' Training Companies in the Reserve Brigades, which were later concentrated into groups under capable officers. Later on still, these developed into the Cadet Battalions, which afforded a means not alone of training officers, but of weeding out undesirable elements.

The training of N.C.O.'s was at first even more rudimentary than that of officers; it was also difficult to find men of sufficient force of character to keep discipline without perpetual appeals to Authority. Men were chosen for these ranks because they *looked* smart, or thought themselves capable of handling other men, and these N.C.O.'s had to pick up their training as best they could in their battalions. It was not until July 1915 that there was established the first school for training N.C.O.'s.

The Fourth and Fifth New Armies were, of course, even worse off than the first three Armies in respect to the training of officers and N.C.O.'s. They were staffed entirely by retired officers. The officer who took command of the 11th (Service) Royal Warwickshires, describes his battalion as raised in October 1914. It was thus five months old and mustered 1000 men and *100* officers. A few of these were retired Regulars or had served in South Africa in irregular formations, but as a whole, officers and men

THE KITCHENER ARMIES

were fresh from civil life. Although the battalion had taken part in brigade or divisional exercises, training had to start from the very beginning with " the first position of the soldier," " right-hand salute," etc. Few of the men had rifles, most of them were dressed in emergency blue. There was hardly any equipment. By the end of May the battalion was equipped and, after about six weeks of intensive training, went to France with the 37th Division, July 28th, 1915.

With the divisions of the Fourth and Fifth New Armies, the system followed was to concentrate the divisions for intensive training at one of the great training areas, Salisbury Plain, Aldershot, etc., which had been vacated by the divisions sent to France. In the case of units which seemed behindhand, experienced senior officers were imported to furbish them up; deficiencies in equipment were made good. The system worked well. There was no fixed order of embarkation. The 36th (Ulster) Division, for instance, although really belonging to the Fifth New Army went to the front in October 1915, many months before the other divisions of this Army. The Division was raised by the Ulster Volunteer Force, and was thus based on an existing military organisation which had commanded great popular enthusiasm. One incident may be quoted:

" Captain Craig,[1] after leaving the War Office, jumped into a taxicab in Whitehall and went straight to a firm of outfitters with which he had had dealings in equipment for the U.V.F. and gave an order for 10,000 complete outfits. Returning to the House he was somewhat exercised in his mind as to where the money was to come from to pay for all this. He spoke

[1] Now Right Hon. Sir James Craig, Bart., Prime Minister of Northern Ireland.

THE FORGING OF THE GIANT'S SWORD

to Mr Oliver Locker-Lampson,[1] one of Ulster's staunchest friends, who pulled out a cheque-book and said:

" 'Don't say another word! There's a thousand pounds to go on with, and nine more will follow in a day or two. This is out of a special fund just available for your purpose.' "

Thanks to the foresight and energy of the leading Ulstermen, the help of the big business houses, and the existence of a framework upon which to build, the Ulster Division had not to endure months of drilling in civilian clothes, in wet weather and in inadequate boots, which marked the early phases of other divisions.

The Ulster Volunteer Force, having no Artillery, the 36th Divisional Artillery was raised in London six months after the rest of the Division. The 153rd and 154th Brigades were raised by the British Empire League—one of the ruling spirits of which was Gen. Sir Bindon Blood—and recruited principally from Croydon, Norbury, and Sydenham; the 172nd and 173rd Brigades were recruited on the initiative of the Mayors of East and West Ham and from these districts. Apart from Artillery, the whole of this Division was raised in Ulster, and training was in full swing by the end of September 1914. Early in July 1915 the 36th crossed to England, to Seaford, on the Sussex coast. Towards the close of July, after an inspection of the Ulstermen, Lieut.-Gen. Sir Archibald Murray, Deputy Chief of the General Staff, reported to Kitchener that they were worthy of a higher place than that which they occupied on the War Minister's private list of the divisions for the front.

[1] Now Commander Locker-Lampson, C.M.G., D.S.O.

THE KITCHENER ARMIES

"It was not Lord Kitchener's fashion to ponder such questions.

"'I'll go and see them tomorrow,' was his reply.

"At half-past four on July 26th came a telephone message that the Division was to parade for Lord Kitchener's inspection at 11 a.m. the following day.

"July 27th was a bright, sunny day. Lord Kitchener came, dashed at the waiting horses with such speed that before anyone could speak he was on the back of one with a very doubtful reputation, by no means intended for his riding, and rode off. . . .

"One incident of this inspection . . . throws an interesting light on Lord Kitchener's quickness of eye for and memory of details. The personnel of the Field Ambulances was of fine physique, the mounted men including many farmers' sons. As the Field Ambulances passed the saluting point, Lord Kitchener turned to the A.D.M.S. with the remark, 'Those men are too fine for the R.A.M.C. You will have to give me two hundred for the Artillery.' The A.D.M.S. replied that he hoped they would not be taken, as they had undergone a very thorough training; to which Lord Kitchener, raising his voice, simply repeated: 'You will have to give me some of those men for the Artillery.'

"A few days later an officer from the Adjutant-General's department came down. He said that, at the moment, men were in fact not particularly wanted for the Artillery, but that as 'K' had ordered it they must be taken." The upshot was that 150 men were drafted to the Artillery. "The sequel came two months later when Lord Kitchener was present at the King's Review. On reaching the 108th Field Ambulance, the A.D.M.S. rode out to take his position behind Lord Kitchener, who turned

THE FORGING OF THE GIANT'S SWORD

to him and asked: 'How many men did you send to the Artillery?' 'A hundred and fifty, sir.' Lord Kitchener, somewhat gruffly, 'I thought I told you to send two hundred.'
"The A.D.M.S. thought it best to leave it at that."

The leading Divisions of the Fourth New Army, the 30th and 32nd, went to the front November 9th and 11th respectively. In December came three more, the 38th, 31st and 33rd—December 1st, 6th and 13th. January 1916—by which time Sir Douglas Haig had assumed command—saw two more Divisions, 34th—January 7th; 35th—January 28th. The 39th Division arrived March 3rd; the 41st, and the earliest of second-line Territorial Divisions, the 61st, came over May 1st, 1916 and May 21st successively. The last New Army Division, the 40th, held back by special circumstances, reached the front June 1st, 1916—exactly one month before the opening of the Battle of the Somme.[1]

Three Divisions, the 58th, 57th and 59th, were sent out to France subsequently, January 20th, 1917 and February 7th and 17th of the same year in the order mentioned. These Divisions were all formed early in 1915.

The full tale of divisions for our National Army was thus built up under the voluntary principle, and conscription, when introduced, was merely a matter of sending drafts to units which were already in good working order. This was undoubtedly the right principle upon which to work. The true magnitude of the Voluntary Effort of the British Empire in the early part of the war has been scarcely realised, but

[1] The 60th Division, a second-line Territorial formation, reached the front June 21st, 1916—*one week* before the opening of the battle.

THE KITCHENER ARMIES

it was *the* decisive influence which made for victory. The vast results attained can best be illustrated by a comparison with the United States. The Americans are a proud and patriotic people who had, moreover, a tradition of conscription. On coming into the war they at once passed a law for compulsory military service, under which between May 18th, 1917 and November 1st, 1918, from a population of 91,972,266 and in a period of eighteen months, they raised a grand total of 3,483,444 men.[1] Excluding the Dominions and India, Great Britain raised between August 4th, 1914 and January 1st, 1916, an equal period, from a population of 41,126,040, and by voluntary service, 2,632,682 men, *i.e.* in proportion to the population nearly twice as many men *volunteered* in Great Britain as were conscripted in the United States. The *British Empire*, within the same period and by voluntary service, raised well over 4,000,000 men. If one takes the total white population of the British Empire, 57,926,180, and compares this with the *white* population of the U.S.A.—over 80,000,000—one discovers that the number of white troops produced by the British population by voluntary service was actually greater than the number raised by the United States by conscription, and, in proportion to the population, was more than half again as large. The United Kingdom herself played a part to which we can always look back with pride. For reasons needless to go into here, large sections of the population of Ireland failed to answer the call to arms with the same enthusiasm as the rest of the Kingdom. The strain of military service thus fell principally upon England, Scotland, Wales and Ulster—a population of some 39,000,000. But the little island of Lewis, which on September 13th, 1914, out of a population of 29,000 souls, had 3500

[1] Including coloured troops.

THE FORGING OF THE GIANT'S SWORD

men serving with the Army or the Fleet, a proportion of 12½ per cent., showed the spirit which animated the whole of Britain. If we include the men who attested their willingness to serve under Lord Derby's " group " system, out of this population of 39,000,000, no less than 5,000,000 volunteered to join the colours, a proportion exceeding 12½ per cent.[1] Before the war it had been held that even with conscription, a *levy en masse* of the population could not produce more than 10 per cent.

These are extraordinary figures. No people in the world has ever shown greater readiness for sacrifice. Anyone who before the war had ventured to predict that the voluntary system would produce such results would have been laughed at as a lunatic. It is hard that the acrimonious controversy anent conscription should have tended to obscure the full wonder and glory of this great national achievement. Not alone did the people of this country raise by voluntary service numbers far outshadowing those produced in America in an equal period of time by means of conscription, but our New Armies were equipped and sent to the front at a speed and in a state of efficiency completely outrivalling the analogous effort by America. Up to January 1st, 1916, for instance, we put in the field fifty divisions, excluding Dominion and native troops, whereas the United States—able to profit from all the " mistakes " made by us in raising our New Armies, to draw upon the highly developed munition industries

[1] The total number of men capable of bearing arms did not exceed 8,000,000, of whom 5,000,000 volunteered, and close on 3,000,000 had actually enlisted prior to January 1st, 1916. Of the remainder, 2,000,000 were " indispensable." Thus, conscription was only really necessary in the case of *one man in eight*. When introduced it was a thoroughly democratic measure, for the vast majority of our manhood were prepared not alone to vote for conscription for others, but *to go themselves*.

THE KITCHENER ARMIES

of Great Britain and France to arm and equip her new levies, and with her full national manhood to draw upon for drafts—could not put into the field more than twenty-four. Moreover, the average British division was in a far higher state of efficiency when it arrived in France than the American formations. To write in this fashion is not meant to belittle or unfairly to disparage the fine effort of America. But it is to illuminate the tremendous energy and practical good sense which went to create the New Armies. The young staff-officer—and many civilians—is apt to look upon conscription as an ideal system under which it is possible almost automatically to create armies. He uncritically accepts popular phrases such as " equality of sacrifice," " scientific organisation," etc., etc. But there can be no real " equality of sacrifice " in war. It is a matter largely of sheer luck whether one man stops a bullet and another passes scathless, the munitions worker or other member of " exempted industries " will never make the same sacrifice in physical suffering or in dangers faced which is made by the soldier in the field. " Scientific organisation " is one of those fine-sounding phrases which cover up a good deal of mental sloppiness. No military organisation is truly scientific which fails to make allowance for human nature, for battles are won *or lost* by *men*. The wise organiser will always strive to adapt his organisation to national characteristics. Methods suitable to one country are not always equally suited to a people of different race and with different traditions behind them. Kitchener, in the methods he took to raise the New Armies, showed great wisdom, and it is an illusion to believe that these Armies could have been raised on the same vast scale, with the same speed and in the same state of efficiency by means of conscription. The only real result of any such

THE FORGING OF THE GIANT'S SWORD

measure would have been to put a damper on popular enthusiasm; the men taken would have been of an inferior stamp; there would have been the same general lack of preparation, but there would not have been the same general spirit of *self-help* which did so much to atone for this. One needs a very strong element of faith to believe that a bureaucracy of elderly, fussy, or incompetent generals at Whitehall, armed with autocratic powers, would have been particularly helpful in the matter of *scientific* organisation.[1] The probabilities are that they would have made an egregious hash of things. The Voluntary Effort of the British people was not, as is so often depicted, a matter of national slackness and inefficiency, but on the contrary a fine and noble performance, the like of which is unknown to any other race. The speed with which our Armies were put in the field was a matter of vital import, for these Armies were just in time to relieve the heroic French troops in the crisis of Verdun, which had put France in imminent peril of a catastrophic defeat.

Conscription, when finally adopted, came at the right time and in the right manner. It came at the right time because conscripts sent as drafts to units in a high state of efficiency and with trained officers and N.C.O.'s can easily be absorbed and imbued with the spirit of the regiment—a very different matter from conscript levies under officers and N.C O.'s as raw as they are themselves. It came in the right manner because it was freely debated in Parliament and passed into law in accordance with

[1] *No* government department in any country could foresee in 1914 the complex economic reactions which the war was to have upon the general social life of their peoples. France and Germany were no better off under conscription as regards the *scientific* allotment of man-power than was Great Britain under the voluntary system.

THE KITCHENER ARMIES

constitutional usage as a supreme act of sacrifice by a free people fighting to defend its freedom. It is to the lasting credit of our people that they had the courage and wisdom to accept this measure, distasteful though it was; it is to the lasting credit of Kitchener that he scrupuloulsy avoided anything which might savour of an attempt to ride roughshod over the liberties of his own country; it is to the lasting credit of the manhood of Britain that when the emergency arose, from out of our small population there were 5,000,000 men who needed no law to teach them Duty.

VII

LOOS AND THE DARDANELLES

THE first great wave of German invasion reached its climax at the Battle of the Marne and recoiled, leaving both armies in an almost equal state of weariness and confusion. Much has been written, and will continue to be written, about the failures of commanders, but the most probable explanation of the general state of disorganisation, alike with Germans and Allies, is that manœuvres, even on the greater scale practised by Continental armies, are no real preparation for the moral strain of handling vast numbers of troops, guns and stores in battle, and that in no army was to be found, at that time, any commander truly capable of handling 1,000,000 men. The terrible *tired* feeling which overcomes the soldier in combat must also be considered. It is safe to say that had either army been able to throw into the crisis of the Marne fighting even 200,000 perfectly fresh, thoroughly trained and well-equipped troops, the Marne would have been either a greater Jena or another Sedan. But it is the most paradoxical feature of a paradoxical war that Germany, the arch-exponent of militarism and conscription, was no better able to produce that *last* ounce of effort which at the decisive moment spells the difference between victory and defeat than were the Allies. So there actually ensued a tactical stalemate which for Germany spelt strategic disaster. The Allies, too exhausted vigorously to pursue, came up against the enemy who had rallied on the line of the Aisne; Joffre and Falkenhayn each called

THE KITCHENER ARMIES

for reserves; each strove to reach the exposed flank of his adversary, and there resulted the Race to the Sea which, culminating in the desperate and bloody fighting of October and November 1914, left both sides stiff with wounds and each claiming victory.

The Germans could point to the fall of Antwerp, and to the fact that they held practically all Belgium and some of the richest provinces of France in their iron hand; the Allies could speak of the " miracle of the Marne "; take pride in the heroic defence of Ypres, and stress the actual tangible truth that the enemy having advanced had retreated—at least in part. Thus, as the year 1914 wore to its close, the mood of the General Staffs in France and in Britain was optimistic. Ignorant of the real situation in Russia, only partially informed even as to the truth as to Tannenberg and the Battle of the Masurian Lakes, they continued to put faith in the Russian " Steam-Roller."

Optimism deepened to conviction when, early in 1915, Przemysl fell into Russian hands, and the armies of the Grand Duke Nicholas came thundering down upon the Carpathians.

Meanwhile, and as part of the general situation, the whole character of the war on the West Front had altered. Germany, no less alive to the menace of the Russian " steam-roller " than were the Allies eager to profit by this, and with Austria's desperate call for help ringing in her ears, was forced to turn her main attention to the East. It became her policy to hold the West Front with the minimum number of troops possible, so as to add weight to the blows she purposed to inflict upon the Armies of the Czar. Her problem was thus defensive, and the urgency of her need led to special measures to economise *men*.

During training in England the relative advantage of siting trenches on the forward or reverse slopes

LOOS AND THE DARDANELLES

was a subject of keen discussion with New Army men. Later on they learnt that discussion was futile; one had to entrench where one could. The flow and eddy of the fighting of 1914 left the two armies confronting one another in a long line of trenches running from the Swiss frontier to the sea, and sited largely in an irregular fashion, without thought for larger strategic or tactical objectives.

This line bulged backwards and forwards without apparent rhyme or reason; here a tongue of " German " territory would project out and form a salient in the Allied lines, there the reverse would happen.

The trenches on both sides were rudimentary as compared to the formidably designed defences of later years, but the Germans, for the reasons given, were the first systematically to improve and develop their defences. Germany, in many respects, had a clear and definite start. First of all she had been forced for years before the war to contemplate special measures of attack against the French fortified frontier; and when later her intention had developed to sweep through Belgium, it had been necessary to think out special measures for dealing with Belgian fortified places such as Liège and Namur. The problems of siege warfare were better understood in Germany than in Britain or France; the value of the heavy gun was better appreciated. Moreover, the great and highly organised German war industries were better able to expand and to answer calls for new weapons than was the case even with France and yet more with Britain. At a Munitions Conference held shortly before the Battle of Loos, for instance, it was estimated that Germany and Austria between them could manufacture 250,000 rounds of artillery ammunition per day, France could produce 100,000, Britain 22,000.

The armies which took the field in France and

THE KITCHENER ARMIES

Flanders in 1914 were pretty much at the same general level in training, equipment and efficiency of leadership. Before the war British, French and German armies had watched one another very closely, and it was impossible for one army to make drastic and revolutionary changes in its equipment or training methods without being "spotted" by foreign rivals.

The proportion of machine-guns, 2 per 1000 rifles, was, for instance, the same in all armies, and the only difference between the British and Continental practice was that we distributed our guns 2 per battalion, whereas French and Germans alike worked with machine-gun companies—usually 6 guns. The Continental system was preferable. It was noticed on manœuvres that many of our battalion commanders did not seem to know what to do with their machine-guns and looked upon them as an encumbrance. The general proportion, 2 per 1000 rifles, was fixed with regard to mobility. It was felt that a larger proportion would mean a heavier demand for ammunition and an increased strain upon supply services. For the same reason and in *all* armies, the heavy gun was regarded primarily as a *siege* weapon, and its use with front line combatant troops in rapid movement as cumbersome. It was less Machiavellism nor super-wisdom, but the grim and awful menace of their general strategic position; the actual danger of being smashed between the Allied hammer and the Russian anvil; which lent to Germany a fierce energy in expanding her forces, a feverish ingenuity in improving her defences. The greatest military empire in the world had her back to the wall, and was fighting coolly but desperately and with a savage cunning to beat off the myriad foes whom her own harsh menace had roused to pull her down. The machine-gun is predominantly

LOOS AND THE DARDANELLES

a weapon of the defensive. The counter-battery work of the heavy gun protects the machine-gun from being smashed up by the field-gun; thus, when it became a matter of organising her lines in France for *defensive warfare*, considerations as to mobility ceased to hamper Germany in equipping her troops with these formidable weapons: the advantages far outweighed the disadvantages. There was thus a steady process by which the German lines in France and Flanders developed into one vast system of fortifications, punctuated by redoubts and heavy batteries, bristling with machine-guns, girdled by broad belts of barbed wire. The British and French leaders, on the other hand, were slow to realise the full change which had come over the general conditions of the fighting. The opening of the Spring offensive of 1915, on the contrary, found Field-Marshal Sir John French and his Staff in a surprisingly optimistic mood. They seem really to have believed themselves about to drive the Germans out of Belgium—in one fell swoop. Some of the means taken subsequently to explain away failure will leave a lasting stain on the memory of those who resorted to propaganda as unjust as it was ungenerous.

The close proximity of the trenches to one another and the special conditions of the fighting led on both sides to the development of new weapons alike for attack and defence. The rifle, for instance, with its flat trajectory was sometimes almost useless against entrenchments—save in the case of keen-eyed, specially trained snipers, vigilant to pick off any unwary wight who showed himself in a careless moment. Even the field-gun could not always reach the enemy's front line trenches, sometimes only fifty yards to seventy yards distant from our own. Thus, there was a general desire for close combat weapons, bombs and trench mortars. These existed at first

THE KITCHENER ARMIES

only in a rudimentary form and were even more dangerous to those who used them than to the enemy. An officer writes:

"Of the many varieties of these weapons and forms of destruction the most famous and durable were the Mills Bomb, the Lewis and Vickers Machine-Guns, and the Stokes Mortar. We feel sure that if Sir Wilfred Stokes, when he so patriotically offered his wonderful drain-pipe to the British Government, had known what a volcano of unpopularity and lava flow of oaths he would call down, not only upon his own head but upon the heads of those unfortunates who were called upon to manipulate his weapon, he would have confined his inventive genius to something which irritated the Hun less, and, consequently, aroused in 'Gerry' less anger in the shape of high explosives thrown back at the imagined location of this flatulent weapon.

"'You! 'Oo are you? The b—— trench mortars! You ain't a-comin' 'ere any'ow! Crimes —here's the Jocks luggin' the gaff up for 'em!'

"'Hey! Are you the gowks that wants tae play about wi' these tin-ribbed polonies?'

"'Hand 'em over, Jock.'

"'Stand by—FIRE!' (Swish—swish!) 'Duck, boys.' (Crack—ss—ss—swish!) 'Into the dug-out.' (Phut!)

"''Oo the 'ell's comin' dahn 'ere? Blarsted wind up! This ain't a Rowton 'Ouse! Tork abaht the overcrahding question! Wot I ses is, damn them flamin' mortars.'"

The earliest types of trench mortar were very unpopular with the Infantry. Any damage they could do to the enemy was a matter of dispute: what was certain was the "retaliation" which would fall to the lot of the unfortunate Infantry—added to the

LOOS AND THE DARDANELLES

uncertainty as to premature bursts. The commander of one of the early trench-mortar companies armed with French 58 mm. weapons writes that they " afforded a certain amount of amusement in the early stages . . . one never knew to a hundred yards where the torpedo would fall." Which required a special sense of humour in the Infantry to appreciate the joke. He thus describes an early incident:

" . . . the fuse had been lighted and we retired some three or four yards away, as was our custom with this weapon.

" Not hearing the usual report on discharge of the bomb from the mortar, I stepped into the trench, and was astonished to see the torpedo lying with fuse pointing at me. Hastily retiring to cover again I waited a minute or two, during which nothing happened. I then recharged the mortar, picked up the torpedo very gingerly, replaced it in the mortar and fired again—this time with great success, a *splendid detonation* resulting! "

The nerve of a lion-tamer was needed to handle such weapons really well and the early bombs were no more satisfactory. At first, jam-pots were used filled with explosives and with a fuse which had to be lighted. Even when more scientific ones came on the scene the early types were very unsatisfactory; they could not be used in wet weather and mishaps and misfires were terribly frequent.

On May 23rd, 1915, the Germans added a new horror to a war rich in horrors by the first use of gas.

The divisions of the New Armies and Territorials had been trained in England in accordance with the recognised precepts of " open warfare," and a considerable apprenticeship was needed to fit them for the very different conditions in France. The system generally followed was to attach each new division

THE KITCHENER ARMIES

for training to older ones. Thus the 20th Division left for France July 20th, 1915. Officers and N.C.O.'s went to the 8th and 27th Divisions for training. Bombing schools were opened, divisional and brigade bombing officers were appointed. The brigade bombing officers picked out men likely to become really expert who were kept for a further course. Others went back to their battalions as battalion or company bombers. No bombs were available for instructional purposes and these had to be improvised. Machine-gun classes were formed, gas-mask drill was strictly practised every day. Between the 2nd and 17th August all units from Brigade H.Q. downwards were attached to the 8th and 27th Divisions in the line.

All ranks were tremendously keen. During the first days of the 18th Division in France the men shaved their heads, blacked their buttons, scrupulously avoided smoking—to discover to their astonishment that pipes were being smoked in the front line. In this particular sector the enemy's trenches were only twenty yards distant. The Germans seemed surprisingly well-informed, and for them to welcome an incoming regiment by its name and number and an ironical shout of "Good morning, Tommy," happened not once but many times. It was only later discovered that they had earth wires and listening posts. At first "spies" were the apparent solution, and an outburst of spy mania sometimes made life burdensome behind the lines. The "spies" took varying shape. Sometimes they were supposed to be clad as British staff-officers. At others to prowl round as Army Chaplains. Staff-officers and chaplains both suffered a good deal when those particular rumours went round. There was much nervousness about German mining. A patrol of the Bedfords reported a German subterranean passage which

LOOS AND THE DARDANELLES

turned out to be a beer-barrel. The Berkshires were alarmed by a mysterious fall of chalk. It was a weasel shifting. The Buffs were roused to watchfulness by a mysterious tapping. There was great excitement. The general came himself to investigate. Then the sergeant-major turned up with an eager smile. It was a man chopping wood.

The near neighbourhood of the enemy lines led to some dangerous errors. An officer took a small patrol one dark night into No Man's Land. He decided to go home, climbed over two belts of wire and said to one of his men: " Go to Company Headquarters and say we're back." Just then an unarmed man with a beard turned up and civilly said, " Gute Nacht." The officer had the presence of mind to reply in kind and hoped to get away unscathed, but the German had recognised them for British; he alarmed his men and fire was opened. The historian of the 18th Division writes:

" Though by the end of 1915 the Division had suffered 1247 casualties, these four months proved to be the quietest and not the least pleasant in its history. Except for the winding ribbon of bare land that marked the opposing trench lines, the Somme country remained green and eye-pleasing. Pozières and Ovilliers, in Boche territory had not yet become crumbled brick-heaps; it was possible through the glasses to pick out the church clock in Pozières, while Ovilliers still hid itself in a bower of trees. The outline of Contal Maison showed graceful and inviting, and though Thiépval, high and forbidding, had its château in ruins, the village had not yet been shelled into an abomination of desolation."

There were not lacking amusing incidents; and others which showed the resource and ingenuity of the New Army men. Sniping, for instance, was a

THE KITCHENER ARMIES

pest and there was one nest which the guns could not cover at ordinary range. Gen. Maxse surmounted the difficulty by cunningly concealing an 18-pounder in a front line trench. The story is told of the Lancashire Division which was taking its first tour of duty in the trenches; the men disgustedly wanted to know " How much further is it to the blinking battlefield? " Of the same Division there is the tale of the Fusilier officer inspecting a battalion and hailed by a sentry to ask when he was going to be relieved—he had been on duty six hours. It was pouring with rain, wet and slimy, and the officer discovered the sergeant cosily ensconced with other men in a dug-out. " That won't do. You mustn't leave a sentry six hours without relief."

" Well, sir, I didn't think it's worth while getting more than one man wet."

But if New Army and Territorials erred from lack of military convention, there were some in the Old Army who went to the opposite extreme. Witness this:

" It is observed that of late the provisions of King's Regulations regarding the shaving of the upper lip have been disregarded. . . . Any breach of these regulations will be severely punished in the future."

" Slang " words such as " dug-out " and " bomb " were prohibited. Instead the words " splinter-proof " and " grenade " were to be used. Thus it came to pass that a young officer questioned by a general: " Captain X., you were in your dug-out when that happened? " answered sweetly, " No, sir."

" *No*," thundered the general.

" I was in my *splinter-proof*, sir."

Up to April 1915 Kitchener and the New Armies were in almost equal measure a target for the refined military wit of G.H.Q. But the collapse of the offensives of Neuve Chapelle and Festubert was

LOOS AND THE DARDANELLES

followed by a depression as profound as the preceding optimism had been unfounded, and then towards the end of May, just after the first two divisions of the New Armies, the 9th and 14th, had made their appearance, there came the succession of sweeping German victories over Russia, finally shattering the hopes built up on the Russian " steam-roller." The truth of Kitchener's forecast as to a long war was at last realised in G.H.Q. and excessive rashness gave place to caution—perhaps equally excessive.

The first three New Army Divisions actually to confront a foe were the 10th, 11th and 13th sent to participate in the ill-omened Dardanelles enterprise. These took part in the Battle of Suvla Bay.

On the West Front, Joffre, eager to help his hard-pressed Russian Ally, undeterred by previous failures, planned sweepingly to break the enemy's lines, a project which for the moment roused little enthusiasm on the part of the British leaders.

Their views were dominated by the munitions problem. The grave errors in staff-work which had led to disaster at Neuve Chapelle seem to have passed almost unheeded. It took years of fighting and a terrible price in blood to teach some of the British leaders that to storm the German trenches more was needed than the process of plastering them with unlimited quantities of H.E. shell.

Serious differences ensued between the French and British Headquarters. Each side had a very strong case. The British maintained that delay would afford time not alone to improve their Artillery and munitions positions, but to train and absorb their new formations; the French pleaded the impossibility of looking on and doing nothing while Russia was smitten hip and thigh; the danger that the Czarist monarchy if thus abandoned might make a separate peace; the certainty that Germany, having

THE KITCHENER ARMIES

disposed of the Russian armies would come to France flushed with victory, refreshed in strength, and cast down a new gage of battle. It was one of those grim, terrible situations such as often happen in war in which the *pros* and *cons* are almost evenly balanced, and the only sure element of a doubtful situation is the dreadful responsibility which weighs upon all involved. To attack with the *possibility* of fruitlessly throwing away men's lives? To keep still with the *certainty* that the enemy, left in peace to develop his plans, will then choose his own time and place for the onset? Given anything like a reasonable chance for success, the instinct of every virile soldier will always be to choose the bolder course.

Whilst the experts wrangled, the attack was postponed, and delay is always a very disastrous element in such circumstances. The Germans worked with feverish energy improving their defences. Civilian populace, prisoners of war, were alike pressed into service, whilst their own troops, conscious that failure might cost them their lives, toiled like beavers on their lines. Lessons drawn from previous attacks were taken to heart; text-books were cast to the winds. From two to four miles in rear of the first line, a second was built, carefully sited wherever possible on the reverse slopes, with a fifteen yard belt of wire so stout that the wire-cutters supplied to French and British Infantry could not pierce it. At that time the practicable range for wire-cutting by Artillery did not exceed 4000 yards. Thus the strong points and redoubts of the second line were effectively covered by the first, and to attack them it would be necessary to bring up Artillery and reorganise the assaulting troops. This would give time to bring up German reserves. It was Kitchener who cast the deciding vote. If the French Army was determined to attack it was impossible for the British

LOOS AND THE DARDANELLES

Army to look on and do nothing. The main operation being in French hands, any British offensive must be subsidiary to this; our function was to draw away as many troops as we could from the front of our Ally. Better to risk a disastrous repulse than to fail to support France in her desperate gamble for victory. What soldier will dare to say that this decision was unjust or ill-founded?

Into the details of the Battle of Loos, September 25th, 1915, it is impossible to go here. It was the first battle fought by New Army troops in France and by universal consent they did well. The 15th Division with superb dash took the Lens and Loos Road Redoubts, Loos itself, and swept on to Hill 70. But senior officers had been shot down, junior officers, ignorant of this, hesitated to reorganise and take command, and upon the mass of men, inchoate, flushed with victory, Hill 70 exercised a magnetic influence. The tendency of some prominent feature of land to acquire a fictitious importance in battle, merely because it dominates the landscape and thereby men's minds, is familiar to soldiers. It happened to French and Germans alike in the struggle for *der rote Berg* at Spicheren in 1870, and it happened again and again to our Regular Army in South Africa. The advance of the 15th Division was deflected to the right, but this would have been but a minor error had fresh troops been available to press home the successes won. On the left, the 9th Division had also stormed grandly forward, carrying the Hohenzollern Redoubt, the Dump and Fosse 8. But now came tragedy; two New Army Divisions, the 21st and 24th, had been kept by Field-Marshal Sir John French in reserve. They were among the last divisions to arrive in France; the men had new boots and were unused to marching on *pavé* roads.

On September 12th Joffre had put it on paper:

THE KITCHENER ARMIES

"It is indispensable that these divisions are put, before the attack, at the absolute disposal of General Haig." On September 18th a difference of opinion arose between Haig and French, Haig urging that two of the reserve divisions should deploy in rear of Vermelles, 2000 yards behind the assaulting divisions. French, without entirely dissenting, assured him that the general reserve would be "brought up energetically once the enemy's defences have been pierced." A renewed request from Haig, September 19th, for the forward distribution of the reserves was replied to by French in the affirmative.

At dark, 7 p.m. of September 24th, the final march of the 21st and 24th Divisions began. It was a very difficult and exceptionally trying progress. The 21st Division moved by various narrow side roads to Place à Bruay, thence in one column on a fair road to Noeux les Mines; the 24th by cramped ways to the north-west corner of Béthune and then on a motor route to Beuvy. But it transpired that a mistake had been made to parallel which one must turn to the early days of the American Civil War where armies were mere mobs and generals civilians in uniform. For the staff-officers responsible for road control had directed the divisions to move by roads marked for traffic " down " from the fighting lines, and the long columns of men, guns and stores were met by a stream of motor and horsed vehicles moving in the opposite direction. "It was like trying to push the Lord Mayor's procession through the streets of London without clearing the route or holding up the traffic."[1] There were constant stoppages by level-crossings to permit the shunting and passage of supply trains. In Béthune, the military police stopped the 72nd Brigade because the brigadier had no pass to enter the trench area. The 64th Brigade

[1] *Official History*, Vol. 4, Loos.

LOOS AND THE DARDANELLES

was held up one and a half hours by an accident to a train. The men as they finally struggled into their allotted areas were dead-beat; they were suffering from lack of food and still more from lack of water; and loaded down in full pack. By special order their cookers had been taken away. There was no thought to *nurse* the men, save them for the coming ordeal, give them a hot meal. The roar of the British bombardment filled the air; to the weary, confused, bewildered, hungry and thirsty men even sleep was denied. It was not until 9.30 a.m. of the 25th that the Commander-in-Chief could make up his mind to "put in" reserves; not until 1.20 p.m. that Haig and his staff feverishly urging for help could know that the 21st and 24th Divisions were on the way but delayed by road troubles; not till 11.15 a.m. that the Divisions even began their march, even then in one case to be halted to let an ammunition column go past. Meanwhile the 15th and 9th Divisions, fighting desperately, had stormed ahead, reached the enemy's second line, and wanted only fresh troops to drive their successes home. *The last ounce of effort.* How much it means in war. How few people in all this talk of divisions, batteries, corps, realise all that even a small body of determined men can do if put in whole-heartedly and at the right moment. Needless to go on further with the Battle of Loos. Counter-attacks pressed the 9th and 15th Divisions back, the men were spent, the enemy, reinforced, was strong, well led, desperately brave. The brigades of the 21st and 24th Divisions, even more weary when they arrived than had they been in battle, could render little real help. Fighting continued with intervals till October 13th. In July 1915, Kitchener had sent wise words to Sir Ian Hamilton:

"Lord Kitchener told me to tell you he had no wish to interfere with the man on the spot, but from

THE KITCHENER ARMIES

closely watching our operations here and in Flanders, he is certain that the only way to make a real success of an attack is by surprise. Also, that when the surprise ceases to be operative, in so far that the advance is checked and the enemy begin to collect from all sides to oppose the attackers, then, perseverance becomes merely a useless waste of life. In every attack there seems to be a moment when success is in the assailant's grasp. Both the French and ourselves at Arras and Neuve Chapelle lost the opportunity." In September 1915 it was the same thing, opportunities missed, persistence in attack which meant merely increased casualty lists. Most of the ground won by the sacrifice of precious lives was lost. Fosse 8, the Dump, Hohenzollern Redoubt, Hill 70, all passed back into German hands. But the New Armies had made their first trial of strength with the enemy and had emerged from this trial with renewed confidence in themselves. The men had been splendid. Even the badgered and be-baited 21st and 24th Divisions fought well.[1] The 14th Division in the subsidiary attack on Bellewaarde Lake took the enemy's front line at three different points and in some places reached his supporting line; the 12th Division played a gallant part on the 13th October in an attack on the Quarries.

Both the 9th and 15th Divisions covered themselves with glory. A Corps Order runs:

"When all did so well it would be invidious to make distinctions. It was difficult to say which had the best right to be proudest, the officers of their men or the men of their officers."

[1] The legend that these weary, famished troops broke has been happily disproved. The reports were due only to a few stragglers. Both divisions fought gallantly in the counter-attack on Cité St Auguste on the day following.

LOOS AND THE DARDANELLES

There was no lack of thrilling and heroic episodes. An eyewitness writes:

"A day or two after the first attack I had occasion to pass over the ground where the 15th Division had assaulted the German trenches. In front of the remains of the work known as the Lens Road Redoubt (Jew's Nose) the dead Highlanders in Black Watch tartan lay very thick. In one place, about forty feet square, on the very crest of the ridge, and just in front of the enemy's wire, they lay so close that it was difficult to step between them. Nevertheless the survivors had swept on and through the German line.

"As I looked on the smashed and riven ground, the tangled belt of wire still not completely cut, and the thick swathes of dead, every man lying as he had fallen, face to the enemy, I was amazed when I thought of the unconquerable, irresistible spirit which those newly raised units of the ' New Armies ' must possess to have enabled them to continue their advance after sustaining such losses."[1]

In that little Highland spear-head, cut off in Cité St Auguste in the September of 1915, there was a forecast of the " infiltration " tactics used with such terrible effect by Ludendorff; polished and perfected by the genius of Foch. The death of Lieut.-Col. Douglas Hamilton of the Camerons is worthy of record.

" Four times he led the poor remnant of his battalion, and some hundred others who had rallied round him against the ever-increasing enemy now holding Hill 70. Then he sank to the ground with the quiet, natural words, ' Colquhoun, I'm done! ' ' Of course,' said Capt. Colquhoun to himself, ' of course he's done. He has had the whole thirty hours of cold, hunger and anxiety, and he has been doubling

---

[1] Maj.-Gen. Thuillier, then C.R.E., 1st Division.

THE KITCHENER ARMIES

on these times ten yards in front of us up Hill 70.' Then perceiving the facts, the two officers still with him bandaged his wounds, but twenty minutes later, with the words, 'I must get up, I must get up!' he passed away."

Describing the attack of the 9th Division, an eye-witness, a very distinguished Regular officer, declared that he would have regarded it as impossible for units with barely a year's service to show such steadiness in their advance.

The impression upon the Germans was profound. Hitherto disposed to ridicule the New Armies, they began to realise in these a grave menace to their own military supremacy. Ludendorff in a letter says: " Lord Kitchener became the organiser of the British Army after England had entered the world-war. He created armies out of next to nothing, trained and equipped them. Through his genius alone, England developed side by side with France, into an opponent capable of meeting Germany on even terms (*vollmächtiger Gegner für Deutschland*) whereby the position on the front in 1915 was so seriously changed to Germany's disadvantage." [1]

The words *in 1915* are significant, and refer to the Battle of Loos, and it was this sense of growing and deadly danger which led Germany in the Spring of the year following to the desperate venture of Verdun.

The 15th Division out of 19,500 men lost 6668 killed, wounded and missing; the 9th Division from a like strength, 5868; the 21st, 3853; the 24th, 3991; and the 12th, in its gallant attack on October 13th, 3225.

---

[1] To the author. See *The Truth about Kitchener*. Appendix I.

VIII
THE PRELUDE TO THE SOMME

THE guns of Loos hushed, public interest switched to the south-east, where Bulgar had joined hands with Teuton to smite down Serbia. The Dardanelles were evacuated, the Salonika Expedition arose phœnix-like from the burnt out hopes of Gallipoli, and in France the armies prepared for a new death-grapple. The bitter, fateful year 1915 drew to its close, and as the autumn leaves scattered and fell from the trees the manhood of Britain came flowing across the narrow stretch of sea. Divisions of the Fourth and Fifth New Armies, raised under the arms of shire or city, nobleman or private gentleman, they poured in an endless stream of gallant youth and determined manhood, bringing with them a glimpse of the pageantry and chivalry of England, the romance of the three kingdoms bound in one, Lord Derby's splendid 89th Brigade—" Pals " from Liverpool, units which nourished strange titles such as " Chatsworth Rifles," Hull and Manchester " City " Battalions, Public Schools and Sportsman's Battalions, Tyneside Scots and Irish, to mention only a few of the fine units whose titles spoke of civic patriotism or local pride. To the jaded war-worn troops in France, the New Armies came as a breath of optimism and a symbol of power, and to their ranks came others from Canada, Australia, New Zealand, and South Africa, the Dominion troops of whose prowess men had already heard. The far-flung British Empire was gathering her strength for a grim and desperate passage at arms, was pouring out her very soul in frenzied

THE KITCHENER ARMIES

preparation; and beneath the chaff and laughter of the New Armies lurked the sense of coming peril, for there was the hint of death in the air and it was but a matter of time ere the mighty guns roused to a crashing chorus.

As the new divisions arrived in France they were quickly initiated into the mysteries of trench warfare, being attached to older units for instructional purposes, usually a battalion to a brigade. Moreover, after the Battle of Loos, older Regular or Territorial units were mingled with the last arrived New Army divisions, the system adopted being to exchange a brigade of the older divisions with one from the new and then to exchange one battalion from this brigade into each of the two " new " brigades. Thus the 12th Brigade from the 4th Division was attached to the 36th Division, being replaced in that Divison by the 107th Brigade. From the 12th Brigade, the 2nd Lancashire Fusiliers were exchanged into the 108th Brigade, and the 2nd Essex to the 109th Brigade. The 11th Royal Irish Rifles went from the 108th Brigade to the 12th Brigade, and the 14th Royal Irish Rifles from the 109th Brigade also to the 12th Brigade. Eventually, the 36th Division under this system had one brigade with two Regular and two " new " battalions, two brigades with one Regular and three " new " battalions. The system was very unpopular and its advantages were more theoretical than actual as, under the conditions of trench warfare, one experienced battalion could not " leaven " three inexperienced ones. It would have been a wiser course to have attached a proportion of experienced officers and N.C.O.'s. With the 36th Division these internal changes, which were very unpopular, lasted only one month, whilst the 107th Brigade was returned to the Division February 7th, 1916. In all, seven other New Army Divisions were treated in

THE PRELUDE TO THE SOMME

this fashion: the 17th Brigade from the 6th Division being exchanged with the 71st Brigade of the 24th Division and then exchanging one battalion each into the 72nd and 73rd Brigades; the 62nd, 63rd and 64th Brigades of the 21st Division exchanged one battalion each for the 1st Lincoln, and 4th Middlesex from the 3rd Division and 1st East Yorkshire from the 6th Division, whilst the 2nd, 3rd, 5th, 7th and 8th Divisions each exchanged a brigade with the 23rd, 25th, 30th, 32nd and 33rd Divisions.

The changes were in most cases temporary and the advantages not all on one side, for the optimism and zest of the newcomers were a welcome tonic to men grown stale in the dreary routine of trench warfare. A brigadier of the 4th Division thus notes his first impressions of the New Armies—seen close at hand:

" The men are extraordinarily quiet, and I thought at first somewhat subdued, and put it down to the big marches they had had. But when I came to talk to them I found they were like new schoolboys, taking in everything, deadly keen and only afraid of one thing—letting down their unit in any way. I have never seen any men with such quiet confidence in themselves, in spite of their efforts to hide it."

Some description of the conditions at the front at that time may be of interest. A division usually had two brigades in the line and one in reserve. Each of the front line brigades had two battalions actually in the trenches and which were relieved at regular intervals, although never the same night, by the two battalions which were in support. The tour of trench duty lasted from four to eight days. Each battalion in the front line had, as a rule, two companies in the line, one in support and one in reserve. It will be observed that a division of twelve battalions

THE KITCHENER ARMIES

—excluding Pioneers—had not more than four battalions actually in the front line, of which only eight companies—out of sixteen—actually held the firing bays. The formation was thus in depth. The front and support lines were held by posts of sections —in the early days, ten to twelve men, about half as many later. These posts furnished each a single sentry by day, double sentries at night. For half an hour before and after dawn the troops would " stand to " in the trenches, and in winter months this was the hour of the rum ration—which in many cases the men refused to take. Each company had one officer on duty in the trench by night and day. The natural order of night and day was inverted in the trenches, for it was during the night that most work was done and all wiring and all patrolling of No Man's Land carried out. Roughly speaking, the battalion in the line was responsible for the work as far back as its own H.Q. with the expert assistance of a few sappers. Behind this area was that of the " resting " battalion—although parties from this had frequently to assist the battalion in the front line also—under direction of the R.E., a field company of which was attached to every brigade. It was very important that the Infantry should understand that the Sappers were assistants and not taskmasters, but it was not always easy to persuade them as to this. Our men did not take kindly to the heavy work of fatigues, labour, and carrying parties. The Germans, in this respect, did better work and the failure of our Infantry to realise the value and importance of the engineer, in the opinion of those best competent to judge, added perceptibly to our losses.

At first, each battalion had two Vickers machine-guns—later increased to four. On November 30th, 1915, these were formed into machine-gun companies as in the French and German armies—one to

THE PRELUDE TO THE SOMME

each brigade. The battalions had each four Lewis guns, one to each company: a proportion doubled later in the war. The machine-guns were distributed in depth further forward than was the case when the Infantry were better supplied with Lewis guns. Machine-gun barrages, telephonic communication linking these guns with battalion headquarters, indirect fire, were scarcely conceived up to February 1916. Machine-gun and Infantry ammunition were stored in boxes let into the parapets of trenches. The size and importance of supply dumps, of course, grew as one went from front to rear.

The Artillery was also in the rear and distributed in depth. If covering two brigades it was divided into two groups, which were commanded at or near brigade headquarters. The original organisation in four brigades of Artillery, one being a howitzer brigade, proved clumsy and extravagant, the howitzer brigade being invariably split up in between the two groups, which meant that it was an administrative but not a tactical unit. The guns were in pits concealed and camouflaged as well as possible. Dug-outs for the detachments were close at hand. Pits contained 200 to 400 rounds of ammunition per gun, also close at hand. At dusk, guns were laid on " night lines."

In May 1916 the divisional Artillery was reorganised, each brigade being made up of four 4-gun batteries, one battery being howitzers. The original howitzer brigade was reconstituted with three 4-gun field batteries, one from each brigade. In March 1916 the " tin hat " was served out to the men. It was at first very unpopular and used mainly as a washing-basin or pudding-bowl. Its value, however, was soon realised. Brigade Stokes mortar batteries were formed at about the same time, the personnel being drawn from each battalion to stimulate *esprit*

THE KITCHENER ARMIES

de corps. Thus the 9th Division formed the 9th Trench Mortar Brigade with three batteries. Heavier mortars were worked by the Artillery. The Infantry had at first three types of mortar, $1\frac{1}{2}$ in., 2 in., 3.7 in.; after a few months only the 2 in. was used.

The system of raids did much to keep alive the offensive spirit of our men and to relieve the tedium of trench warfare. They were also a very valuable means of training and produced a school of daring and thoroughly competent leaders. An officer writes:

" . . . few realised what such an operation involved in the way of preparation; the study of ground, compilation and issue of maps, siting of mortar and machine-guns; digging of mine-galleries; cutting of wire; placing of barrage; getting up of bombs, gas cylinders, medical stores, signalling apparatus; deductions by the Intelligence branch of the General Staff from aeroplane photographs; and not least, the rehearsal on similar ground behind the line by that body of troops selected to play their little part in the tactical operation."

There were two types of raid, " raid and stay," " smack and back," and it was sometimes smack and back and smack again. Raiding was a grim and desperate business. If successful, there was mention in despatches, decorations. But they were not *all* successful.

" Some little thing forgotten; some little piece of preparation not perfected; and the whole operation was inevitably a fiasco. In one raid, perhaps, the Artillery observer, owing to ground mist and after many hours of watching with tired eyes, thought that the shrapnel had done its work and cut a path for the Infantry through the enemy's wire. And it was not so! In another, the boy with ' one pip ' guiding

THE PRELUDE TO THE SOMME

his platoon on his compass bearing, had not remembered the existence of a 'true' and a 'magnetic' north and led his men too far to the left.

"Memory asserting itself had made endeavour to correct his bearing and complete his task, but had not only thrown himself in desperation and reckless gallantry on the uncut wire to hang there a corpse for many days, but had at the same time sacrificed his platoon to the murderous chattering fire of the enemy machine-gun nests."

In another raid it was necessary to clear our front supporting lines and to explode a monstrous mine. To protect the raiders against *débris* they were concentrated in the supporting line whilst the garrison holding the front line were in strong dug-outs. But the effects of the explosion were greater than had been anticipated, and in the dim light and with tautened nerves, the raiders mistook the confusion of *débris* between our support and front line for No Man's Land. The captain in command could see the yawning mouths of dug-outs, lights, and hear voices. He thought they were Germans, organised a party, attacked them with bombs, entered the dug-out revolver in hand, to find no enemy but the torn and bleeding bodies of our own men. An error of judgment. "In this experimental stage of the war when we were testing our New Armies, such incidents have occurred over and over again." Some officers were too lazy or too careless carefully to study their work. *Daily Intelligence Summary* would be cast aside with a hasty glance and labelled *Comic Cuts*. But, "there was no doubt that the officer or N.C.O. who conscientiously did his job as a leader spent his time in remorseless, restless study, not only of the art of war, but of enemy practice and ruse, and of map and plan and photograph. Only such leaders could expect success; and even they could not be sure."

THE KITCHENER ARMIES

It was inevitable that in the rush of a mighty expansion and amid the general dearth of officers, a certain number of commissions should have been granted to men unsuitable in type and capacity, and that a certain friction should arise between Old Army and New. The friction was social as well as military. There were many New Army officers and Territorial officers who, whilst brave men and capable leaders, could not reach to the social standards of the pre-war Regular officers. Whilst training in England, instances occurred of officers in uniform dashing along on motor-bicycles with flappers on pillion—instances reported to the Army in France with some embroidery. In France, moreover, there were many occasions in which the conduct of New Army officers roused the older types of Regular officer to horrified protest. But occasions of really gross misconduct were happily rare, and the effervescence of youth and ignorance of conventional military usage had more to do with sins against discipline and respect for the uniform than deliberate wrongdoing. The attitude of G.H.Q. towards the New Armies, however, was not at first exactly sympathetic, and there were not lacking certain staff-officers who showed a greater disposition to dwell upon the alleged deficiencies of the New Armies in these respects than was either wise or fair. As regards the general run of Regular regimental officers, the New Army men soon reached a sympathetic understanding. The men in the front line were more concerned with military qualifications than any others, and the keenness of the newcomers, their enthusiasm and readiness to learn, far outweighed any social deficiencies which may have cropped up here and there. It took longer to establish really cordial relations with the Staff. First of all the Regular regimental officer was usually a man who knew his

THE PRELUDE TO THE SOMME

job, whereas a large percentage of the Regular staff-officers lacked this very necessary qualification; secondly, many of the staff, lacking close and personal touch with the fighting troops, were a little apt to overrate the value of the manners and mannerisms of the parade-ground and officers' mess, and to forget that the qualities to inspire and lead men in battle are the only qualities which really count in war. One doesn't know who was the inventive genius who coined the phrase " Temporary Gentleman." But it was a terribly snobbish phrase and perhaps those who used it most frequently and most loudly were themselves " gentlemen " only in virtue of the King's Commission which they unworthily held. All classes and conditions of men joined up in the New Armies alike in the commissioned ranks and as private soldiers. Many who were of humble origin reached high command. Others, of the public school and 'varsity type proved failures, for war is a very searching test and one which rides roughshod over conventional standards. Generally speaking, the " public school and 'varsity " type produced good leaders, brave and capable officers. The professional and business type were, however, no whit inferior, nor had the older universities or public schools any marked superiority over men from Glasgow, Sheffield, Manchester, Liverpool or Aberdeen—to mention only a few. As the war proceeded and death thinned the ranks, the lower middle classes and working classes also produced men who dropped their " h's " and whose table manners left something to be desired, but who were excellent regimental officers.

If among the Regular officers of our Army there prevailed a certain corporate spirit, and a tendency to look with patronage upon the newcomers, this was not unnatural and scarcely militated against efficiency.

THE KITCHENER ARMIES

A corporate spirit is inevitable with every body of men banded together in one profession: it is to be found with doctors and barristers just as much as with professional soldiers. Generally speaking, the best elements of Old Army and New quickly fraternised and reached a basis of good comradeship in the thought that they were all *soldiers*. Friction which occurred subsequently was largely a matter in which the best types of Regular officer sympathised with his comrades of the New Armies and Territorials, for it was a matter which affected all regimental officers alike; the poor quality of the Staff, and the unfair distribution of rewards. A Regular officer, a battalion commander, writes:

" I suppose it is in the nature of things that people in snug billets (in the full meanings of that term!) should be looked upon with disfavour by the men who lived in constant danger and discomfort. And if in addition the former got the pick, and a monstrously large pick, of all the decorations and promotions, their unpopularity was the more natural, especially amongst the Captains and Subalterns, who, as Lord Rawlinson is credited with saying, won the war.

" Nevertheless there must be a Staff College. There must be Staff Officers, and I think the matter goes further than in this most unfair distribution of rewards. The most general complaint about these Officers is that they soon get out of touch and sympathy with the fighting men, and the older they get and the longer they remain on the Staff the greater becomes this aloofness. This danger was recognised many years ago and it was then decided to follow the German example and return all Officers to duty with fighting troops after each tour of Staff Service. I suppose this wise proceeding was carried out for

THE PRELUDE TO THE SOMME

a bit; but it is common knowledge that it didn't last long, and the permanent, or semi-permanent, Staff Officer soon appeared again. Everyone with pre-war knowledge of soldiering knows how these fossilised limpets, entirely destitute of any human feeling, clung to such a sanctum as the War Office, from which they were at intervals dragged, only to snuggle down again at once into some other equally lucrative Chair of Office. An interview with these people was always a terrible trial to the fighting man with a small income—if he had a large one he was, of course, independent of them. It's not at all easy to suggest a remedy for this state of things. Unfortunately it is in human nature that the strong should domineer over the weak, that the rich should stick to their riches, and that the outlook of the one should be out of touch with that of the other. Your suggestion that character should receive more attention in the selection of Staff Officers is excellent, and if that could be done no doubt a great advance would be made. As it is, I can only suggest, as a partial remedy, the attaching of the Staff to fighting troops at frequent periods of their service and that a larger proportion of Staff appointments should be allotted to the Infantry arm of the Service.

" In war, the grumbling about the stupidity, the ignorance, or the callousness of certain Generals and Staff comes mostly from the Infantry, for the simple reason that it is the Infantry that usually suffers most from these faults or mistakes. Men with a thorough knowledge of the virtues and shortcomings of the foot-soldier (The Queen of Battles) are seldom unpopular. I don't think it is a coincidence, only, that the Army with the finest reputation on the Western Front was commanded by an Infantryman, whose Chief of Staff was also an Infantryman. I

THE KITCHENER ARMIES

think it is doubtful whether any one of the other Armies would, for instance, have stood the ordeal of the Passchendaele operations and retained its spirit to the extent that did the II Army. I can call to mind no instances in the past history of our Army, where outstanding deeds of valour and endurance were performed by forces not led by Infantry Generals. I don't refer to isolated acts, but to the more prolonged operations which called for determined and sustained effort. Wolfe, Moore, Wellington (and his Generals like Craufurd), Clyde, Haig, and Buller are good instances of the power such leaders had to get the best out of their men; and although the last named, like so many who were dashing leaders in their youth, failed as a General in later years, yet I instance him as one never heard any grumbling about the bull-like rushes he made against the Tugela line (1899–1900), and the quite unnecessary loss of life that they occasioned. Probably his men realised that it was with the (mistaken) idea of saving their lives that he continually broke off actions, that were not immediately successful, and all knew that his personal courage was of a high order and that he never asked them to do what he would not himself have done. Haig was a Cavalryman, but his personality, courage, and calm control of the I Corps at the First Battle of Ypres mark him as the successful leader of men. Wolseley, an Infantryman, and probably the most efficient British General of the Victorian era, was never called upon to show his power of leadership under difficult conditions, neither was the Artilleryman, Roberts. The greatest soldier of all ages, Napoleon, also an Artilleryman, was always in the closest touch with the fighting men. From the day when by his personal example and leading he inspired his Infantry to victory at Lodi (1796), till he reviewed his Guards

THE PRELUDE TO THE SOMME

on the field of Waterloo, his life on service is the story of the front-line troops.

"With all these examples before us, it is difficult not to come to the conclusion that close and frequent contact with the Infantry should form a much more prominent part than it has done in the training of Generals and Staff. After all, the human is the most important element in War and the foot-soldier is the most essential part of that humanity. I am convinced that until this fact is duly recognised and acted upon in all Command and Staff training, and its lessons properly applied to the battlefield, discontent will prevail."

With an army as hastily improvised as were our Armies of the Autumn of 1915 and Spring of 1916, the problem of producing thoroughly trained and qualified staff-officers was one which at best bristled with difficulties. Take a man of good natural qualities and sound general education, give him six months of really intensive training with all the stimulus of war, and there is no difficulty in producing an officer capable of handling say a hundred men in battle. But multiply this hundred by *another* hundred, produce a force of 10,000, and the problem of leadership to be solved assumes quite a different scale and complexity. It is necessary to work out railway movements and approach marches by road, one must arrange the movement of supply, transport, medical and ammunition columns, provide for the interaction of arms, infantry, cavalry, artillery, aircraft—and in modern warfare tanks—one must arrange reconnaissance, intelligence work—under certain conditions engineering problems must be tackled. To do all this successfully requires years of specialised training—and the assistance of a carefully selected *team* of specialists. Moreover, it is safe to

THE KITCHENER ARMIES

say that the greater the size of an army, the more hastily it has been improvised, the greater the need for a highly trained staff. For the difficulties to be solved increase *disproportionately* to the size of an army, and whilst a highly trained regular army may possess sufficient elasticity to recover from initial errors in leadership—as the French did at the Marne after the disasters of the August fighting—there will always be the danger that a hastily improvised army will go to pieces after a first disastrous shock. The rapid expansion of our Army in France (within less than two years from four divisions at Mons to fifty-five at the Somme) in any case far exceeded the number of trained staff-officers available, and the difficulties were accentuated by the poor quality of many, if not most, of the Staff College trained men, and the failure, in this most important factor, to pursue a far-sighted policy or to make the best use of the resources to be drawn from the New Armies and Territorials. From the days of Wellington, who complained bitterly as to his staff-officers, staff-work has always been a very weak element in a British Army, and the root cause has always been the same, social influences outweighing the claims of military capacity. A Regular officer of great experience writes somewhat caustically:

" Some relics of feudal times still lingered in our Army. No one was supposed to be fit to occupy the position of an army officer unless he lived in a certain style and spoke with an approved accent. Much of the happiness of the first few years of a young officer's life depended on the amount of his private means. . . . The overgrowth of perpetuated privilege with its resultant power has made itself clear in the case of our cavalry, whose insistence upon young, and at the same time propertied, officers has culminated in their holding nearly all the most important and best

THE PRELUDE TO THE SOMME

paid positions in our Army. The pre-eminence gained by an oligarchy of officers of this arm, seems almost to discredit Euclid's up to now undisputed axiom that the whole is greater than the part."

In 1914 we had 146 battalions of Infantry and only 31 regiments of Cavalry: under a fair system of promotion three times as many Infantry officers should have been in high commands as was the case with Cavalry. These proportions, however, were actually reversed; thus we reached the ludicrous situation that in a war in which the part played by Cavalry was infinitesimal as compared with that played by Infantry, Artillery, and Engineers, Cavalrymen virtually monopolised all the higher commands. But the same vicious system extended all through our Army. Officers, with powerful social patronage behind them, would go to Camberley, emerge with the magic letters *p.s.c.* attached to their names, pass from one staff billet to another, and be finally pitchforked into a high command with no genuine practical experience and after a system of training which produced excellent office-men but very bad soldiers. This system cost us so terrible a price in blood at the Somme that no apology is needed for dilating upon it here: it was a system hateful to the Regular Army as to the New Armies and Territorials, and one which undoubtedly brought Staff College into bad odour with the rest of the Army—perhaps unjustly. A Staff College training cannot, at best, be more than a theoretical training; a man with such training, and however able he may be, is no more fitted to command troops in battle, against an enemy as formidable as were the Germans, than is a youngster fresh from a business-training college fitted suddenly to take charge of some great business firm. Henry Ford has some wise words to say which everyone, soldier or civilian, would do well to take to heart:

" An educated man is not one whose memory is trained to carry a few dates in history—he is one who can accomplish things. A man who cannot think is not an educated man, however many college degrees he may have acquired. . . . There are two extremes to be avoided: one is the attitude of contempt towards education, the other is the tragic snobbery of assuming that marching through an educational system is a sure cure for ignorance and mediocrity."

It is unfair to judge any institution by its failures. Whether in fleets or armies the officer trained specifically to *think* war will never be a very popular figure among officers who have not had the advantage of such a training. If a distinguished general, not himself a *p.s.c.*, was once heard to declare that the principal value of a Camberley trained man depended upon how quickly he could manage to *forget* what the august institution had taught him; if another declared of a certain officer that if X. ever *had* had any sense Staff College seemed to have educated it out of him, such comments should not be taken too seriously. Taken as a body of men the Camberley trained officers did good work. The trouble was that their training had failed to conceive of any vast expansion of our armed forces or of a war fought under the conditions we had to face. Thus a Dominion general declared bluntly that the classically phrased products of the minds " polished in the science of war " were as much use to him and his men as the cuneiform inscriptions on an Assyrian monument. It was, however, with the Dominion troops that the Camberley men did their finest work, and the tragedy was that it was so long before they were suffered to do the same sort of work with New

THE PRELUDE TO THE SOMME

Army troops and Territorials. The Dominion Governments were in a position to put pressure upon our own General Staff. They insisted from the outset that the Camberley men should be used primarily as *teachers* to develop local talent in the way of producing trained staff-officers. Had the same system been used from the beginning with the New Armies some of our worst errors might have been avoided. Instead of this we had a solid phalanx of Regular staff-officers, mostly men of mediocre ability, and no attempt was made to look for New Army men with special qualifications—who, after an apprenticeship, could have done the work much better.

Seen in its true perspective, the war on the West Front was a long drawn-out duel between methods and resources in attack and defence which in many respects recalls the long drawn-out duel between gun and armour at sea. The trench system represented a system of *armour*; the gun was a means of paralysing this armour, the Infantry were a means of exploiting and extending the gains of the gun. But parallel with this major duel between gun and fortification there developed various subsidiary means of attack such as gas, liquid fire, tanks. Every new means of assault developed by the Allies meant a " counter " by the Germans in the way of improved means of defence; the struggle continued on an ever-increasing and more complex scale ; new calls were perpetually made upon the ingenuity of the peoples, their wealth and readiness to make sacrifices for the common cause. In this grim and desperate *race* between means and methods of defence and those of attack, Germany at first kept the upper hand. She was usually quicker to devise improved **means** of defence than were the Allies quick to produce more powerful means of attack. In fact it was not until 1918, and not alone when she was at the end of her

THE KITCHENER ARMIES

tether in industrial resources and in man-power, but had chosen to throw all the advantages of her strong positions aside and to challenge a decision in open fighting, that the balance of advantage in attack swung round to our side, and we were able to administer a *coup de grâce*.

Towards the end of 1915 Field-Marshal Sir John French was replaced in command in France by Gen. Sir Douglas Haig, and Gen. Sir William Robertson went to become Kitchener's right hand at the War Office. At home there ensued a valuable tautening up of administrative methods. The first rush of improvisation was over, the munitions problem was well on the way to satisfactory solution, hutments had been built upon a vast scale, the new recruits could be equipped with quarters, uniforms, boots and rifles. The Young Officers' Training Companies were now grouped into Cadet Battalions, six schools were opened for N.C.O.'s, training manuals were simplified, lucidly written pamphlets became available dealing with trench warfare; the training of the Army in England was brought more into line with that of the Army in France. It was not until after Kitchener's death that there was instituted the most drastic and far-reaching of the measures associated with the name of Sir William Robertson, the " pooling " of the Reserve Battalions. Yet this system which produced the drafts for our Army in the later phases of the Somme offensive, and during the whole of the Flanders offensive, is of sufficient importance to be briefly alluded to here.

It will be remembered that in pre-war days the only machinery set up for providing drafts were the Special Reserve battalions. Kitchener, in April 1915, had converted the original Fourth Army into a new series of Reserve units known as the Service Reserve

THE PRELUDE TO THE SOMME

Battalions. The locally raised units were also asked to form two reserve companies per battalion and these companies were grouped into battalions known as Local Reserve Battalions. The Third-Line Territorial Battalions were similarly to provide drafts for First and Second-Line formations. There were thus Special Reserves, Service Reserves, Local Reserves, Territorial Reserves, the difference between whom, however, was more in name than in kind, whilst the difficulties inherent in working with the county as an administrative unit became quickly manifest. The association of many counties with their battalions was of the most slender description; thus the 9th (Service) Battalion, the *Devonshire Regiment*, had only eighty men from Devon, most of the men being Londoners or from Birmingham. Innumerable other instances could be quoted. The upshot was that thinly populated counties could not maintain their quota of battalions whilst others had an excess of recruits. Robertson sharpened and intensified the system of " recruiting blocks " introduced by Kitchener. Thus on September 1st, 1916, the 16th and 17th Battalions the *Durham Light Infantry* became the 1st and 2nd Training Reserve Battalions; the 11th (Reserve) Battalion North Staffordshire Regiment and 31st (Reserve) Battalion Northumberland Fusiliers became the 4th and 86th Training Reserve Battalions. Robertson was forced by the logic of hard facts to go even farther in disregarding the Territorial system than Kitchener. He even dropped Territorial titles altogether. In July 1917 there was a further reorganisation of reserve battalions, these being divided into four classes according to the category, age and training of the recruits. The 4th Training Reserve Battalion was renumbered the 258th, and the 86th the 273rd. In October 1917 it was decided again to affiliate all these battalions to

THE KITCHENER ARMIES

line-regiments, but this was done in entire disregard of the origins of the battalions. Thus the 258th—originally the 11th (Reserve) Battalion, *North Staffordshire Regiment*—and the 273rd—originally 31st (Reserve) Battalion,*Northumberland Fusiliers*—became the 51st and 52nd (Graduated) Battalions, the *Durham Light Infantry*.

"Young Soldiers' Battalions" were formed at this time to which were posted lads of 18 years and one month, later increased by one month, who were then sent by companies, after four months' training, to one or other of the Graduated Battalions. After seven months' further training they were then old enough and fit enough to be sent abroad. In March 1918, however, this system had to be modified, lads of $18\frac{1}{2}$ years being sent to France.

The history of the 11th (Reserve) Battalion *Black Watch* is a similar story. On September 1st, 1916, it became the 38th Training Reserve Battalion; in August 1917 this title was changed to the 202nd Infantry Reserve Battalion. On November 1st, 1917, the New Army Reserve Battalions of all Highland regiments were telescoped into two battalions "which for some arbitrary reason," complains the historian of the *Black Watch*, were called the 51st and 52nd Graduated Battalions *Gordon Highlanders*.

Perhaps the most significant thing about this study of the evolution of the drafting system is that Robertson, with all the powerful aid of conscription at his elbow, found himself unable to use to profit the Territorial scheme bequeathed by Lord Haldane. The real author of this scheme, it may be said, was a staff-colonel who had never commanded so large a unit as a brigade, and who was about as qualified to provide a basis of national military organisation for a world-wide war, lasting many years, involving millions of men, and directed against the greatest

THE PRELUDE TO THE SOMME

military empire in Europe, as to pass an expert judgment upon the canals of Mars.

Despite conscription, the improvement of training conditions at home, and the general tautening up of the drafting system, it was noticed that the quality of the drafts sent to units at the front grew steadily poorer.

In December 1915 an Allied Council of War was held in Paris to arrange a co-ordinated offensive by France, Great Britain, Russia and Italy, and on the 19th of the same month Haig and Joffre agreed upon a combined attack along a front of forty-five miles from Gommecourt to Lassigny. The French were to use thirty-nine divisions, the British twenty-five; powerful Cavalry forces were to exploit the gap made, and the Allied Armies pushing through were to wheel, British north, and the French south. The blow was to be directed at the *German Army* rather than at fixed territorial points, and Joffre suggested preliminary offensives with limited objectives to wear the Germans down before the main attack. Haig, towards the end of January, discussed with Allenby a limited offensive in the THIRD ARMY area of the Somme region and agreed to attack with fifteen to eighteen divisions, to be increased to twenty-five if Russia attacked in the Spring. The Czarist monarchy was not, however, expected to be ready until June, and the main attack of the Allies was therefore fixed for July. The British Commander-in-Chief agreed that two weeks before this another " limited " attack should be made, and Rawlinson, put in command of the newly formed FOURTH ARMY, was sent to Flanders to study an attack there.

Haig and Joffre proposed, Falkenhayn disposed. February 21st, 1916, the German Crown Prince opened the Verdun offensive, knocking these far-reaching schemes grievously awry.

On February 9th, 1916, Kitchener paid his last

THE KITCHENER ARMIES

visit to the Army in France. Word had reached him that the new Commander-in-Chief had faith in a process of piercing the enemy lines with " mathematical exactitude," and that far-reaching schemes were in the air for a " break-through battle " upon a tremendous scale. The War Minister devoted his last opportunity of meeting face to face the man into whose hands had been entrusted the responsibility of leading the greatest Army ever put by the British Empire into the field, to giving a grave and solemn warning which he repeated to Haig's principal staff-officers:

" The war is not against the men immediately opposed to you, it is against the German nation. The Allied armies must press against the German line, and strike it hard and repeatedly: some day the front will waver and bend, but let me never hear from any one in France any mention even of the words ' piercing the line.' "

The Commander-in-Chief and his staff-officers listened with scepticism. Four months later, three weeks after the icy waters of the northern sea had passed over the head of the great soldier, the " mathematical " schemes for piercing the German line collapsed in a holocaust of broken, bleeding bodies, a riot of blood, ruin and death.

It has been left for Lord Grey, a civilian lacking in technical knowledge of war, but possessed of profound knowledge of human nature, to pass upon Kitchener a wise and temperate verdict.

" We can see in the light of after-knowledge the mistakes that actually were made; we do not know the mistakes that might or would have been made by the Cabinet, had someone other than Kitchener been at the War Office." [1]

[1] *Twenty-Five Years*, Vol. II, p. 72.

THE PRELUDE TO THE SOMME

To realise the true magnitude of Kitchener's services to the Empire and to his Cause it is necessary to reflect upon what would most likely have happened had he not been there.

So far as concerns the mobilisation and despatch of the Expeditionary Force no great difference would have occurred. The difference would have been felt mainly in the arrangements made for future expansion. Next to Kitchener, the soldiers whose views would have been accepted as authoritative by the Cabinet and the country would have been Field-Marshal Sir John French, Sir Henry Wilson or Sir Charles Douglas, the then Chief of the Imperial General Staff. All these, however, were firmly convinced that the war would be over in six months, and their one thought would have been to take every officer or man who could have been of use in training an army to fight in France. Thus we should have had a War Office staffed by men old, infirm, out of date or lacking in prestige; a Territorial Force enlisted only for Home Defence, sketchily trained, armed with obsolescent guns and rifles; and a Special Reserve only capable of filling the gaps in our existing tiny Regular Army for three months. The *Diaries* of Sir Henry Wilson, the recorded views of French, put it beyond dispute that up till April 1915, G.H.Q. was firmly convinced that our small Army, plus the French Army and the Russian "Steam-Roller," was going to drive the Germans out of France. They did not want New Armies, they did not want even Territorials—save as battalions sandwiched into Regular brigades; they were content that the Old Army and Territorials should be kept up to strength. Can anyone imagine Mr Asquith's Cabinet countenancing sweeping schemes for the expansion of the Territorial Force, or drastic measures of conscription in the teeth of the judgment

THE KITCHENER ARMIES

of their most trusted military advisers? It was not until the disastrous defeats of Russia in June, July and Autumn of 1915, that either G.H.Q. or the Imperial General Staff realised the fallacy of their early views, and that armies would be needed upon an infinitely vaster scale than anyone had anticipated. Here is a simple sum in Rule of Three: If Kitchener, setting to work with Herculean energy on the very day he entered the War Office, firing the whole country, rousing the whole country to eager and enthusiastic co-operation, needed ten months before even the first of his New Armies were ready to cross the sea, and close on two years to get his armies into full working order and in a reasonable state of efficiency, what chance would the General Staff have had of solving this problem successfully, starting nine months later, bringing to its problem rusty generals, a strictly *official* mind, and with the country swept bare even of the limited number of officers and N.C.O.'s seized upon by Kitchener to train his New Armies?

Again, the poverty of the land in regard to supplies of guns, rifles, uniforms, equipment, munitions, boots, training quarters, etc., and our limited resources for manufacturing all these requirements, only became clear even to Kitchener himself when he set actually to raise his Armies; but they would have been experienced in equal measure by any Government or General Staff which had set itself subsequently to raise armies upon the same vast scale. The only difference would have been the loss of the priceless months during which all these deficiencies were remedied.

Lacking as we did the rousing of the national spirit to danger by an actual invasion, to call men to arms meant a vast recruiting campaign, in which civilians such as Lord Derby and the Press and public came powerfully to Kitchener's aid. But it must never be

THE PRELUDE TO THE SOMME

forgotten that the impulse for this campaign came from Kitchener; it was because of his prestige and the trust felt by civilians in him that they rose with so fine a spirit to his aid. This mighty impulse affected the Territorials also, and it is difficult to say how this Force would have worked had Kitchener not been there. The historian of that fine corps, *The Royal Scots*, writes:

" No one knew precisely what would be the effect of a general European War, but most people took it for granted that the fighting on land would be carried out by professional soldiers, assisted perhaps by volunteers, as had been the case in the South African War, and that the worst that could happen to a civilian would be that he would probably be called upon to dig more deeply into his pockets to meet the expenses of the contest. Fortunately there was a national leader to show what required to be done. Lord Kitchener, brushing aside the airy optimism that predicted a short, sharp struggle, solemnly warned the nation that it was on the threshold of a long and doubtful conflict and that the numbers of the fighting forces must be augmented beyond precedent without delay. . . . The institution of the New Armies created much stir among Territorial troops, many of whom were not content with the passive rôle assigned to them under the regulations of 1908."

The regimental historian of *The Devonshire Regiment*, speaking of the Territorial Battalions of this regiment, expresses a view identical with those of Territorial historians, such as the *London Scottish* already quoted:

" The response naturally varied in different units; there were officers and men in the Territorials who had joined the force as a Home Defence Force,

THE KITCHENER ARMIES

which, indeed, was all it was supposed to be, and were not prepared, or were not able, to undertake other obligations. In August 1914, too, it was not wonderful if many had, as yet, failed to realise what the war involved. Some months were to pass before optimistic visions of seeing the Germans back over the Rhine before the New Year were to give place to the realisation of the deadlock along the unbroken trench line from the Yser to the Alps." [1]

No one can doubt that, had the Territorials realised the national danger, they would have rallied as manfully to their country's cause, whatever leader we may have possessed; but, lacking the right leader to kindle their hearts, it is doubtful if they would have universally accepted the obligation for foreign service. Some battalions would have done so. Territorial companies could have been formed for Regular battalions as was done in South Africa. But there, at least during the first nine months of the war, the thing would most probably have ended. Even if one takes a large view, and considers that all Territorial units would have volunteered, this would have meant at most fourteen divisions ready by June 1915, at least six of which must have been kept back for Home Defence, leaving eight for France—assuming none were sent to Egypt, India, Gibraltar or Malta. By June 1915, Kitchener had the equivalent of seven Territorial divisions in France, besides thirty New Army divisions formed or forming and twelve *second-line* Territorial divisions.

There's no doubt about it. The scheme prepared by Lord Haldane and his military advisers, excellent as far as it went, would have been no substitute for Kitchener's New Armies. By the time they had awakened to what was really needed, the opportunity

[1] *The Devonshire Regiment*, p. 60.

THE PRELUDE TO THE SOMME

to raise these Armies would have passed. The General Staff, setting itself in the Autumn of 1915 to expand the Territorial Force, to convert it into a foreign service army upon a vast scale, would have had to face even greater difficulties than were faced by Kitchener in the Autumn of *1914*; and even with conscription to help them they could not have got these armies ready in time. For in February 1916 there developed the great German offensive of Verdun, of which it has been said by competent critics:

" Verdun had come within reasonable distance of knocking out France for good . . . it marked the culminating point in the fighting spirit of the French Army."

In this great crisis France was saved from decisive defeat because our Armies were able to put into line fifty-five divisions. These divisions held off German divisions; they enabled the *whole* of the French Army to be concentrated against a part of the German Army; the counter-attack of our Armies ultimately broke the back of the German onslaught on Verdun. But it is taking a very optimistic view of the Haldane scheme to believe that we could have had in the field, say fourteen first-line Territorial divisions and six second-line divisions by February 1916; the grand total of divisions available would not have exceeded thirty under the most favourable conditions, many of which would have been even more hastily raised and more imperfectly trained than were the New Armies. The loss of a whole year would, moreover, have been acutely felt in the munitions programme. Heavy guns and machine-guns cannot be conjured up at a moment's notice. The upshot would have been—too late! France would have been smashed at Verdun. We should have lost the war.

THE KITCHENER ARMIES

Nobody wants to be unfair to Lord Haldane and his military advisers, nobody wishes to disparage or to belittle the gallant Territorials. But some measure of justice and of generosity is due to the memory of the great soldier who died in his country's service, but who, before he died, could feel that the foundations of victory were well and truly laid. The drumfire of journalism, the whizz-bangs of propaganda can exalt the mediocrity and belittle the genius, but such a judgment will not stand. Poet or peasant, soldier or priest, it is by a man's work that his life is judged, by his services to his fellow-men. The final and lasting verdict upon Kitchener will always be this—*he delivered the goods*. Having set himself to produce his New Armies he successfully accomplished his task; he had his Armies ready in time to play a decisive part in the war. And the plain, average, sensible man or woman will reach the conclusion that this after all is the only thing which really matters.

IX

THE SOMME: OPENING PHASE

As the deep-toned baying of the German guns arose around Verdun it was clear to all that the war had reached another great crisis and that the hour of trial for the New Armies was at hand. The first result was that the line held by the French Tenth Army was taken over by the British, who now held a continuous stretch reaching to its junction with the French Army at the Somme. Division after division of the French were hurled into the fighting and furious attacks varied with desperate counter-attacks. Marshal Pétain had grimly announced *ils ne passeront pas*: the words found an echo in the hearts of his troops, and a surge of battle endured whilst the world marvelled—and waited, sick with suspense, for what the coming day might bring. Kitchener at the War Office was in full accord with Joffre that a premature offensive by the British Armies before the newly formed divisions had settled down, or the munitions programme was fulfilled, would do more harm than good; nor did the French generalissimo, conscious of our difficulties, unfairly press his own desperate need. Whilst making no secret of his own desire that the British offensive should be hastened to April, he remained serenely calm; no voice of panic came from this grand and mighty figure; he forebore by word or deed to press the British leaders to do that which their better judgment condemned. But as the Spring flowers passed away and the days lengthened there was a tautening up of the British Armies, a quiet deadly earnest in the

THE KITCHENER ARMIES

spirit of the training, and uncoiling themselves like some slow-moving but massive growth the British Armies moved Somme-wards. Away back in England men and women toiled fashioning the mighty guns, the mountains of shell, the deluge of bullets soon to be belched out upon the German lines: at night here and there, officer or man would lie in wakefulness, sensing what lay in store, wondering how he would meet the ordeal, desperately afraid of being afraid. But outwardly it was all laughter and jest and confidence. 1916. The wonder year that was to free France. Vengeance for the disasters of 1915. If there were many who, as Spring brought forth buds and blossoms, secretly wondered " Shall I live to see the falling of the leaves? ", these were thoughts one kept in the inmost recesses of one's own soul. The New Armies, the cream of Britain's manhood, the flower of her race, how blithely they marched to the Somme! What splendid youth and power there was about those khaki columns winding into Picardy: what mettle and fire in those gallant boys and men, old in years but young in spirit, who marched to death as blithely!

" The whole hinterland behind the trenches," writes one who was there, " was a hive of industry and traffic. Swarms of troops from every part of the kingdom were to be seen in every village; at night the roads groaned with the passage of guns of all sizes and of transport carrying every conceivable variety of material, and the whole countryside was covered with dumps containing R.E. material, bombs, shells, and stores of all kinds. Hospitals and aerodromes formed additional villages in the district. The back areas of the Somme in the Summer of 1916 were the busiest centres of activity in the whole world. It was a wonderful exhibition of the resources

THE SOMME: OPENING PHASE

of the British Empire, and a visible proof of the diligence with which workers at home had applied themselves to the manufacture of munitions of war. It was not a feverish bustle that one witnessed, but a steady and systematic application of labour; every movement was directed by an organisation that was not surpassed by any other nation in war. The whole of the work performed by Britain in its administrative arrangements has probably never been appreciated at its full value. It had a most heartening effect upon all who saw it, and gave the men an inspiring confidence in the determination and ability of the Allies to achieve complete victory."

The arrangements for the supply, transport and feeding of our Armies from the very outset were in the hands of specially qualified civilians who were doing work not dissimilar to that which they did in peace. These services all functioned admirably. Failures in staff-work mainly concerned *combatant* functions, *i.e.* arrangements in the timing of approach marches and conditions under which these were made, operation orders, failure carefully to co-ordinate attacks. Kitchener in his message to Col. Dallas on October 5th, 1914, had written: "Warn everybody to keep movement of troops absolutely secret. Try and bring off a complete or partial surprise on enemy's left; for this purpose movement of troops from sea-coast should be as much as possible at night. Am sending flying squadron, which will, I hope, protect troops from too inquisitive enemy's aircraft." But in 1916 G.H.Q. was far from having grasped the importance of secrecy, camouflage or surprise in war. An officer writes: " G.H.Q. seemed to think in 1915–7 that stamping everything ' Secret,' documents, envelopes, maps, was all that was necessary to keep our battle intentions secret.

THE KITCHENER ARMIES

" How could they be secret when in the projected area of operations we were building new roads and battery positions beneath the Fokker and the Albatross? When we were registering new batteries by wireless every day, and omitting to change or in any way to control our wireless call-signs so that the Germans, by intercepting our messages, knew of every fresh battery we brought up? When we constructed additional casualty clearing stations, and dumps and hutments, in the zone behind where we proposed attacking? When our reconnaissance and photographing machines were concentrated in one specific zone? When our signal traffic was allowed to increase in volume locally out of all proportion to other normal sectors of the front? When the whole rearward zone of our contemplated attack was literally criss-crossed with Decauville light railways? When movement of troops and transport was permitted by day and also train movement? When an advanced G.H.Q. was planted down weeks beforehand behind the very sector where we proposed attacking, for all the world to note, when . . . but one could go on indefinitely.

" We wrote our intentions on the ground, in the air, everywhere, but we changed for dinner."

With that uncanny knack of his of seeing into the heart of a problem at a glance, Kitchener, in October 1914, had already put his finger on the very thing in which our Army was most deficient—the failure to appreciate the overwhelming importance of secrecy and surprise in attack. As our Armies wound down the valley of the Somme they were like some slow, powerful, heavily muscled mastodon. And it happened, not infrequently, that French peasant girls or waitresses in cafés, chaffingly informed the troops where they were going, matters supposed to be a profound secret, the penalty for betraying which was death.

THE SOMME: OPENING PHASE

The Verdun offensive had greatly modified Haig's plans. Originally the Battle of the Somme was to have been a huge drive along a front of forty-five miles by an army of fifty divisions. But the French share was reduced to five divisions instead of thirty-five, their frontage of attack to eight miles instead of thirty, and even this on July 1st was reduced by two miles.

The British attack was to take place with nineteen divisions, and six in reserve. There were five Army Corps, reading from right to left, the XIII, XV, III, X, VIII, the whole under the command of Sir Henry Rawlinson.

And now, before we follow these British divisions on that clear, sunny, but fateful morning of July 1st, 1916, something must be said as to the character of these troops and as to the character of the man who was to lead them in this grim and frightful ordeal.

The Armies of the Somme, in the true sense of the phrase, were *all* New Armies. In the Regular battalions, a few officers and N.C.O.'s here and there were all who survived of the original British Expeditionary Force. Not only the men in the ranks, but the major proportion of officers and N.C.O.'s had joined up under arrangements made by the great War Minister. The same thing applied to the Territorials. The percentage of all ranks in these fine divisions who had enlisted in pre-war days was infinitesimal. Most of the officers and men came from the second-line units, built up under the *ægis* of Kitchener, and in accordance with the administrative measures which he had introduced. The Armies of the Somme formed a homogeneous national volunteer Army, and any distinction in the efficiency of divisions was a matter primarily of the divisional commander and his staff. The British Army followed a vicious system, which was to use the *Army Corps*

THE KITCHENER ARMIES

purely as a clearing-house for divisions. With the Canadian, and subsequently the Australian Army Corps the divisions were kept together, which meant that they were accustomed to *work* together; the divisional commanders and their staffs knew one another and their Corps Commander and Corps Staff, a thing which made for good team-work and a general standard of efficiency. But an Imperial division—to use the phrase applied by the Dominion troops to those from the United Kingdom—might be attached one day to the II Corps, a week later to the XI Corps and a month later to the III Corps. This system made an Army Corps a mere hotchpotch of divisions, which were being perpetually moved from one Corps to another. Thus the Corps Commander and his staff were not accustomed to work with the divisional commanders and their staff, and this, although in some cases the worst effects were obviated by good will, was unquestionably a very serious handicap upon efficient leadership.

In practically all divisions divisional schools had been established, which were an invaluable means by which company and battalion officers could get not alone a theoretical and practical training in their profession, but—and this is even more important—they could get to know one another and the officers of other arms, and acquire the spirit of divisional *esprit de corps* and of team-work.

By July 1st, 1916, the worst evils of improvisation, as regards battalions, brigades and divisions, had been successfully surmounted. Division for division, our new troops were fully a match for French or Germans, brave and well led though these undoubtedly were. During the battle some extraordinarily brilliant performances were given by divisions, arguing a standard of staff-work and battle discipline unparalleled in history, and the like of which has never been wit-

THE SOMME: OPENING PHASE

nessed even from highly trained professional troops. But the evils of improvisation continued to be felt in the higher commands, and were undoubtedly aggravated by the vicious system described above. Some of the Army Corps leaders were quite incapable; even the most capable were hampered by lack of touch and of close sympathy with their divisional commanders.

Gen. Sir Douglas Haig, who now commanded our Armies, is a figure about whose head has been wreathed bitter controversies. By some he has been acclaimed as a heaven-sent genius; by others condemned as a dull and plodding mediocrity. The truth is probably between these two extremes.

From the accounts of his most sympathetic biographers he seems to have embraced the profession of arms in a very casual fashion, and to have joined the Army in a spirit which might fairly be described as that of a young man at a loose end and with nothing better to do. This in itself scarcely suggests a *great* soldier. For the artist in war, like the artist in painting, music, or literature—who begins writing or daubing or strumming on a piano even before he reaches his teens—starts with the love of his art born in him. Instances can be quoted of a man like Cromwell, with great military capacities lying dormant, and revealing themselves under impulse of strong emotion. Other instances can be quoted of a man of high social position called upon to hold command and doing well in the field not because of any *genius* for war, but because he had good natural parts. But one cannot think of any really great soldier *sauntering* into the practice of his art. However, Haig joined a Cavalry regiment, and did well without inspiring any particular enthusiasm on the part of his men or his brother officers—who described him as cold, dogmatic, intolerant, lacking

THE KITCHENER ARMIES

in sympathy for others. Then, we are assured, "his ambition awakened," and he decided to go to Staff College—because he had observed that men with *p.s.c.* had a better chance of preferment. In this he showed judgment. His career after leaving the institution was that of the "permanent" staff-officer who marches from one staff-billet to another. Prior to 1914 his war experience was very little. He took part in a skirmish in Kitchener's Soudan campaign, became a staff-officer to Egyptian Cavalry, then chief staff-officer to French's Cavalry Brigade at Aldershot, and when this went to South Africa in 1899, shared as a staff-officer in the Battle of Elandslaagte and the operations around Colesberg. Needless to say, however, the responsibility—and credit—for these operations rested with French, and Haig's only experience of even semi-independent command was as a column leader in the Guerilla War. As to any achievements against the wily De Wet, history is silent. But we have the negative evidence that if he did nothing very brilliant he at least escaped ignominious defeat.

The Chief of Staff to a successful general is bound to come in for his share of *kudos* and rewards. Haig, who had never commanded a squadron, received command of a Cavalry regiment, and this was his last experience of regimental work. Thereafter his career was a long succession of Staff appointments, which he wound up in 1913 by being given command of the 1st Division at Aldershot. On the outbreak of the war, however, when, at the last moment, the decision was taken to form Army Corps, Haig was appointed to command one of these.

It is no unfair criticism to say that Haig's career had been such as to render him in 1914 rather a successful military academician than a thoroughly trained and efficient leader for great armies in battle.

THE SOMME: OPENING PHASE

He was a man who read much, studied deeply, and who, cool-headed, resourceful, self-reliant, morally and physically fearless, had natural qualities of command. If reading, reflection, natural qualities could qualify a man to handle masses of troops in battle, Haig would have been an excellent leader. The trouble is that they *don't*. Study, reflection, natural qualities will carry a man far on the road to success in war. But they will not carry him *all* the way. No imagination can forecast the terrible reality of battle, no man can expect to gain a true, practical and vivid insight into the difficult problems of the supply of armies or movement of masses of troops, guns and stores, on a basis of experiments with non-existent troops against an imaginary enemy. Staff-rides, war-games, are very valuable training, but they cannot substitute manœuvres with full scale bodies of troops; the man who has learnt how to handle a brigade both practically and theoretically will always be much better off than the man whose soul is wrapped up in the movements of Army Corps—but who does not know how to handle a brigade. The most disastrous thing about Haig's training was that it had put him out of touch with the fighting troops. It had given him a false scale of values. He saw men in battle as prettily coloured blocks of red or blue or green on large scale maps, and he failed to realise that all these blocks were made up of living and breathing men. A man possessed of a greater fund of human sympathy, a broader and more tolerant spirit might perhaps have overcome this difficulty. But Haig's own temperament was such as to accentuate the deficiencies of his training. Cool, aloof, deeply intellectual, there was about him no spark of personal magnetism, nothing which could fire men's minds or arouse them to enthusiasm. The historian of the 33rd Division has something to

THE KITCHENER ARMIES

say, the truth of which is so apparent to every thoughtful soldier that no apology is needed here for quoting it in full:

"Previously, as part of a Division, Brigade, or Battalion, or even as an individual, one had felt oneself a definite unit of the army. One now seemed to be engulfed in the colossal panoply of war. A man seemed to lose his identity as an individual. Divisions were swallowed up in terms of Corps and Armies. Probably, for this reason, from this point of the war one seemed no longer to regard death as individual. Death claimed so many friends and men one had never seen before. Reinforcements would arrive; one never knew their names, they disappeared so quickly through the Dressing Stations, or to swell the number of the little wooden crosses. The individual man was gone. His soul survived despite the orders which moved him from point to point in the battlefield, not as a man but as a molecule in a body of 120,000 troops. This remarkable fact must be appreciated. For it was a factor which from this point began to influence the whole of our national life until it had laid such a grip upon us that in the later days of the war we were in peril of coming entirely under the spell of the Military System. Conscription, Bureaucracy, Officialdom, must all have started from this point when our Government began to think in terms of Armies and not in terms of Platoons.

"The personal equation is a definite force in an army. A high moral is its strongest quality. Individual moral is the germ of its success. It was left to the regimental officer who understood this to see that so great a quality did not perish whilst the Staff, of necessity, became absorbed in questions of Grand Tactics and Strategy. In our national life

THE SOMME: OPENING PHASE

also it was left to the Little Man to preserve this quality in the national heart, whilst the bureaucrat and official chivvied him from pillar to post in a mad endeavour to turn a free people into a militarised and bureaucratic state. We do not blame the bureaucrat. In his neglect of the idea of a National Ideal he was only attempting to perform a task of which he had had no previous experience. Probably few other than the humble recruiting officer at home, before the days of conscription, and the Regimental Officer in the field, fully realised that an appeal to the soul of our Ideal, of which there was the germ in every Briton's heart, could make men do what rules and orders and laws could never accomplish.

" We had lost sight of the greatest factor of success in leadership—leadership in war, no less than leadership in industry. The personal equation was lost, where, with a great civilian army, it should have been paramount. In the armies of France—the civilian force of a Republic—the personal equation was the keystone of their training, efficiency, and *esprit de corps*. In our Army such expressions as "*on vous aura!*" and "*ils ne passeront pas*" were seldom heard. Marshals Foch and Joffre referred to their troops in the inspiring and personally affectionate term "*Mes enfants!*" Such terms of affection were mostly deprecated in our Army. Those officers who knew the value of perfect camaraderie and were daring enough to practise it, did so in the teeth of active opposition. Yet there must have been many who felt it strongly. We are not the cold, unbending race we are so often supposed to be. Even the American can now appreciate this. But we are invariably fearful of exposing our hearts. Common danger forced this. The Higher Command, who rightly were not called upon to sit freezing in a bitter wind in the hell of a bombardment, could

THE KITCHENER ARMIES

seldom feel how this new Freemasonry bared the soul of spoiling conventionalism, and left the heart of peer and peasant stripped naked before its God. It could think in no terms less than divisions; and so it forgot man and his throbbing heart, his soul; his weakness and his love—a love passing the love of woman . . . the Freemasonry of the Trenches has its various degrees. The Grand Master was no more necessarily General or Commanding Officer than private soldier."

It was a strange paradox which gave the command of these keen, eager, enthusiastic volunteer armies to a man who was the archetype of the purely professional soldier. It never seemed to occur to Haig or his staff-officers that the highly intelligent, sternly determined men of the New Armies might be responsive to a more sympathetic handling than the old type of Regular soldier, or that men tackled in the right spirit by a man who knows how to handle *men* will achieve more and suffer more than for a commander who treats them as automata. There were other Regular officers who did not make this mistake. Take Maxse's orders before the storming of Thiépval.

" (*a*) The summit you are asked to capture provides the enemy with his last remaining observation posts over the Albert Area. By capturing its crest we shall deny observation to the Germans and enlarge the scope of our own.

" (*b*) Great importance has been attached to Thiépval by the Germans, who have issued frequent orders to all concerned to hold it ' at all costs.' They have even boasted in writing that it is impregnable. The 180th Regt. of Würtembergers have withstood attacks on Thiépval for two years but the 18th Division will take it tomorrow."

THE SOMME: OPENING PHASE

Note that touch, " The 180th Regt. of Würtembergers have withstood attacks on Thiépval for two years but the 18th Division will take it tomorrow," with its subtle play on divisional *esprit de corps*.

The British soldier does not expect to be addressed as *mes enfants*; he would laugh if he were; he is not susceptible to phrases anent glory. But it is ludicrous to write and talk as if men from the greatest democratic Empire in the world cannot appreciate a rousing speech or an appeal in terms of their own national sentiment. The phrase, " England expects that every tank will do her damndest " has been officially denied, but nothing did more to kindle enthusiasm. " St George for England and may we give the Dragon's Tail a damned good twisting " may not be a very lofty sentiment, but it is the right way to talk to men about to venture their lives in a desperate raid on the enemy. Even Haig at last realised the need to speak to his men in terms which they could understand and to which they could respond. " There is no other course open to us but to fight it out. Every position must be held to the last man. There must be no retirement. With our backs to the wall and believing in the justice of our cause, each one of us must fight on to the end."

Some men did not get the order till the battle was over; others complained that they had no wall to put their backs against. But, generally speaking, the effect was excellent.

The above criticisms should not be taken as an attempt unfairly to belittle Haig. He had great qualities; no man has ever had a harder task to perform or has been less qualified by previous experience to perform it. He has been termed a " text-book soldier," and perhaps he failed at the outset to realise the value and need of the *personal* touch in war; but " wearing out " as a policy was

THE KITCHENER ARMIES

fundamentally sound; we could not have won the war without it. The trouble was that Haig pushed this theory to an unwise degree. Few soldiers will support the prolongation of the Flanders offensive after the weather had broken, mud had produced an enemy more formidable than the Germans, and Ludendorff was free in any case to draw fresh men and guns from the East Front. But Haig's worst enemies have never accused him of lack of moral courage, readiness to accept defeat or failure to keep his head in an emergency. All these are qualities which count for much in war. In the Battle of the Somme he took big risks, made some errors in judgment, and paid for these with the lives of his troops and in loss of reputation. But the general who in war fears to take risks will fail to accomplish much; the qualities which led Haig to disregard the advice of others, to dare and partly to *fail* on July 1st, 1916, were the very same qualities which in the Autumn of 1918 led him to break the Hindenburg line and end the war at a stroke, also in the teeth of those who would have dissuaded him. We must always be chary as to how we condemn a general for taking risks, or because he is man enough to stand by his own opinions. Kitchener rightly described his New Armies as a gigantic experiment. All war is experimental. It is absurd to suggest that the soldier can study his profession as the mathematician studies mathematics, the chemist studies chemistry or the physician medicine. The mathematician can always *do* his sum and prove it; the chemist can test his theories by laboratory experiment; the physician can base his practice upon clinical research. But there are no actual means by which the soldier can test the character and resources of the enemy other than *fighting* him; and by the time he has committed himself to battle

THE SOMME: OPENING PHASE

it is too late to withdraw: he must either win or admit defeat. The public is deluged with a mass of *scientific* military criticism—mostly rubbish. When we call a soldier *scientific* we do not mean that he is a scientist in the sense that Edison or Marconi are scientists. We are merely using a popular colloquialism to indicate a man who is a cool-headed, determined gambler, a master of the tricks of his trade, who after weighing the chances and counting the risks, reaches his decision and backs his judgment with his own reputation and the lives of his men. War is very far from being a matter of mere luck. It is a matter of shrewd surmise, thorough knowledge of ground and of weapons, knowledge of men. But there will always be a gambling element in every military operation, there will always be an element of *judgment*. For it seldom or never happens that any commander is in possession of a superiority so overwhelming as to render success a mathematical certainty, or knows exactly what is in the enemy's mind or the means at his disposal.

So, in considering Haig, let us above all things avoid the cheap wisdom which comes after the event, or the awe-inspiring criticism which, starting with the hair-raising declaration that he had a " polygnathous jaw "—whatever that may be supposed to mean—proceeds sweepingly to condemn him as " a poor offensive general." A general either knows his job or else he does not. If he does, then whether he attacks or defends he will be successful. If he *does not*—then he will get beaten either way.

Although one of the phrases most often on his lips was, " the spirit quickeneth," the conviction seems with him to have been more intellectual than actual. His own character was too reserved and too *hard* for him to feel sympathy for the frailties, passions and virtues of the " common " man. His

THE KITCHENER ARMIES

mind was willing but his soul was weak. Haig had never *suffered*. His career had been a succession of easly triumphs, and it needed the agony and humiliation of 1918 to wrench from his cold, reticent nature the cry of agony which first established a real bond of sympathy between the Commander-in-Chief and the men he led.

It must never be forgotten that Haig developed tremendously during the war. Underlying an exterior, outwardly narrow and conventional, there was in this Scottish soldier a spirit of fanaticism akin to that of the Covenanters. He was a military Torquemada, as prepared cheerfully to burn at the stake himself as ruthlessly to burn others—in defence of his own ideals. His soul might be compared to an oxy-acetylene gas flame which, narrow but intense, will cut through the toughest steel. He may not have been a genius, but, after all, geniuses don't grow on rose-bushes and it is too much to expect that a British Fleet or Army will *always* be commanded by a Nelson or a Marlborough. If a general is cool-headed, capable, resourceful, that is as much as we can reasonably expect—and the soldier will be satisfied. Haig's narrowness in some respects gave him added force in others—and a man of his type would be a very ugly customer even for Napoleon to face in battle.

Haig was big enough to face disaster and to face this unappalled; he was great enough to see his carefully worked out plans for the Somme collapsing in ruin before him, and to gather up the loose and blood-stained ends of battle—and go in again. He kept his courage high, and a heart for battle under conditions which would have broken the heart and nerve of a weakling, and if he made mistakes he redeemed these by successes; this very *regimental* Regular officer ultimately found the key to the souls

THE SOMME: OPENING PHASE

of his men. In ending this study of the man who led the New Armies through mud and blood to victory, one may well paraphrase the words applied by Grey to Kitchener. Everybody can see in the light of after-knowledge the errors he made; no one can know the errors which might have been made by a different commander.

Picardy, the scene of the Somme fighting, is one of the fairest lands of France, open, bountiful, fit mother for a race of deep-breasted women and stalwart men. At that time of midsummer few could have foreseen the ruin which war was to bring to this region and the dreary waste of fetid leaden mud into which that smiling landscape was to dissolve. What most caught the eye was the range of high land from Thiépval to Combles, a bastion throwing out spurs and valleys and a series of ridges to Cambrai. The western slopes were steep and rugged, but north-eastwards the ground fell in gentle swells to Bapaume. This great bastion, protected by nature from attack from the west, had been in the enemy's hands since the retreat to the Aisne, and had been fortified with all the wit of a race schooled in war, all the resource and device of a highly industrialised empire. Concrete gun emplacements with chambers for gun detachments, deep under the ground, proof against the heaviest shelling; broad stretches of barbed wire covering trenches labyrinthine in their multitude and complexity, with spacious dug-outs as laboriously as cunningly devised, affording sure refuge from the fierce bombardment soon to play upon the enemy's lines; the whole system skilfully co-ordinated so that it made of the series of chalk hills and valleys one vast fortress system. " To win a detail of it was to win a slaughter pen enfiladed from both flanks. It had to be smashed through from stage to stage on a wide front." Where generations of

THE KITCHENER ARMIES

farmers had scraped away the muddy soil from their cart-tracks sunken roads had emerged, sometimes twenty feet deep, ideal communication trenches for our desperate and determined foe. Rain was frequent in the Somme valley even in summer, and every shower made the chalky marl soil treacherous and slippery. Save where the Thiépval ridge reared its head, the northern half of this area is marshy at all times. The German defences comprised two wide belts of what were in reality permanent fortifications running along the Thiépval-High Wood-Ginchy-Guillemont ridge. Behind these lines stretched a third running from Miraumont through Flers-Lesbœufs-Morval to Sailly-Saillisel. This, known as the Flers line, was incomplete when the battle opened.

To many people, and even to many men who took part in it, the Battle of the Somme seems a mere tangle of names and a bewilderment of confused fighting. The public has a vague picture of terrific losses incurred without apparent rhyme or reason, " Wearing Out " and mud. The somewhat disingenuous style of Haig's despatches strengthens the popular confusion, for every commander who in war has won successes and sustained failures will be disposed to dwell upon the successful side and strive to strike a balance in which success outweighs defeat. Thus, Haig invites us to regard the Somme and Flanders offensives, and the Amiens operations of 1918, as one great battle. But although these great events undoubtedly interacted upon one another, one might say just as much for the Battle of the Marne of 1914 and go on to include Tannenberg and the break-through at Gorlice. In fact the whole war must then be regarded as a single vast battle. Some people might suggest, and logically enough, that this is the true view. But if the whole

THE SOMME: OPENING PHASE

is made up of many parts, still there are certain phases of this titanic conflict which have a character individual to themselves. Falkenhayn's successful Roumanian Campaign of 1916 was destined disastrously to affect the policy on the West Front in 1917; but it was fought under conditions of rapid manœuvre, utterly dissimilar to those of the Verdun offensive, also planned by Falkenhayn. To reason from the one set of operations to the other would be very unsound criticism. So with the Battle of the Somme. It was a battle which had its own special character equally distinct from the Flanders offensive which succeeded it, or from the brilliant counter-strokes of Autumn 1918. The true aim and object of the Somme fighting may be thus described. The two great German lines of defence up to the Flers line constituted what was till then the strongest fortress system ever raised by man; it was *packed* with strong points, fortified farms and villages, easily defensible woods, well-sited and well-defended batteries and machine-guns, hedged in by wire. Now, had Haig's object been the comparatively modest one of " killing Germans " or " wearing out " pure and simple, the reduction of this fortress line, whilst a very difficult achievement, would not have been one of insuperable difficulty even for our improvised Armies. It would have meant a process of siege and sap, a grinding, continuous pressure all along a broad front—in fact, a system of attacks with limited objectives such as the brilliant series of operations of September 25th, which culminated in the storming of Thiépval. The disadvantage of any such procedure was that the enemy could build, continually, fresh defences behind his front lines—against which must be put that the strain on his *moral* and resources by any such system of attack could not be kept up indefinitely. But what Haig actually had in

THE KITCHENER ARMIES

mind was not to *eat* into the enemy's lines, but to *rush* them. The real object and aim of the three great attacks of July 1st, July 14th and September 15th was to pierce the enemy's fortified belts with such speed that he would have no time to build other fortified lines in rear; the way would be open for our Cavalry to get through; our Armies pouring through the gap would wheel northward—and the French south; the enemy would be swept from France. There thus entered into all our attempts to overrun the enemy's fortified lines, a definite *time factor*. The Commander-in-Chief and his Staff insisted upon the need for *speed*. It happened again and again that divisional commanders, appealing desperately for heavy Artillery to shell enemy strongholds which they foresaw could not be taken by Infantry alone, were denied this because it would have meant loss of time in bringing up guns, and *time* seemed to the Higher Command the most vital element.

The Battle of the Somme can thus be divided into three distinct phases in each of which the *principles* governing the attacks were the same, although the methods used continually varied and were improved.

Let any thoughtful reader ask himself what these attempts *rapidly* to pierce strongly held fortifications really meant. They meant bringing forward an array of guns so numerous and powerful as to crush these fortifications by an overwhelming blast of fire; they meant the closest possible co-operation between Infantry and Artillery to cover the Infantry at every stage of the attack; they meant pushing forward this array of guns with such speed that the enemy's second line could be battered down before he had time to build a third. But to do all these things successfully meant staff-work and team-work developed to the very *nth* degree; it meant to achieve what the

THE SOMME: OPENING PHASE

Germans with their highly trained staff, skilfully devised Artillery tactics, thoroughly trained Infantry had failed to do at Verdun; what the French under leaders of the calibre of Foch and Pétain had failed to do in their Champagne and Artois offensives previously; what Ludendorff with all his undoubted genius for war, and with "calibration" and "infiltration" to help him, shrank from attempting in the Spring of 1918; and what Haig himself, with staff-officers, corps commanders, divisional commanders, who were the survival of the fittest after four years of war, highly developed Artillery tactics and highly developed tanks, shrank from attempting in the Autumn of 1918. Read this:

"The derelict battle area which now lay before our troops, seared by old trench lines, pitted with shell-holes, and crossed in all directions with tangled belts of wire, the whole covered by the wild vegetation of two years, presented unrivalled opportunities for stubborn machine-gun defence. Attacks carried out on August 13th proved the strength of these positions and showed that the enemy, heavily reinforced, was ready to give battle for them. I therefore determined to break off the battle on this front, and transferred the front of attack from the Fourth Army to the sector north of the Somme, where an attack seemed unexpected by the enemy. My intention was for the Third Army to operate in the direction of Bapaume so as to turn the lines of the old Somme defences from the north."

This was a period when "wearing out" might have been assumed to have had its maximum working. The enemy were reeling back after a terrific defeat, worn by four years of desperate fighting. But when the German reserves had appeared, good troops, in a position easily defensible, Haig was by now too

THE KITCHENER ARMIES

wary to attempt to *rush* them by a frontal attack. He broke the battle off, switched his power from right to left and smashed in on their flank from Arras, where they were not expecting him. Not until it had become manifest from various symptoms that the enemy were by now growing rapidly demoralised did he attempt to do again what he had tried to do in 1916 against thoroughly trained, thoroughly alert and well-prepared Germans, which was to *rush* at their strong lines, without surprise or even an attempt at manœuvre, and try to break these by sheer weight of men and guns and metal.

Thus our New Armies of 1916 were asked to do what the most highly trained troops in Europe, and under the most capable and experienced commanders of their day, had tried to do in vain, and to do what Haig himself in 1918 regarded as possible, if at all, only at such a price as to make victory worthless; to *rush* strongly fortified lines held by a brave, resolute and well-equipped foe, without any attempt at surprise or manœuvre, but by the element of sheer weight and power. The true marvel will always be, not that we failed in breaking through, but that we came within a narrow margin of doing what no other troops in the world could have done. Nor could there be a surer test as to the extraordinarily high quality of the New Armies. Three times our troops rose up in a mighty avalanche of men, guns and metal against the German fortifications; three times they battered into them like a gigantic battering ram; three times the Germans' positions cracked and splintered under the shock. They cracked and splintered—but they did not quite give way.

Nevertheless, these tremendous blows, if they did not actually break through the enemy's lines, had far-reaching effect. Hindenburg writes:

THE SOMME: OPENING PHASE

" On the Somme the struggle had now been raging two months. There we passed from one crisis to another. Our lines were permanently in a condition of the highest tension." And Professor Oman quotes another German writer:

" The loss of ground was of no strategic importance. But the importance of the course of the fighting must not be measured by this. The great losses in men, the heavy expenditure of material, ate only too deep into the strength of the German army. The mighty material superiority of the enemy did not fail to have its psychological effect upon the German soldier. The enemy commanders may put this down on the credit side, as a profit of their attrition purpose. . . . The Old Army disappeared in the long drawn-out battle."

The tremendous attack of July 1st, 1916, was ushered in by a mighty cannonade. For six days and nights our guns rose in swelling chorus, thundering out the challenge of the Anglo-Saxon to the Teuton: 12-in. guns reared their monstrous necks from the street corners of Albert, 15-in. howitzers squatted in the fields around, 6 in., 4.5's, " whizz-bangs " stretched in a long curving line over a sixteen-mile front. The voice of the cannon blended into a rushing cataract of sound in which the note of individual calibres could not be distinguished. The earth trembled as if under the hammer-blows of some superhuman smith and at night the flashes of the guns made darkness visible. Whilst the bombardment endured, officers studied trench maps and plasticine models of the ground to be fought over, and gleefully renamed to suit their fancy the enemy's positions they thought to overrun. The divisions, trained for months beforehand over dummy trenches,

THE KITCHENER ARMIES

were already in position, the 30th Division on the extreme right joining hands with Foch's gallant men, then the 18th, 7th, 21st, 34th, 8th, 32nd, 36th, 29th, 4th and 31st Divisions. Behind them were the 9th, 17th and 48th Divisions in reserve. Further to the left the 56th and 46th Divisions with the 37th in reserve, were to make a subsidiary attack on Gommecourt.

Down on the enemy's lines beat the hurricane of shell, tearing huge craters in the soil, throwing up fountains of displaced earth, covering his front with smoke and dust, causing it to belch as if a vast array of factory chimneys were on fire. High in the air swept the airmen, ranging far and wide over the German positions, photographing, reconnoitring, signalling the effects of the fire, bombing. But bad weather, driving mist and rain hindered their activity. Beneath the soil toiled miners driving their galleries, packed with explosives, 'neath the enemy's lines; at night crept the patrols examining the German wire, testing the effect of the guns, whilst machine-guns and Artillery played with synchronised bursts of fire, even at the danger of killing our own patrols, to prevent the enemy from repairing it. Raiding parties, with bomb and revolver and ammonal torpedoes, sprayed themselves over No Man's Land in the blackness illuminated but by the fire of our own guns. By night and by day, above the earth and underneath it, the work of preparation went on.

Describing the bombardment one who was there writes: " The results, as witnessed from our observation posts, were excellent. All wire that could be seen was effectively cut. As one watched the big shells bursting, sending up huge columns of earth, day after day, it appeared as though no life could endure in that tortured blasted area." The same observer speaks of the ominous Schwaben Redoubt,

THE SOMME: OPENING PHASE

sixteen rows of wire in the first line; five rows along the second.

The barrage used in covering the attack was not, however, the true " creeping barrage " used at that time by the French. There was a final intensive bombardment of sixty-five minutes, after which the barrage " lifted " to play on support lines and reserves. These wide " lifts " were perhaps responsible for much of our losses.

The Infantry took position on the night of the 22nd-23rd. Describing the assembly of the 36th Division in Thiépval Wood, the writer quoted says:

" These troops had a purgatory to endure. For the most part in the narrow slit assembly trenches, with the rain pouring steadily down upon them, they were under furious German bombardments that wreathed the wood in smoke and flame and made the crashing of great trees the accompaniment to the roar of bursting shells."

Owing to the sheets of rain and heavy cloud-banks, however, the attacks, planned originally for the 29th June, had to be postponed, a delay which, whilst necessary, was unfortunate, as it led not only to a slackening of our bombardment to economise shell, but gave to the enemy a chance to relieve some of his nerve-racked garrisons. Inter-brigade reliefs were carried out in our own front line. Meanwhile, behind these the work of preparation went on, the accumulation of stores in special dug-outs, the establishment of command and dressing stations, the widening and improvements of assembly trenches, all the vast paraphernalia for a " set-piece " attack, work which had been in hand for long previously.

" So close were the big convoys to the German trenches that extraordinary precautions to avoid noise had to be taken. Wheels were bound with straw and old motor tyres, steel chains replaced by leather straps, boots, like those used in rolling a cricket ground, placed over the horses' hoofs. And it was an amusing sight to see an A.S.C. driver frantically clinging to the nose of some sociable horse that desired to greet new acquaintances with a friendly neigh."

The assaulting troops began their approach to the trenches on the 30th. The final stages of the attack were covered by a hurricane bombardment of trench mortars and the explosion of several mines, the principal against Beaumont Hamel. This is what happened to the 31st Division:

" . . . but the same explosion warned the Boche that zero was at hand, and with one roar their guns broke out into a triple fire-curtain on our front line, supports and reserves, hurling a deadly avalanche of shells up to the highest calibre; their masked batteries opened, and with absolute accuracy of aim poured hell and destruction on our trenches, crowded with men who were now on the point of climbing out. Our front line trenches, Russian saps, and advanced communication trenches literally disappeared and with them the major portion of the two leading Battalions and 'D' Company. A few of our men broke past our wire, fewer still crossed No Man's Land, and only a mere handful reached the German lines. Some of 'D' Company struggled on and vanished into Pendant Copse and were never seen again, and a very few stumbled up the heights of Serre, and these stout hearts now lie buried there. . . .

" Meanwhile the hostile trenches could be seen thick with men, who, immediately the barrage had lifted and passed beyond them, stood breast high to repel our assault. . . . The ferocity and volume of

THE SOMME: OPENING PHASE

the Boche batteries was as overwhelming as it had been unexpected."

The men of the 36th Division moving against Thiépval ridge formed up in No Man's Land facing their objectives, covered by intensive fire and a smoke barrage from the mortars.

Here is a description of what occurred:

"Zero! The hurricane Stokes bombardment ceased. The Artillery lifted off the first line. The whistles of the officers sounded, and the men sprang up and advanced at a steady marching pace on the German trenches. Those who saw those leading battalions move to the assault, above all their commanding officers forbidden to accompany them, received one of the most powerful and enduring impressions of their lives."

Col. Macrory, 10th Inniskilling Fusiliers, writes of " lines of men moving forward with rifles sloped and the sun glistening upon their fixed bayonets, keeping their alignment and distance as well as if on a ceremonial parade, unfaltering, unwavering."

Gen. Ricardo, formerly of the 9th Battalion of the same regiment, tells us:

" I stood on the parapet between the two centre exits to wish them luck. . . . They got going without delay; no fuss, no shouting, no running, everything solid and thorough—just like the men themselves. Here and there a boy would wave his hand to me as I shouted good luck to them through my megaphone. And all had a cheery face. Most were carrying loads. Fancy advancing through a heavy fire with a big roll of barbed wire on your shoulder!

" So they bore on upon the German lines, while behind them, from Thiépval Wood, rocked by

THE KITCHENER ARMIES

exploding shells, sheeted in the smoke and flame of bursting shrapnel, fresh troops issued and followed upon their advance in little columns."

North of the Ancre not even these brave men could do much. The German machine-gunners trained their weapons on the gaps in the wire, from Serre German guns vomited death into their ranks. They swept fearlessly to death, and as with so many of the New Army battalions, the trail of bodies lying face to the foe and growing ever thinner and thinner marked their glory and their death. South of the Ancre, with dreadful losses they took all their objectives, but now came one of those tragedies of vacillation and inco-ordination which marked that luckless day. At 8.32 a.m. it became apparent to Gen. Nugent that the failure of the divisions on either hand, no less gallant, to reach their impossible objectives, rendered an advance by the remnants of the 36th on their final objectives, a suicidal attempt. His G.S.O., Col. Place, telephoned to the X Corps H.Q. to ask permission to stop the advance on the last line. The reply was that a new attack was to be made on Thiépval and by the VIII Corps north of the Ancre. Three-quarters of an hour later the message came that these plans had been altered and the further advance of the 107th Brigade (36th Division) could be stopped. But the message came too late. The attack had begun, runners, messengers, desperate volunteers failed to get through, and the brigade marched to certain destruction.

Another officer of the 31st Division describes his experiences:

" At 7 p.m. the assaulting troops moved off from Warnimont Wood to march to the assembly trenches behind John Copse and Mark Copse. No music as they slowly wended their way down the woodland,

THE SOMME: OPENING PHASE

All faces expressed determination. A lump rises in the throat. What were the thoughts of these wonderful soldiers who kept their anxieties to themselves?

"The 1st of July 1916 will be remembered as one of the saddest and most tragic, yet withal one of the most glorious pages of Sheffield history, for on that day there fell in battle the largest number of Sheffield men ever known."

He tells with unstudied eloquence of " . . . the toilsome journey through the trenches half-full of water; see again the tired slumberers of the dawn, the beautiful summer morn, the faultless parade on the parapets, see again those brave comrades mowed down as grass before the scythe and those odd parties crossing the German trenches, alas! never to return." And, "the welcome sunset and more welcome shades of night, which enabled the living and hysterical wounded to reach our lines, some by crawling, some by crouching runs, and some by painful dragging of bodies.

"About a hundred gallant men of the East Lancashires, favoured, perhaps, by some curve in the ground, got past more than one line of trenches, and a few desperate individuals even burst their way as far as Serre, giving a false impression that the village was in our hands. But the losses had been so dreadful that the weight and momentum had gone out of the attack, while the density of the resistance thickened with every yard of the advance. By the middle of the afternoon the survivors of the two attacking brigades were back in their own front line trenches, having lost the greater part of their effectives."

Another officer describes how the men assembled for the attack at 3.45 a.m. There was a delay of two and a half hours in the badly battered trenches. At daylight, 4.5 a.m., the enemy began to shell John

THE KITCHENER ARMIES

Copse; this was three and a half hours before the attack began and it almost seemed as if he had had warning. At 7.20 a.m. our own bombardment reached its zenith. The massed guns, great and small, thundered hard and the noise, no longer a gigantic discord, became a terrible rhythm like some " superhuman machinery." It drummed in the ears till the men were nearly deaf. At 7.29 a.m. the enemy started his counter-barrage and gradually brought it on to our own front line. And we get the illuminating revelation, " The German front line was manned about one per yard by men who had either been lying behind the parados of the fire-trench or who had emerged from shelter." At 7.30 the signal for attack came; it was impossible in the tremendous din to pass the word and the officers must give their orders by signs. Our barrage lifted, the first and second waves moved to the attack, the third and fourth climbed the parapet:

" All halted—up there in face of the enemy so that they could get into line, then started across the open in section columns. It was a wonderful sight, the waves of humanity going steadily and grimly across No Man's Land. They were advancing just ' as if they were on parade.' They had to pass through a terrible curtain of shell fire, and German machine-guns were rattling out death from two sides. But the lines, growing ever thinner, went on unwavering. Here and there a shell would burst right among the attackers, and when the smoke cleared slightly, the line would be still thinner. Whole sections were destroyed; one section of fourteen platoon was killed by concussion. . . . The left half of ' C ' Company was wiped out before getting near the German wire, and on the right few of the men who reached the wire were able to get through. As

THE SOMME: OPENING PHASE

soon as our barrage had lifted from their front line, the Germans, who had been sheltering in dug-outs, immediately came out and opened rapid fire."

The attacking troops were simply wiped out, the few who survived taking refuge in shell-holes in front of the German trenches until they could get back under cover of the night, and what these men went through neither tongue nor pen can describe. At 8.45 a.m. the enemy's barrage was exceptionally intense. The 13th York and Lancaster incurred frightful losses in an attempt to support the 11th East Lancashire. The German Artillery were exceptionally well served and invariably concentrated on the trenches where troops were massed. At 8.22 a.m. a message came to this battalion from the brigade inquiring as to strength, state of ammunition, bombs, and Lewis guns. The answer ran: " Strength of battalion ten men unwounded, these being runners or signallers. No Lewis guns, 3000 rounds S.A.A., 350 bombs."

The experiences of the 34th Division were no whit dissimilar. Emerging from their dug-outs the German machine-gunners spat out death whilst their gunners, in previous days silent, almost as if contemptuous of our great array of guns, became active as if imps from hell stirring up a witches' cauldron to spew destruction at our men. Gen. Ingouville Williams wrote pathetically of his troops: " My division did glorious deeds. Never have I seen men go through such a barrage of artillery. They advanced as on parade and never flinched. I can't speak too highly of them."

The 20th and 23rd Northumberland Fusiliers were literally wiped out, their gallant commanding officers, Lieut.-Cols. Lyle and Sillery, were killed at the head of their men, and the progress of these battalions could be traced for days afterwards by a trail of bodies growing ever thinner and thinner, *each man with his face to the foe.* The 21st and 22nd Battalions of this regiment fared only slightly better, the 15th and 16th Royal Scots had *heavy loss*, the 10th Lincolns and 11th Suffolks were practically annihilated. A handful of desperate men managed to seize Wood Alley and captured Scot Redoubt, other men as brave and determined ventured through a volcano of shell with bombs, ammunition and supplies—at the cost of one man out of every three. The dead lay in regular rows for days afterwards. That brave and resolute soldier, Ingouville Williams, soon himself to die in battle, could not restrain his tears when that night he visited the gallant handful who had won a foothold in the enemy's lines. " Well done, lads, well done, you've done *damned* well." The brigades of this division averaged 3000 men apiece, of which the 101st Brigade lost 2299; the 102nd, 2334; the 103rd, 1968; a total of 6591 out of some 9000 officers and men. The 36th Division lost in two days 5500 officers and men from a similar strength. Many battalions had almost disappeared. The 9th Inniskilling Fusiliers had *no* officers and 80 men of other ranks. The 15th West Yorkshire—of the 31st Division—out of 25 officers lost every man; the 16th and 18th Battalions were little better off. Of the 94th Brigade, the two splendid leading Battalions, the 11th East Lancashire, 12th York and Lancaster, had whole companies exterminated. The Sheffield " Pals " Battalion lost on this day 12 officers and 60 per cent. of other ranks out of a total of 789. The losses of the Brigade were 2000 from a total of about 3000.

The Germans had believed the Artillery preparation south of the Somme to be a *feint* and the attack from this direction came as a surprise. The

THE SOMME: OPENING PHASE

French XX Corps swept forward in a grand sweep almost to Peronne; the 30th Division and 18th Division each reached their objectives with sharp fighting but without much loss. The Germans here were unprepared. Probably, but for the "limited objective," these Divisions could have pierced right through the German second line and have taken ground—with ease—which cost us in subsequent days desperate fighting and a terrible price in blood. But in the centre and left of the attack, where the Germans were ready and waiting for it, we sustained the most disastrous repulse of the whole war. The authors of *Sir Douglas Haig's Command* write:

" The troops detailed for the assault reached and entered the enemy's positions along practically the whole line of attack, but no adequate arrangements were made or at least none were properly carried out for clearing up and securing the ground won. All along the front parties of our troops succeeded in pushing forward to great depths across the German positions, but these advanced bodies lost touch with or were not properly supported by the troops behind them. The enemy was able to reoccupy trenches that had been overrun and, being no longer driven to ground by our bombardment, succeeded in too many cases in holding up our reserves and reinforcements." And we get an illuminating explanation that the "action of the II American Corps in the attack on the Bellicourt tunnel defences on September 29th, 1918—an attack supported by a far vaster weight and intensity of Artillery fire, employing gas as well as high explosive shell—is an interesting parallel and instructive commentary upon the failure of the left of the British attack on the Somme on July 1st, 1916. The Americans . . . were engaged against an enemy whose *moral* had been shaken by

THE KITCHENER ARMIES

repeated defeats and was on the point of breaking down utterly."

The " inexperience of the troops," " wet weather," and the " Machiavellian intrigues of Mr Lloyd George " have all, perhaps, been a little bit overdone. The true cause of the failure of most of the " mopping up " parties on July 1st was the enemy's fire from which the troops in rear suffered even more than those in front, and which made " carrying parties " or even messengers a matter of desperate volunteers. The troops detailed for " mopping up " were mostly shot down. It is no ungenerous reflection upon the men of the gallant American II Corps to state that had our New Army divisions possessed the same advantages in their attack on July 1st as were possessed by the brave but very ill-trained American divisions, we should have had no difficulty in taking the Somme lines. Most of the battalions which fought on that day had been embodied for periods of eighteen to twenty months, many months of which had been spent in France, in the fighting line or close to this. After making all allowance for deficiencies of instructors and equipment, eighteen to twenty months' training with all the stimulus of war and men of quality of the New Armies is equal to at least three years' training in peace. When in South Africa at Colenso, the Tugela, the Modder River, and Maagersfontein our highly trained professional Regular troops were asked to storm Boer lines, not one-tenth part as formidable as were the German defences on the Somme, they failed disastrously. Nor were they very successful in night operations such as Spion Kop. Those who know the Old Army from personal experience—and who are second to none in their love and admiration for it—will always feel some scepticism as to whether any of our

THE SOMME: OPENING PHASE

1913 divisions could have achieved some of the difficult deployments made by New Army divisions in pitch blackness and under fire. Very awkward errors were sometimes made on manœuvres in broad daylight and in profound peace. There was one incident—not so long before the war—in which two Cavalry regiments blundered into one another, were unable to check their speed, and became involved in a "charge" in which several men were injured.

A more just and temperate explanation of the disasters of July 1st is that of the historian of the *Thirty-Sixth Division*:

"Artillerymen of the higher ranks were to some extent carried away by the weight of metal for the first time at their disposal, and carried away other arms by their new enthusiasm. The heavy gunners believed and proclaimed that no life could endure their fire and that the battle would resolve itself by the Infantry to take over shattered and undefended trenches. They had not realised that the machine-guns would be comparatively safe under their bombardment, and that it would take but a few seconds to bring them into action when the barrage was past. . . . But no explanations that can be found stand without ample tribute to the fighting qualities of the German soldier. The dash and bravery of the counter-attacks of the bombers moving up from the valley merit high praise. The highest, however, must be reserved for the machine-gunners, who had sat for days in their dug-outs without fresh food, the very earth shaking to the thunders of our Artillery, and then came up and brought their guns into action at the right moment. . . .

"We had realised that defence with the machine-guns had beaten attack, and had begun the process of increasing the quantity and improving the quality

THE KITCHENER ARMIES

of mechanical accessories. It was still, however, to cost thousands of lives before the factories could produce sufficient of the latter, or the higher commands reach the ratio between Infantry force and mechanical aids necessary to the prosecution of a given operation."

Perhaps it is wiser to see the explanation of the ill-success on the left and centre in our own deficiencies and in the high quality of our foes than to be perpetually engaged in recriminations directed against all and sundry, including our gallant Allies.

It is pleasant to read the tribute of the 36th Division to their gunners, London men raised in the Summer of '15, but whose work we are assured " could not have been bettered." One battery of the 172nd Brigade in Hamel, far forward, although exposed to fire, did yeoman service.

The final verdict will always be that no troops on earth, however brave, well-disciplined or well-trained, could have done more than was done by our Infantry on the Somme, few other troops could have done as much, and the records of human heroism in battle will never produce a finer story of courage and constancy rising supreme over death.

Men from the 34th Division reached Contalmaison, parties of the 36th Division got to Grandcourt, and a brigade of the 49th Division was able to attack from the north the fortified village of Thiépval—to which our troops had already penetrated from the south and west. Groups from the 29th Division achieved the southern portion of Beaumont Hamel; others from the 4th Division had attacked the German support lines and pushed beyond Pendant Copse, south-east of Serre. The Germans were observed to turn their guns on Serre itself and it is possible that men from the 31st Division reached this village.

THE SOMME: OPENING PHASE

The morning of July 1st found G.H.Q. in a very optimistic mood. The objectives given for the troops on the centre and left of our attack were very far ahead. The historian of the *Thirty-Fourth Division* thus describes what this Division was asked to do:

" This meant an advance of about three thousand five hundred yards, on a front of about two thousand, capturing two fortified villages and six lines of trenches, which it was known were well provided with deep dug-outs, and made as strong as our industrious enemy could make them after two years of constant labour. Truly might the representatives of Army Headquarters, who came to address the officers, tell us that if we carried out the whole of the programme we should do uncommonly well, and that we ought not to be disappointed if we only achieved a partial success."

Cavalry were massed in readiness to exploit the gains won, and these masses of horse, with their demands for forage, cumbered up the few roads available and were a grievous burden upon the already overtaxed administrative services.

But as the day wore on and the stream of messages flowed in with their disastrous tidings of death and defeat, Haig must be admitted to have shown a spirit inflexible and indomitable; his decision was immediate and his judgment sound. The weight of the attack was to be swung from left to right to press home the gains of the 30th and 18th Divisions. Renewed attacks on the centre and left were to pin the enemy to his ground to prevent him from massing his reserves. But opportunities in war are but fleeting and must be seized at once. The difficulty of fighting a battle to fixed plans, rules and schedules was never more strikingly illustrated than in the

THE KITCHENER ARMIES

events of July 1st. For the success here shows not alone that it *would* have been possible to surprise the enemy, but that such a surprise could have been made overwhelming had there been troops available to exploit it. The strongest fortifications in the world are of little avail unless men are there to man them. Fresh divisions following hard on the heels of the XIII Corps, a more daring and more elastic leadership, would have gone right over the German second line.

The divisions shattered in the fighting of July 1st were transferred to Gough's Reserve Army, their torn brigades replaced by fresh ones; thus a brigade from the 37th Division went to the 34th, including a certain battalion, the 11th Royal Warwicks, from the diary of whose commander one gets a vivid insight into the realities of war. Gough was ordered to continue a " slow pressure," whilst to the right wing of the fighting streamed every man and gun from Haig's reserves. But the Germans streamed thence also, and Maltz Horn Farm, Trônes Wood, Contalmaison, Bailiff Wood, Ovillers, all became the scenes of desperate, bloody fighting. Haig's object was to gain a jumping off ground for a smashing blow at the enemy's second line; the enemy was fighting to gain time; attack varied with counter-attack and every step won was paid for in blood. Take what happened to the 12th Division on the left of this new series of attacks. The 2nd and 19th Divisions were to push on to La Boisselle, the 12th to capture Ovillers. The X Corps on the left was to capture the Leipzig salient. The attack was timed for 3.15 a.m., July 3rd, under cover of smoke from the left and an intensive bombardment of one hour. The 12th Division had been in Fourth Army Reserve and to reach its objective meant a considerable march.

THE SOMME: OPENING PHASE

But, at the last moment, a message came from the X Corps H.Q. that their attack was postponed—too late to check the advance of the 12th Division. German guns and machine-guns from the left were free to enfilade the boys from the eastern counties, sending a swathe of death through the leading battalions, sweeping down all supporting parties, shooting down the men carrying reserve bombs, ammunition, and materials for consolidation.

The divisional historian gives, among others, the following reasons for ill-success:

". . . Also by the attack being carried out in the dark by troops who were hurried into the fight without being well acquainted with the terrain leading to loss of cohesion; by the Artillery bombardment destroying the wire and the trenches, yet failing to reach the deep dug-outs, which remained unharmed; and by the recent storms making shell-holes and trenches in places almost impassable."

A renewed attack was made July 7th by the 36th Brigade. It was before Ovillers that the 8th (Regular) Division had sustained its frightful losses, and the 35th and 37th Brigades had suffered heavy punishment two days later, and the spirit in which the men of the 36th Brigade went forward may be gleaned from the following extract from a soldier's diary:

"Hear our brigade is to have a chance to take Ovillers. Hurrah! . . . We are all proud to know the G.O.C. has given us this task. Boys are determined not to fail, and no grumbling is heard when our rest is cut down to twelve hours."

Such was the dash and daring of these splendid men that the 36th Brigade swept right over the German lines, reached to the outskirts of Ovillers

THE KITCHENER ARMIES

and actually managed to maintain themselves there, their commander having wisely trained his men to use German bombs and rifles and supplies of these being found in captured German dug-outs. Thus our men held on, turning the enemy's weapons against himself, enduring his fire, resolute against imminent death, and so added a strip of the Somme line to the gains of our Army. But in the 36th Brigade, out of 66 officers in 3 battalions, 60 fell; and out of 2100 men, 340 were hit by shell-fire before they left our own trenches; 1260 were hit by machine-guns in No Man's Land. Of 500 men who reached the village, 150 became casualties in the subsequent fighting. The total loss of the 12th Division in the Somme battle from July 1st to 8th were 189 officers, 4576 other ranks, mostly Infantry, out of a total strength of some 19,000 and 13 battalions = about 12,000 men.

On the right of the line Trônes Wood changed hands repeatedly as attacks and counter-attacks swayed the battle-line; Contalmaison on the left shared the same fate; and there was a grim struggle for Mametz Wood,[1] a key position, for its possession

[1] There is a certain discrepancy between the account of the fighting for Mametz Wood given by the authors of *Sir Douglas Haig's Command* and the account of the divisional historian of the Thirty-Eighth Division. Professor Dewar and Col. Boraston speak of repeated attacks by this division which failed, and of an order to attack which was disregarded. The divisional historian speaks of Mametz Wood as being considered so strong a position that the original scheme was to work round it; he mentions only two " small attacks "—apparently to pave the way—and his account of the final assault and capture of the wood certainly does not suggest a division which had suffered serious disasters. Needless to say, there is no mention of any order to attack being disregarded. The authors of *Sir Douglas Haig's Command* attribute the failure of the Break-Through Battle of July 14th to the three days' delay in taking Mametz Wood. The reader must draw his own conclusions as to which account is the

THE SOMME: OPENING PHASE

by the enemy would have exposed our troops in their planned advance against the enemy's second line to a counter-stroke from Germans massed under its shelter. But it was not until July 12th that this position was finally taken by fighting in which the 17th, 38th and 7th Divisions all shared.

The thoughts of the British Commander-in-Chief and his staff continued to be dominated by the vision of a Break-Through which would open the way for his Cavalry and bring sweeping and sensational success. For the second time the battering ram was to be swung against the German lines. Speed, speed, was the cry which sounded—speed against the watchful, wary foe.

"The unsatisfactory result of the fighting in Trônes Wood," writes the historian of the 9th Division, "affected disastrously the plans of the Corps for an attack on the enemy's second system of defences. Every day gained by the enemy added to his strength. On July 7th the Division had received instructions for operations to be undertaken against Longueval and Delville Wood on the 10th, but the original scheme presupposed the capture of Trônes Wood, consequently the date had to be postponed and the arrangements modified. The task of the XIII Corps was probably the toughest on the whole front. It was to secure the ridge running from Waterlot Farm to Bazentin-le-Grand, and the key of this ridge, Longueval and Delville Wood, fell to the 9th." For the first time we hear the ill-omened name Delville Wood—rightly called *Devil's* Wood by the men and destined to be the graveyard of so many of our best and bravest.

most credible. It will be observed that the historian of the *Ninth Division* attributes the failure of the attacks of July 14th to the delay in capturing *Trônes* Wood.

THE KITCHENER ARMIES

A daring scheme was put forward to save time, that most vital element.

" It was realised that the Germans were expecting attack. To keep them in uncertainty as to the exact time of the onslaught, their lines were heavily shelled every morning by the Artillery, and to gain the full advantage of surprise what was virtually a night attack was planned. The British Army might be unimaginative and unenterprising in strategy, but it was bold and audacious in the use of tactical expedients. A night attack demands the most careful arrangements by the Staff and a high standard of discipline on the part of the troops engaged."

Two divisions were to be deployed over the long stretch of No Man's Land, in one case meaning an advance of 1000 yards before they could even be formed for assault. They must then advance about a quarter of a mile by creeping and crawling, retaining their formation as well as possible, and this must be done in pitch blackness without a single error—for a single error might mean a hurricane of shells beating down upon the massed troops and a confusion of tortured, broken bodies. The men who were to achieve all this had become soldiers only after the war.

" The ground in front of our lines had been thoroughly reconnoitred by patrols, and during the night a strong line of scouts was to go up the crest of the rise in front of the enemy's trenches. These men were to be supported by Lewis gun detachments, and the exposed right wing was to be protected against an attack from Trônes Wood by a chain of posts, which the Highland Brigade was to establish in 9.2-in. shell-holes, previously made for this purpose by the Artillery. Thus covered, the brigades detailed for assault were to form their leading battalions in waves of attack on the south-west slopes of the plateau." During the night of the 13th-14th,

THE SOMME: OPENING PHASE

after the covering parties had taken position, the Brigade-Major of the 26th Brigade with the adjutants of battalions and forty markers went out to mark the ground. The plan was to work from the left of each battalion. Sixteen markers commencing from the rear were posted in pairs at seventy yards distance. As each pair was posted, one man moved off at right angles with a tape about 150 yards long, and thus fixed the right of his wave or platoon. The most advanced pair of markers were about 500 yards from the enemy's lines.

Then at 12.25 a.m. the battalions by companies in single file, moved out to line on the markers, and as each platoon reached its left marker, it wheeled to the right and fixed bayonets. Other brigades arranged their deployment with slight variations, but upon the same principle. Thus Major Teacher, the Brigade-Major of the 27th Brigade, with one officer and two N.C.O.'s of the 90th Field Company R.E. worked from the centre. The first tape, fifty yards long, was laid on a compass-bearing previously taken, others were put in prolongation of the first until the line was 1000 yards long—the work having taken forty-five minutes. Then the front tape was laid off at right angles, the flanks of each battalion being fixed. When the tapes were in position the right and left markers for each unit were posted. Despite the darkness and intermittent shelling—which cost the life of Lieut.-Col. H. L. Budge of the 12th Royal Scots and four others—this difficult deployment went off without a hitch and the brigade was formed ready for the assault by 2.45 a.m. Zero was fixed for 3.25 a.m.

Haig himself thus referred to this fine achievement:

" The decision to attempt a night attack of this magnitude with an army, the bulk of which had been

THE KITCHENER ARMIES

raised since the beginning of the war, was perhaps the highest tribute that could be paid to the quality of our troops. It would not have been possible but for the careful preparation and forethought, as well as thorough reconnaissance of the ground made personally by divisional, brigade and battalion commanders and their staffs."

The night of July 13th-14th, 1916, the desperate bloody fighting of the days which ensued, are a picture difficult to focus, so dark with horror, so rich in heroism that its lurid colours bewilder the observer; the mere chronicle of the gallant and the ghoulish becomes a wearisome repetition. Certain figures and incidents stand out, not because they were braver than others or because the ordeal to be endured was more terrible, but because there is in them a certain dramatic touch. Maxwell,[1] leading Maxse's men to the reconquest of Trônes Wood, cool as ice and fierce as flame, the spirit of war incarnate. As he strode into the wood, " British Warm " on arm, revolver in hand, he said quietly to the padre whom he passed on the way, " I am going this night to instil the spirit of savagery into my battalion." In all the darkness, confusion and deadly menace of that fighting he kept his head and his battalion in hand, organised a line of men to beat the wood from one end to the other, rightly surmising that the line of shooting men, offering no " bunches " to their fire, would be demoralising to the Germans. There loom out the desperate attempts to storm Longueval, which the pounding of the guns had but converted into a fortress impregnable to Infantry, a confusion of tangled and

[1] Brig. F. A. Maxwell, V.C., C.S.I., D.S.O., then a Lieutenant-Colonel. He had been Kitchener's A.D.C. in South Africa in 1900 and was killed in 1917.

THE SOMME: OPENING PHASE

jumbled masonry in which the defenders could lurk undetected by our men and which needed really to be pulverised by heavy guns before it was " ripe " for Infantry assault. But heavy guns there were not, and time was denied, so the ruins of the village became littered with the bodies of Scots and South Africans. And, a name of imperishable memory, stands Delville Wood, the graveyards of South African Brigade and of the 53rd Brigade of Maxse's men.

" It was two days and nights of the grimmest kind of warfare, for the Boche shelling did not cease, and the enemy poured in reinforcements in desperate attempts to recapture the stretch of tangled undergrowth and shell-smitten trees that he had lost. The wood was littered with wounded and dying men, hundreds of them—men of the South African Brigade as well as 53rd Brigade men, and Germans too. There was great difficulty with regard to water. There was only one well in the wood, and that was close to where the enemy was strongest; while the Berkshires received no food supplies the whole of the time they were in the wood. The hand-to-hand fighting between small parties was of so desperate a nature and the German attacks were so persistent, that non-combatant David Randell, padre to the 10th Essex, who was with Col. Scott and the battalion headquarters party, armed himself with a rifle to be ready for all emergencies. . . .

" Capt. Ackroyd, the medical officer of the Berks, was a heroic figure during those two days. The fighting was so confused and the wood so hard to search that the difficulties of evacuating the wounded seemed unconquerable. But Capt. Ackroyd, bespectacled and stooping, a Cambridge don before he joined the forces, was so cool, purposeful and methodical, that he cleared the whole wood of wounded, British and Boche as well."

THE KITCHENER ARMIES

Into the confusion of this tangled wood fighting, with its deadly play of bomb, bayonet, bursting shell and rattling machine-gun, comes trotting a squadron of the 7th Dragoon Guards.

"It was a memorable occasion, as it was the first Cavalry advance since the beginning of trench warfare; gunners, Infantry and returning wounded each gave us a cheer as we went past them. The valley showed the intensity of the fighting; there was not a square yard of ground that was not broken up with shell-holes; the trees in the woods stood blackened and broken, stripped of all their leaves and branches; dead and wounded, British and German, lay on every side; here and there a wrecked German gun, with the mangled remains of a team that had striven in vain to withdraw it; further on three or four burnt-out railway trucks stood among the *débris* of a siding." One troop actually charged German machine-gunners bolting from dug-outs, cut down fifteen, and took thirty-two prisoners. But the anticipated Break-Through had not arrived yet and, cursing their ill-luck, they trotted back again.

There is the sweeping onrush of Sixt von Armin's men of the Magdeburg Corps and that wonderful charge by the Cameron Highlanders. "For all who took part in that attack this was the most thrilling moment of the war. For the space of a single second both sides hesitated, so dramatic was the meeting, and then from the left of the 26th line came the rousing command ' Forward boys!' and the Highlanders surged on like an irresistible wave."

Far away in G.H.Q. the mind of Haig, sternly purposeful, was bent on seizing High Wood and the ridge crowned by this which, two short miles from our old positions, would threaten the whole German battle line, and open to our arms the slopes and spurs falling north and east to the Ancre, with Bapaume

THE SOMME: OPENING PHASE

gleaming in the distance like some prize of victory. Squadron leaders of the 4th (Queen's Own) Hussars had been sent to reconnoitre north of Longueval on July 13th, and on the 15th British and Indian Cavalry " stood to " at fifteen minutes' notice throughout the day, ready to sweep like a living torrent of men and horses let the gap once be made. They " stood to " all the long day while the tide of battle raged and the glittering prize seemed almost in reach. Then came heart-breaking disappointment. The Germans clung desperately to their corner of High Wood; patrols reported the Flers line in such an advanced state of defence that heavy guns would be needed to smash it. Sixt von Armin's counter-stroke came crashing on our lines. " In France, the most difficult part of an attack was not the winning of an objective but the keeping of it after it was gained. The Germans knew all about the art of war. Their counter-stroke on July 18th was admirably planned and skilfully carried out." Most of the gains made were stubbornly maintained but the enemy had won time, which was what he most urgently needed. For when our divisions, exhausted and battle weary, had been relieved by others, there faced them defences so formidably planned that to " rush " them would have been madness. The First Phase of the Battle of the Somme was over.

X

THE SOMME: LAST PHASES

" . . . the real trial of strength between the opposing armies had now come. It was therefore decided to adopt slower methods, and orders were issued that our troops should limit their efforts for the present to securing with as little delay as possible certain definite points, the possession of which would enable us at a later date to renew the attempt to break through the German lines."

Thus Haig in his Official Despatch. The description is perhaps a trifle euphemistic, for an attempt to break the enemy's lines had been definitely made and as definitely defeated. There followed a period of ding-dong fighting, local attacks with local objectives to clear up salients in our own lines and to pave the way for a new attempt in grand style.

The casualties for the first four weeks of July fighting totalled some 156,000 men, of whom about 20,000 might be written off as part of the " normal " drain of trench warfare, leaving 136,000 as the price of the Somme. The German losses in this particular period of the fighting were certainly nothing like so heavy.

But drafts from home quickly made good the gaps in shattered battalions; at the end of August, and despite all his losses, Haig's " bayonet and sabre " strength was still 650,000 out of 660,000 with which he had started, the supplies of heavy guns had increased from 730 to 950 with munitions and other weapons in proportion. Moreover, the terrific British offensives, if unsuccessful in smashing through,

THE SOMME: LAST PHASES

had been successful in relieving the pressure on Verdun, and the French Army, recovering from its exhaustion, could take an increasing part in a renewed offensive. Valuable lessons had been learnt in the matters of staff-work, the co-ordination of attacks and *liaison* between Infantry and Artillery. Thus, as the July days wore on and August suns faded, despite all the disasters of previous offensives, optimism reigned at G.H.Q. At the opening of the battle, July 1st, 6 German divisions with 62 battalions had been in line against our troops, by July 16th, 8 fresh enemy divisions had been drawn into the fighting, by the end of July there were 18, and by the end of August, 30.

In the matter of attracting and pinning down the enemy reserves, Haig's sledge-hammer had been undoubtedly successful.

Preparations for what was in reality the third Break-Through Battle began early in September. An officer from the 39th Division, newly drawn into the Somme area, writes on the 2nd September:

" The relative quiet of June was far behind us. Here were camps crowded into every bit of cover and even straying out into the open, endless horse-lines, newly made roads, and the troops of innumerable battalions we had never seen before."

From another, this time a Regular, we get a vivid picture of Bernafoy Wood as it appeared to troops newly arrived:

" On reaching the wood the peculiar pungent smell of decomposing horse-flesh would greet one's nostrils and add to the depressing, unnatural feeling which seemed part of the Somme. Bernafoy Wood was a nightmare. It was nothing but charred, shorn stumps devoid of vegetation, with fresh breaks and

THE KITCHENER ARMIES

bruises on the ghastly remnants of one-time trees showing like white streaks visible for some distance through the darkness. The effect of shrapnel on these truncated remains reminded one of a devil's tattoo. And the sound of numerous small bullets pattering off the bark and rattling to the ground brought home to us poor struggling humans that we were always under fire. . . .

"The instructions to the Battalion contained an injunction that ' it was to evade the enemy's barrage as much as possible,' a thoughtful piece of advice to a battalion that had been out since 1914 and might be expected to splash about gleefully in torrents of projectiles."

There is an equally vivid description of the attack on Guillemont which was one of the preliminary phases to the planned renewed great offensive:

"No one who was present on that wonderful September 3rd will ever forget the picture at the moment of attack. Just west of Guillemont ran a small valley or depression. At 11.50 a.m. it appeared just a mournful, battered strip of France, bare and absolutely devoid of life. In a flash the whole scene had changed. At 12 noon to the crash of a bombardment, the place swarmed with living beings, soldiers of the 18th Royal Irish, Connaught Rangers and Munster Fusiliers, line after line moving eastwards as though on parade and gradually disappearing into the smoke and dust which enshrouded what had once been Guillemont."

This battalion was reduced to 15 officers and 289 men, but Guillemont was taken.

In the Battle of September 15th, 1916, the fighting on the Somme reached its highest tide. The account given by the authors of *Sir Douglas Haig's Command*

THE SOMME: LAST PHASES

illuminates the high hopes with which it was planned. They claim for the Allies a four to one superiority in Infantry, superior Artillery and the supremacy of the air; they assert that the enemy was showing signs of demoralisation, that there was little depth or strength in the defences behind him, that his reserves were weak and completed by units which had already suffered. Once more the Cavalry were warned to "stand to," once more the Commander-in-Chief went "all out" for victory. Tanks, newly devised, crude in design, were to be used for the first time in battle. But the tremendous blow, while it broke through the enemy's positions on a wide front, shared the fate of previous offensives. The enemy clung desperately to certain key-positions. Flers was taken, but the Quadrilateral, sited on the reverse slope of a false crest line, held out, "C" line was still in his hands. Then the heavens opened and down came the rain. Whether, even without this, Haig would have succeeded in his larger designs will always be a matter of conjecture. As will be seen, the account given in *Sir Douglas Haig's Command* as to the enemy's demoralisation and the weakness of his positions behind is somewhat over-coloured. The probabilities are that even had the attack been renewed, as planned, on September 21st, the system of defence by "shell-hole areas," introduced by Ludendorff, the formidable nature of which, at the time, had not been grasped by our Higher Command, would have made the German positions a very tough nut to crack. We should have taken them, but at such cost to ourselves, meaning a state of such exhaustion and confusion in our own Army that any attempt sweepingly to exploit our successes would have been unlikely to succeed. The result, most probably, would have been to make a bigger bulge in the enemy's lines. The criticisms on Haig, however,

THE KITCHENER ARMIES

for using his tanks instead of keeping them secret until 1917, and then using them in masses as an overwhelming surprise to produce a " world-shaking victory, " are very unsound. First of all Haig could not foresee in 1916 a whole lot of things destined disastrously to affect the Allied plans for the Western Front for 1917, such as the fall of Bucharest and collapse of Russia; secondly, on September 15th, 1916, he was not *tinkering* with the enemy but was putting in everything he had to win a decisive victory; every Commander-in-Chief, under such circumstances, will want to use *every* weapon; thirdly, the 1916 tank was at best a very crude affair, slow, terribly vulnerable to Artillery, and with its endurance limited to that of the track-pin—a matter in most cases of forty-eight hours at an outside limit. Finally, nothing *keeps* in war. It is very unlikely indeed that we could actually have produced masses of tanks and kept them secret for another year.

If it is doubtful whether even fine weather would actually have realised the gleaming mirage of the complete " Break-Through " which filled the hearts and minds of G.H.Q., there can be no doubt that the loss of four days and the sodden condition of the ground substantially reduced the gains in terrain and in prisoners which it is reasonable to believe might have been made. The historian of the Rifle Brigade gives a sober and balanced picture of the renewal of the offensive, September 25th:

" Cavalry was hurried forward to go through the gap. But it was not yet a gap and the conditions were none for Cavalry. On the III Corps front the line was taken forward to the neighbourhood of Le Sars, and the Reserve Army attacking from Courcelette to the Ancre, stormed Thiépval and pushed forward up the Spur above it. Still no

THE SOMME: LAST PHASES

decisive victory. Combles, now almost surrounded, was evacuated by the enemy and entered by the Allies on the 26th. Still, however, no decisive victory. Despite the British preponderance in men and material, despite the loss of large numbers of prisoners and heavy casualties, the resistance of the enemy was stubbornly maintained. . . .

" The advance was now developing rather north-east than north. The main objective of the Fourth Army was the ridge projecting north from the Morval Spur between Les Bœufs-Gueudecourt and Le Transloy-Beaulencourt. The enemy's principal defensive line was now a strongly wired trench system sited on the western slope of the high land between Bapaume and Sailly-Saillisel. This system was in the neighbourhood of two thousand yards; and the aim of the operation was to advance within striking distance, in order that a later operation might break it. The ridge that formed the British objective, though considerably lower than the main ridge for which they had battled since July 1st, was a formidable piece of ground to attack, seamed with sunken roads, torn by repeated bombardments and the operation of the weather into a wilderness of viscid mire, and intersected with trenches or fragments of trenches excellently sited for fire effect . . . the series of advances behind Artillery barrage, and the terrific Artillery preparation for the battles, in which the enemy trenches had been systematically obliterated, had proved the total inadequacy of trenches against an organised attack. But the very vigour of the bombardment had provided its own reply. The whole area was riddled with shell-holes which, with a small amount of work, gave equally effective cover as a trench whilst being undistinguishable in appearance from the surrounding country. The German reply to the British Artillery

THE KITCHENER ARMIES

was organised shell-hole defences. It took some weeks to realise what had happened, and even longer to evolve a new tactics in answer. The main defensive line continued to be made and wired in rear; but, in place of a front line, the enemy held an area of shell-hole defences, organised in depth, of which the chief defensive weapon was the machine-gun. This gave no target for the Artillery: it was difficult for the tank to detect: the very Infantry were often unaware of its existence until a tornado of machine-gun fire had broken their attack and dispersed them."

Our experiences in South Africa against Boer riflemen in rifle-pits almost on the flat, and the failure of the Artillery to deal with these, may illustrate the formidable nature of such a system of defence.

At all events the fighting when renewed was grim and desperate:

" Those who were under cover with the wounded were so harrowed by the suffering and so sickened by the smell of blood that it was a question whether the wet and cold outside were not preferable to the stench inside."

That gallant Rifleman, 2nd Lieut. Purvis of the 9th Battalion Rifle Brigade, deserves mention here. His son, Capt. J. R. Purvis, was killed September 25th, 1915. Mr Purvis, well over 60 years old, a retired naval officer and ex-planter, determined to carry on his son's work. By some miracle he " wangled " past the medical authorities, got a commission, and the September fighting actually found him commanding his son's company and doing brilliant work. He was severely wounded, and the femoral artery severed, September 15th, 1916.

And now we come to that most brilliant feat of

THE SOMME: LAST PHASES

arms, the Storming of Thiépval. Grim and lofty and on the left of the Somme fighting, the wit of man has never devised a place of arms more formidable.

" The steadily rising ground was crowned by an intricate system of trenches, redoubts and strong points, including Wonder Work and the Leipzig Redoubt, which commanded an enormous area of approach and field of fire. This fortified system contained the series of elaborately equipped dug-outs which were afterwards so well known. The Mirror dug-out alone could hold an entire company and give them beds too. They were, moreover, so deep and strongly constructed as to be invulnerable to Artillery."

Various divisions, British and French, had looked at the place for two years; it had been repeatedly and unsuccessfully attacked from the west, and the gallant men of the 36th Division had even won foothold to be bloodily hurled back. But the progress of the fighting now rendered it possible to attack Thiépval by Infantry from the south, whilst guns played upon it from the west.

General Maxse went about his task coolly and methodically:

" The secret of successful attacks in modern trench warfare," he wrote in his report, " may be summed up in two words—previous preparation. Without it the bravest troops fail and their heroism is wasted. With sufficient time to prepare an assault upon a definite and limited objective, I believe a well-trained division can capture almost any ' impregnable ' stronghold, and this doctrine has been taught to the 18th Division. Indefinite and frequently altered objectives involve wasted energies and diminish the confidence of the troops. Hurried

THE KITCHENER ARMIES

attacks launched on the spur of the moment possess certain attractions for dashing platoon commanders, but they usually fail because they necessarily lack organised cohesion."

The 18th Division benefited, of course, by the fighting of other units and experiences gained by this. The attack was to form part of a combined operation with the Canadian Corps on the right and the II Corps on the left. There was also the great advantage that the Artillery covering the assault had been long in action and were familiar with the terrain; there was thus no time lost in getting staff-work done. Nevertheless, great pains were taken in making brigade, battalion and company commanders familiar with the ground to be fought over and the approaches to this. An excellent lecture by Brig. P. Howell, G.S. at Corps Headquarters, on the local situation, helped greatly in causing brigade, battalion and company commanders to realise the importance of the mission charged to them. They felt that they were being taken into the confidence of the Corps H.Q. In the preliminary bombardment care was taken to avoid destroying certain hostile trenches which our men were determined to occupy and consolidate. Some special communication trenches in the German lines were spared for similar reasons.

The preparation of the attack needed four nights of intensive digging, in improving assembly trenches, etc., work magnificently done by two battalions of the 55th Brigade, Sussex Pioneers, and all R.E. Companies under supervision of Col. H. G. Joly de Lotbinière, D.S.O., C.R.E.

By a bold innovation Gen. Maxse fixed the hour for " zero " at 12.35 p.m., a time when the enemy would not be expecting attack. He always maintained

THE SOMME: LAST PHASES

that " zero " should be reckoned *backwards* from sunset so as to give the men time to reach their objective and then consolidate in this without the ordeal of an " observed " barrage.

The opening of the attack caught the Germans unawares. On the right the Suffolks swept forward and were met by half-dressed, unarmed Germans emerging from dug-outs. Some surrendered, others hesitated and were shot. The battalion swept forward moving, as was described by an airman, " as if glued to the barrage." Schwaben, Zollern and Bulgar trenches were seized with sharp fighting.

On the left the 54th Brigade had to storm a nest of 144 deep dug-outs covering Thiépval from the west, besides a nest of similar defences around the Château of Thiépval. By 3.35 most of these objectives had been gained with confused, tangled, desperate fighting. The Germans still held the north-west corner of Thiépval, the 11th Division had not entirely cleared the high ground to the right of the 18th. It is difficult clearly to describe what happened; the day's fighting abounded in grim incidents. When officers were shot down, the initiative of privates and N.C.O.'s again and again saved the situation. Private Edwards, dashing alone to bomb German machine-gunners, converted a doubtful episode into a success. Private Ryder did the same thing under similar conditions. Lance-Corporal Tover of the Royal Fusiliers took a machine-gun single-handed, bayoneting two men. The most desperate fighting was in Thiépval itself, and here quarter was neither asked nor given. There was a grisly episode of a large dug-out where the enemy were ensconced with two machine-guns. They refused to come out unarmed. The dug-out was set on fire. Four tanks had been detailed to take part in the attack, of which only two reached Thiépval,

THE KITCHENER ARMIES

where they stuck in the mud and were useless—although one managed to give some help to the Fusiliers by the Château before subsiding on her side. By nightfall three battalions of the 54th Brigade, all mingled together in such wise that it was impossible to sort out platoons, companies and battalions, were stretched in a line occupying Thiépval save the high ground in the north-west corner; the Essex on their right were badly used up; the Suffolk on *their* right were in touch with the 11th Division. The problem was now to consolidate the ground won, relieve tired troops by fresh ones, and arrange for an immediate attack on the remaining corner of Thiépval. Col. Maxwell, V.C., D.S.O., whom we have already met about to " instil the spirit of savagery " into his men, took command and with Major Charrington and Capt. Johnston to help him, formed the scattered men of three battalions into a double defence line around the Château which became a keep. The machine-guns from the stranded tank were taken out and it was garrisoned by twenty men. But the problem was still to relieve the tired and disorganised troops. The 146th Brigade of the 49th Division had been put at Gen. Maxse's disposal; the Bedfordshire, the reserve battalion of the 54th Brigade, had been in dug-outs in Thiépval Wood; they were now to be replaced by the 7th Royal West Kent. There then occurred what Maxse in his report described as " the finest example of efficiency and battle-discipline which has been seen in the 18th Division during the course of the Somme and Ancre fighting in the last five months."

It was necessary to extract three tired battalions from their battle position and put one battalion in their place. This had to be done in pitch blackness by troops who had never seen the locality, but had to get to it through a hostile barrage. Lieut.-Col.

THE SOMME: LAST PHASES

Price, commanding the Bedfords, and Col. Maxwell made such excellent arrangements, and these arrangements were so well carried out by company officers, that before day fresh Bedfords instead of three spent battalions were confronting the enemy.

" The Bedfords got their orders about midnight and in the profound darkness, lighted only by the bursting of shells, with no guides to meet them, following a line that had been run across to the château in dayling by the signallers, they went up in ' sneak formation ' and arrived 3.30 a.m."

Col. Maxwell, in a letter to his wife, wrote:

" I cannot but wonder at the behaviour of the battalion. If there were ever an occasion when things might have gone wrong, and the attack died or fizzled out, that one occurred on the 26th. The ground was made for skulking, and every yard of it afforded opportunity for men to drop down unseen and stay there without being seen. If I saw evil and wicked sights in Trônes, I saw more and varied ones at Thiépval."

Meantime, the plan of attack had been made; two companies of the Bedfords were to rush the Germans with the bayonet.

" What had to be done on September 27th had to be done quickly and before daylight. ' C ' and ' D ' Companies of the Bedfords went forward under Capt. L. H. Keep and, thanks to Capt. Johnston and Lieut. Sulman, both of the Fusiliers, who knew the ground and gave invaluable assistance, both companies were got into position by 5.45 a.m.

" There was no chance of any help from Artillery. The business was one for the plain fighting man on his own. From the very start a most determined resistance was encountered, and although the left company managed to make steady progress the right

THE KITCHENER ARMIES

ran up against a machine-gun, snipers and standing patrols established in shell-holes, all of which they dealt with.

"A little later, about 7 o'clock, the right-hand platoon of the right-hand company was held up by heavy rifle and machine-gun fire from several strong points. The moment was a very critical one, and 2nd Lieut. Tom Edwin Adlam, who commanded the platoon, seeing that time was the most important element in the success of the attack, dashed out across the open under all the fire that had checked his platoon, and gathered up his men from the shell-holes for a combined rush. He could throw a cricket ball about a hundred yards. So he got together as many German bombs as possible and started a whirlwind attack upon the enemy with these. Thanks to his powers, he could fling a stick-bomb farther than an ordinary Mills, and he pulled off all his equipment to throw the better, and bombarded the Germans furiously. Wounded in the leg, like Widdrington, he kneeled and 'fought on his stumps,' and even in that posture managed to out-throw the Germans. Finally he snatched an opportunity to lead in his platoon, killed or captured everybody who stood up to them, made his objective by 8.30, and exploiting his success went on and gained a further 300 yards. Wounded as he was, he continued at the head of his men all day and the next, when he was wounded again."

Mr Adlam at that time was twenty-two years old, and had been only two months in the trenches. Before the war he had been a schoolmaster and a sergeant in the Territorials.

By 11 a.m. on September 26th the last strip of Thiépval was in the hands of our men, and a fortress which had defied the Allies for two years had been taken. The total casualties were 1456 of all ranks,

THE SOMME: LAST PHASES

killed, wounded and missing, and it is one of the few cases in which it is possible to state quite definitely that the defence was costlier than the attack, for including 4 officers and 606 men, prisoners not far short of 3000 Germans fell or were lost to the German Army. That fine regiment, the 180th Würtembergers, well redeemed their pledge to hold Thiépval to the last, for few surrendered and most died fighting.

To the thoughtful soldier, the storming of Thiépval by Maxse's men of the 18th Division will always rank as one of the finest episodes, if not *the* finest episode of the war, for it is an operation which, achieved against an enemy brave, determined, well posted and well prepared, shows every virtue which the soldier loves: shrewd appraisement of the enemy's power, cool-headed, methodical preparation, nice adjustment of the means at hand to the end in view, mastery of *men* as well as of machines of battle. The manner in which—despite all forethought and preparation—the situation was repeatedly saved by the initiative of subordinate leaders illustrates the limitations upon the plans and foresight of the commander. For there is no man, however gifted, who, dealing with a well-matched foe, can foresee *every* element of a changing situation. The unexpected will always crop up, elements of confusion and inco-ordination will arise, and it will then depend upon the general spirit of the training and the elasticity of the system of command how far the subordinate leaders are able swiftly to decide and boldly, but not recklessly, to dare.

" Teach, drill and practise a definite form of attack so that every officer and man shall know it thoroughly. On this basis of theory and knowledge common to all, any brigade, battalion or company commander varies his attack formation to suit any condition which may be peculiar to his front and to his objective."

Here we have it, the spirit of *battle discipline* which seeks neither to reduce men to machines nor to cramp their initiative, but to co-ordinate their efforts and to introduce and to enhance the spirit of teamwork.

Hard on the storming of Thiépval comes another epic, the seizure and defence of the Schwaben Redoubt, a tale to which no pen can do justice, and neither painting nor playwright can reveal in all its mingling of the horrible and the sublime: the brilliant work of daring patrols,[1] the taping out of assault lines in darkness under fire, the fierce deadly rush of bayonet-man and bomber, covered by the smashing, creeping barrage.

" The men fought with a deadly purposefulness which was irresistible. And they kept their heads. Sergeant C. Palmer, who brought up a Lewis gun, fired his first shots from it with the muzzle close up against the breast of a German and he mowed down others at close range. ' I was so close,' he said afterwards with an explanatory gesture, ' that I could see their tunics shaking like *that* as the bullets went through them.' " Then comes the holding of the captured redoubt against the desperate, determined foe.

" Men are to be informed by their immediate superiors," ran a captured German order, " that this attack is not merely a matter of retaking a trench because it was formerly in German possession, but that the recapture of an extremely important point is involved. If the enemy remains on the ridge he can blow our Artillery in the Ancre valley to pieces and the protection of the Infantry will be destroyed."

---

[1] Particularly one by Capt. H. J. Impson.

THE SOMME: LAST PHASES

Between September 30th and October 5th, ten times the enemy came surging on:

"The trenches, knee-deep in slimy mud, were thick with British and German dead; the ground was so torn and shattered that every landmark almost had disappeared and it was practically impossible to derive assistance from maps. Tremendous shelling went on day and night, and there was persistent rain. Schwaben Redoubt may have had dry days, but the 18th Division saw it only in the autumn and the winter. It took ten hours to get the rations up from 3000 yards away. Many of the severely wounded Boche as well as British, lay in the deep dug-outs: the shelling was so heavy and the going so muddy and treacherous it was impossible to shift them. As the fighting went on and our casualties increased, there were even cases where, in order to make room for our own wounded, dying Germans had to be lifted out of dug-outs and laid in the open while German shells were falling all round. The Berkshires had one wounded Boche who became a sort of mascot, being handed over to each relieving platoon, until eventually he was got away by the stretcher-bearers."

In the capture of the Schwaben Redoubt 1990 British and some 2500 Germans fell.

An officer from the Division who took over from Maxse's men describes Thiépval at this time:

"It was an Abomination of Desolation. There was not a blade of grass, not a bush, not a trace of the original landscape, and two demolished tanks half-overturned formed the only substantial objects in this terrible landscape, while the shell-pocked ground was covered with every conceivable form of war material—rifles, equipment, tattered uniforms,

THE KITCHENER ARMIES

battered helmets, ammunition, bombs, boots and machine-guns, all mixed up with the *débris* of what had been probably the finest system of trenches ever made . . . we were caked with mud, crawling with lice, had not shaved, washed or removed our boots for ten days, had had no sleep for two nights and little the night before."

Haig, constant in purpose, inflexible in resolve, continued his efforts to break the enemy's line. A renewed attack by the Fourth Army took Le Sars, October 7th, and made a shallow bulge, but wet weather and the system of organised shell-hole areas had enabled the defence to gain on the attack. The terrific bombardments had upset the drainage system of the country, the heavy traffic had worn the bottoms out of the roads. The attacks of October 12th, 18th, 23rd and November 3rd were made under conditions which beggar description.

" During the remainder of October it may almost be said to have rained without intermission, but the struggle was grimly maintained. To some extent the blows that followed in quick succession on the 12th, 18th, and 23rd must be regarded much as the struggles of a man who, having waded into a bog, is plunging and floundering to clamber out on firm ground beyond. The French had a definite tactical objective in the high ground of Sailly-Saillisel which enfiladed the British line, but when that had been gained the Allies can hardly have expected to progress much farther. The tanks were already useless on the treacherous ground. The men employed in the assault stumbled exhausted into their assembly positions, and at zero slithered and slipped, staggering under the weight of their equipment, through sludge and water in their effort to keep up with the barrage. The dash of the battles of September was irrevocably

THE SOMME: LAST PHASES

gone. But the winter was approaching fast; and it seemed to be worth almost any sacrifice to get out of that awful mud before it came. Let but the Fourth Army come to within striking distance of the Le Transloy line (as it came to be known) and they would break through once again on a wide front and find themselves in open country. What perhaps was insufficiently appreciated was that, in the existing conditions of warfare, the open country was a mirage, that with each successive advance must inevitably recede farther and farther away. By virtue of the contending artilleries they took their mud with them. Unless there could be a break-through of such breadth as to penetrate beyond the shelled area, there could be no escape from it. And unless the enemy could be kept on the run there was equally no escape; for directly the line halted the mutual bombardment would be resumed and the mud would reappear.

"Why, it may be asked, advert to this aspect of the Somme battle? In justice to the troops, the 4th and 8th Divisions contained some of the Regular battalions of many of the finest regiments of the British Army. Both of these Divisions had been shattered in the Battle of July 1st. Both, however, retained a leavening of officers and N.C.O.'s schooled in the 4th Division at Le Cateau and the Marne and the two Battles of Ypres, and in the 8th Division at Neuve Chapelle and Fromelles and Le Bridoux. They were reinforced by picked men from the Reserve battalions. The units were commanded by the cream of the Regular Army. In the light of all the experience gained in the great offensive they were intensively trained to resume it. And they returned after the triumphs of the Service Divisions to failure once again. In the tasks that they were asked to perform no human beings could have succeeded."

THE KITCHENER ARMIES

On October 21st, a fine day, the Fifth Army snatched an advance, but the results of the battle of October 23rd were " meagre," and that of November 5th was a repulse. The 9th Division attacking the Butte de Warlencourt, October 18th, found that " all firmness had been soaked out of the ground, which became a sea of pewter-grey ooze, and even the lightly equipped runners sank with each step beyond the knees in mud and took fully four hours to struggle over 1000 yards . . . the long muddy slope up to the Butte was thickly strewn with British and German dead and in the more forward trenches corpses of all units lay sprawling, wedged in by the slime that coated them. In the open near the Snag, a long line of men of the London Division, each on his face, was grim evidence of a gallant charge and the accuracy of the enemy's machine-gun fire. . . . The air was rank with the odour of death. To the eye, ear and nose the whole place was repellent and it required extraordinary strength of mind even to appear cheerful amid such ghastly surroundings."

Men, guns and horses wallowed in a sea of mud, and whilst wallowing to attack, the enemy's fire scourged them pitilessly. One gets a grim picture of Hébuterne—Suicide Corner—where the same traffic-control policeman was never seen twice.

" At 4 p.m. daily an unending procession of Infantrymen would be seen tramping through the gloom of a drenching November afternoon along the Sailly-Hébuterne road, for all roads lead to Rome—Suicide Corner; mixed with these would splash along ammunition columns for the guns, pontoon wagons carrying elephant shelters or rails, G.S. wagons with wire and timber, limbers with rations, pack-animals with anything, and probably some lorries with gas-cylinders, gas-shells or gas-bombs, of which one or more might be leaking slightly. The

THE SOMME: LAST PHASES

mud can now be passed over only in silence. The whole column moves on slowly with frequent checks, as double banking is not only forbidden, but is impossible owing to the returning stream of men and transport. The majority of us will probably admit that we only had two wishes: first, that the 18- and 60-pounders firing across the road would have sufficient elevation to clear our heads; second, that there would not be a check at Hébuterne Corner. By about 6 p.m. there would be, in addition to the garrison and front-line troops in Hébuterne, well over 2000 men, all moving forward towards the line on their thousand and one duties, and at the same hour 'Gasper,' the code word for 'wind favourable for the discharge of gas,' would be received at the various Orderly Rooms of the unit from which those parties had been found. At once mounted orderlies and cyclists would hurry at full speed into Hébuterne to warn and bring back their respective parties. Wagons, vehicles of all sorts, animals and men had then to turn round in the narrow *débris*-strewn, shell-pitted village streets and get clear of Hébuterne, parties would be broken or cut in two by converging transport, and could only be got together again by the exertions of the officers, non-commissioned officers and the men themselves. And this did not happen one night, or two nights, but night after night; yet it was entirely unavoidable, the working parties must carry on, and the gas must be discharged when possible; and the fact that night after night parties returned to their units without a straggler speaks much for the self-discipline of the British soldier and the resourcefulness and powers of control possessed by the British officer and non-commissioned officer. . . . When the rain streamed down and the clouds hung low the deeds done were marvellous. In No Man's Land the shell-holes were filled with water, the mud stretch hid the empty tins, the old sand-bags, the strands of barbed wire that tripped the infantryman, and the mud itself clogged their steps so that thay walked slowly and painfully, dragging their feet like old men. In the trenches—wet ditches that could not be properly drained—men crouched down in the rain among boxes of bombs and ammunition. They whispered or ate or fell into uneasy doze, waking suddenly with startled expression—waiting for the time they would be relieved.

" Along the roads the great weapons of war passed each other in the streaming nights, the flare from a match lit up the sweating horses and wet-faced men, and was reflected dully by the grey guns. In one place a huge tractor had slipped off the side of the *pavé* into the mass of mud and the traffic was blocked for a mile each way. One by one lorries crawled round it, while men tried to heave the great engine on to the road again, finally pushing it down altogether into the mud, where it wallowed without delay to the current of traffic.

" There were times at Hébuterne when men fell into sumps and were almost drowned. They had to be rescued by ropes slung under the arms. . . . Regularly men had to pull their legs along with the aid of their hands, and left boots and gum-boots in the mire and clay."

A sober regimental historian tells us:

" The back of the front behind the Somme during the winter of 1916–17 is not likely to be forgotten by those who went through it, for sheer undiluted misery and discomfort it was impossible to beat. We none of us were well and we were seldom warm. One lived and slept and moved in mud. Everything that one touched was muddy, and after a time one's mind got into very much the same state.

THE SOMME: LAST PHASES

"In these uncomfortable and depressing surroundings the men who formed the New Armies, from whom Regular and Service battalions were now alike recruited, displayed a height of spirit worthy of the men who saw through the winters of 1914 and 1915. Whatever the weather, whatever the state of the road, it was rarely that a battalion marched at ease (whether from or to the trenches) without a catch of song. Sullen looks were rare and even the mildest insubordination rarer."

In the 11th Battalion, "One man died from exhaustion in the dug-out of the support company commander, and Capt. Hollond, the commander of 'A' (right front line), stayed throughout the whole night of the relief endeavouring to extricate one of his men who had stuck in the mud of a front-line trench."

With these pictures of suffering, death, misery, mud and of the spirit which rose superior to them all, the Battle of the Somme draws to its close. There was fighting on the Ancre in November, but the attempt to Break-Through had been abandoned ere then and these operations served but a local purpose, brilliant though they were. In a period slightly exceeding four months of terrific fighting ninety-seven German divisions had been in action against our troops, of which thirty-eight were put in twice and four for a third time.

The cost to our own Army had been severe. The official figures run:

Fourth Army . . .	277,134
Fifth Army . . .	57,681
Third Army (July 1st-2nd) .	7,847
	342,662

THE KITCHENER ARMIES

In the period from June 24th to November 22nd the 18th Division lost, in its 13 Infantry battalions, 414 officers and 11,219 men, *i.e.* every battalion had to be " remade." The 7th Royal West Kent lost 32 officers and 1055 men, the 7th Queen's lost 47 officers and 1626 men. The 12th Division, from July 1st to October 20th, lost, all told, 11,124 officers and men killed, wounded and missing. The 15th Division, not so heavily engaged, lost 6828 men in its Infantry battalions alone from July 1st to November 1st. The 9th Division lost 314 officers and 7203 men, July 1st to July 20th, 1916, and 118 officers and 3137 men from October 12th to 24th, a total of 10,872 officers and men in the Somme fighting. This meant that every battalion had to be filled with recruits anew. For the whole period of the war the losses in these Divisions were:

18th—550 officers and 13,000 N.C.O.'s and men killed or died of wounds. (No figures for wounded or missing.)

12th—2105 officers; 46,038 other ranks, killed, wounded or missing.

15th—1525 officers; 33,767 other ranks, killed, wounded or missing.

9th—2493 officers killed, wounded or missing; 52,122 other ranks.

The losses sustained by the German Army in the prolonged agony of the Somme are difficult to surmise. The official figure of 180,000 is undoubtedly an under-estimate, as it does not include " lightly " wounded who figure in our own returns. Professor Oman, in a lucidly written and powerfully reasoned study, reaches the conclusion that the German losses were slightly heavier than our own.[1] This may,

[1] *The World Crisis*, by Winston Churchill. A Criticism. The German Losses on the Somme.

THE SOMME: LAST PHASES

perhaps, be too favourably estimated from our own standpoint, but although at the outset our tactics were faulty and our losses unduly high, the progress of the battle marked a steady improvement in the means, methods and co-ordination of attacks, whilst the Germans were forced continuously to expend themselves in costly counter-attacks. In what may be called the middle phase of the Somme, the enemy undoubtedly had even heavier losses than were sustained by our troops, although with the improvement of his defensive system and the handicap of weather conditions the concluding phases of the fighting were again costly to our own side.

The subsequent decision of the enemy to retreat is, however, incontrovertible evidence that he dreaded a renewal of the onset.

The historian of the 9th Division writes temperately but with force:

"As the war recedes into the past and as the emotions roused by it subside, the tendency is to linger on the splendid and spectacular advances of the latter part of 1918 . . . after August 1918 the Germans were men without hope, and to deduce our lessons of the war from the last four months of fighting would be the height of folly. . . . The wearing-out battles, when the foe was encountered at the zenith of his strength, with all their disappointments and mistakes alone made possible the gigantic advances at the end."

Ours was an amateur Army led by amateurs; the mistakes made were largely unavoidable; the courage shown was great.

XI

THE PASSING OF THE KITCHENER ARMIES

OUR story is ended. As the battle thunder of the Somme died down into the daily rumbling of the Western Front there remained of the men who had joined Kitchener's Armies but enough to leaven with their own brave spirit the levies who came to fill their shattered battalions. The Volunteer Armies had played their part, and it was a part glorious and mighty. They had stepped into the breach and held the foe in play; had met him breast to breast in the full swing of his victorious onset; in the full pride of his power. An irregular scrap of earth, twelve miles wide by seven deep, each step paid for in blood and won in face of the flower of the German Army, rested in their hands. This strip had held the strongest fortifications ever conceived, manned by a foe well-led, well-trained, well-equipped, fierce and determined. The fortifications had been stormed, the enemy hurled back, his fighting spirit subdued. And as day by day, week by week and month by month the khaki lines shot-torn, scourged by weather as by man, came ever anew to the attack, a consternation seized upon the hearts of the German leaders, for these were troops of a type they had never met before. The genius of Ludendorff, the prestige of Hindenburg might snatch a temporary respite, but these leaders themselves felt their country's cause to be in desperate danger. They dreaded a renewal of the onset, and chose rather to withdraw their lines and play the gambler's hazard of the unrestricted U-boat war.

PASSING OF THE KITCHENER ARMIES

There are those who can see in the Battle of the Somme but an orgy of useless butchery, lice, animalism and mud; but there are others, viewing things perhaps in truer perspective, who can see in this long-drawn-out grim and pounding struggle the most wonderful battle epic known to mankind, a story of which the background changes from July suns and autumn tints to a sea of pewter-grey mud, but emblazoned upon which at all times stand out a series of flaming pictures dazzling and bewildering in their glory of achievement. Napier, in one of his most thrilling passages, writes of the Fusiliers at Albuera:

" Then was seen with what a strength and majesty the British soldier fights. In vain did Soult with voice and gesture animate his Frenchmen; in vain did the hardiest veterans break from the crowded columns and sacrifice their lives to gain time for the mass to open out on such a fair field; in vain did the mass itself bear up and, fiercely striving, fire indiscriminatingly upon friends and foes . . . nothing could stop that astonishing Infantry. No sudden burst of undisciplined valour, no nervous enthusiasm, weakened the stability of their order; their flashing eyes were bent on the dark columns in their front, their measured tread shook the earth, their dreadful volleys swept away the head of every formation, their deafening shouts overpowered the dissonant cries that broke from all parts of the tumultuous crowd . . . the mighty mass, breaking off like a loosened cliff, went headlong down the steep; the rain flowed after in streams discoloured with blood; and 1800 unwounded men, the remnant of 6000 unconquerable British soldiers, stood triumphant on that fatal hill."

These, and the Charge of the Light Brigade at Balaclava, in which the losses were about the same,

THE KITCHENER ARMIES

were the heaviest losses known in previous wars to our Old Army. There was scarcely a battalion of the New Armies on the Somme which did not sustain heavier losses—and continue to go on fighting.

To take a few instances at random: the 8th Norfolk, going into battle in the opening phase of the Somme, with 34 officers and 890 men, lost 23 officers and 638 of other ranks; the 8th East Surrey, from 29 officers and 883 men, lost 14 officers and 769 men; the 6th Royal Berkshire, from 22 officers and 754 men, lost 18 officers and 575 men; the 7th Queen's, from 31 officers and 951 men, lost 27 officers and 741 men. These were not extreme cases. In many instances battalions lost *every* officer and were reduced to 80 men or so, and this handful went on fighting. The " life " of a subaltern on the Somme was estimated at three weeks. Companies were led by sergeants; private soldiers and lance-corporals in many cases took the lead and saved a doubtful situation by daring initiative; men who had been schoolmasters, clerks, haberdashers, navvies, showed all the qualities of the born fighting man. In those days when the movements of the barrack-square were a real preparation for battle, our Fusiliers at Albuera were the best trained and most highly disciplined troops in Europe: our New Armies on the Somme were citizen-soldiers to whom drill was something alien, the military career but a temporary and, as they hoped, fleeting episode. The hoofs of the Light Brigade re-echo in immortal verse, but theirs was a swift ordeal and one which came to men specially trained to meet it. Our New Armies on the Somme had to face an ordeal not of minutes as with the Light Brigade, nor of hours as with the Fusiliers, but of days and nights of battle, stretching in some cases almost to a week. Incidents which in other days roused a whole Empire to enthusiasm,

PASSING OF THE KITCHENER ARMIES

such as the Defence of Rorke's Drift, the Blowing-up of the Kashmir Gate, the Storming of Delhi, were to the New Armies a mere matter of course. They happened so often that a couple of lines in an official report was all that was ever heard. For every man who won the V.C., a hundred others earned it, and most of these others fell.

Let those who will tell of the heroism of the knights of old or sing the praises of the professional soldier. The New Armies can tell a tale which will out-glamour all their glories and which will pass to the chronicle of the world's most heart-stirring themes. Is it a matter of " two o'clock in the morning courage "? Think of that night relief by the Bedfords in pitch blackness and on strange soil. Think of the battle discipline it meant; the sheer quality of *guts* those men had; think of the fierce bayonet charge at dawn which put the last corner of Thiépval in our hands. Is it a matter of cool disciplined valour? Methodical preparation for attack? What can rival the taping-out of assault lines in darkness and under fire; the massing of whole divisions for attack where a single error could spell annihilation? Yes. That splendid little band of Regular officers who taught the New Army men their trade, the New Armies who were such apt pupils, such fine raw material, can stand together and challenge comparison with any feat of arms known to history—and find none to rival their own deeds.

The tremendous struggle of 1914–18 was the first great trial of the British democracy in war, and it can be said that democracy emerged well from this ordeal. A system of government which counts the grocer, the butcher, the tailor, the clerk, the university professor, all as equal citizens, is limited to the general fund of common sense which is to be found in the community. It cannot be expected to rise much

THE KITCHENER ARMIES

above the average in the matter of foresight and preparation, but it has the great advantage that it cannot fall much below this level. In those matters the importance and necessity of which was clear to the average man or woman, such as the Navy, there was no lack of preparation. And if there was lack of preparation with the Army—and there *was* lack of preparation—it must never be forgotten that the general mass of soldiers were themselves at fault in their estimate of the magnitude of the problem we should have to solve and the conditions under which we should be called upon to solve it. Even Lord Roberts based his plea for compulsory service upon the danger of invasion—and the country had been taught to regard defence against invasion as, primarily, the business of the Fleet. There is not a line extant to show that any member of the Imperial General Staff—who were the professional military advisers to the Crown—had expressed dissatisfaction with our actual scale of military preparation, or had impressed upon Government as a matter of urgent, vital need, that greater preparations should be made.

But when the voice of the guns made danger manifest, when in Kitchener democracy had found a leader in whom it could trust and who was worthy of its trust, there was no backwardness in answering the call. On the contrary, the underlying strength and elasticity of our system of government revealed itself, for the whole nation worked together and we had in the New Armies what was in reality a national surging to arms which focussed itself around the personality of a great leader.

If we take the simple standpoint that however wise a man may be he cannot be wiser in *all* than the whole body of his fellow-citizens, it follows that an excess of knowledge in any one subject is likely to be paid for by a *deficiency* of knowledge in others: the

PASSING OF THE KITCHENER ARMIES

specialist, whether soldier, sailor, lawyer or doctor, is a specialist only in these particular subjects; take him out of these, and he ceases to be a specialist and is then only a layman. Thus a system of Government, such as democracy, which gives to all free opportunity to state their various standpoints, and proceeds to reduce these to the common denominator represented by the general fund of common sense of the community, has the advantage of *elasticity*. Errors cannot be avoided, but their worst consequences can be redressed. Seen in its true perspective, the whole story of the New Armies represents the effort by a democratic people to redress an original error: lack of peace-time military preparation, and in this effort the democracy was successful. On the other hand, when we contemplate that huge and mighty German military machine we see errors made by the German leaders no less serious than those made by our own, but we do *not* see the same elasticity, the same great *reserves* of strength and energy, which, in our own country, went to produce the New Armies.

A process of military improvisation can never be anything else but wasteful and costly. Not even Kitchener with all his vast genius, and with the vast resources of the British Empire at his back, could crowd into two years the work which should have been spread over twenty: the New Armies were costly, not alone in money, but in life. But it was a matter of making the best of a bad job. The choice was not between well-trained armies and hastily trained armies, but between hastily trained armies and no armies at all. And no armies at all would have meant a defeat, the full consequences of which, to the world and to ourselves, have scarcely yet been realised. Of the officers and men of the New Armies who went through that grim and awful

THE KITCHENER ARMIES

ordeal on the Somme, it is safe to say that few have today feelings of hatred for our vanquished foes. No men have ever fought better—or for a worse cause. A triumphant Germany would have been an outrage and an oppression upon the free spirit of mankind. In Germany herself, social life would have crystallised into the adoration of the military caste. To the vanquished it would have meant enormous war indemnities, economic treaties enforced at the sword's point, strangling the free economic development of our people, the perpetual menace of renewed attack crystallising the social life of our own people into a counter-militarism.

From all these things the New Armies saved us. The learned doctors of war damned them solemnly by bell, book and candle—which worried them about as much as the Pope's Bull against the Comet. They trusted to Kitchener as he trusted to them, and between them they won the war—and salvation for mankind.

This liberty which is our boast and pride is, after all, something more than an empty phrase. It is a living force, a spiritual flame, a rare and precious heritage. It means the free intercourse of man with man, the right of the humblest to work his way up to the highest dignities our Empire affords on the score of his own unaided merit, the free play of the social conscience to redress social wrong. Those who see in that terrible Battle of the Somme nothing but an orgy of blood and death, mud and killing, have failed to realise the true spirit of our men, that which nerved them to dare and to endure more than men had dared or endured till then. For there fired them that flame of righteousness which kindles every virile man against something which is foul and threatening, which has again and again nerved men to suffer and to die, and which, when it has passed away, will leave of life itself but the dregs—flat and tasteless.

God grant that no such a danger may menace the world again! And may He send also that should the emergency arise, there will still be found men of our race to strike a blow for freedom—and women to cheer them on.

On that grim battlefield the crosses lie strewn thickly, the graves of Kitchener's men. Their memory lives in empty chairs and fumbled tear-stained letters. But theirs is a story sorrow can but sanctify, nor will Time obliterate it, nor will its gorgeous colours fade. Chivalry will take it to her bosom, Romance will lend to it her soft engoldenment, History will enmesh it with her fairy-like enchantment. No poet need sing this story, no playwright to declaim. It lives on in terms of human agony and bursting, broken hearts. Yet those who have stood beside the body of some dearly loved friend or comrade may feel that Death may sometimes come pityingly as a refuge from greater ill: surely if aught can engentle his touch or soften his visage, it is to die with work accomplished and to know the work well done. Worthily to cross the threshold and for a worthy cause is not the hardest fate which can befall a man. In no better way can his soul win Redemption. And if to die for others is to find Grace with God, then may we hope that He will have Mercy upon those who fell in Battle, and pardon their trespasses and the trespasses of those left behind, and Grant unto the Dead who Sleep, and the Living who Mourn, a common Resurrection.

FINIS

APPENDIX

THE BRITISH EMPIRE IN THE WAR

It was intended originally to include in the present work some account of the evolution of the Dominion Troops. Considerations of space, however, have rendered it impossible to deal with these Forces in a fashion truly worthy of their great feats of arms, which can be better dealt with by their own historians. The following brief notes are intended merely to convey to the general public some idea as to the pre-war organisation of the Dominion Armies and their vast expansion during the war.

Canada, with a population, according to the 1911 census, of 7,206,643, maintained a very considerable force of Militia, consisting of " Permanent " and " non-Permanent." The " Permanent " Militia were virtually Regulars and, comprising units of Infantry, Artillery, Cavalry, Engineers, etc., provided schools for the training of officers and N.C.O.'s for the " non-Permanent " Militia.

The " non-Permanent " Militia comprised:

    27 regiments of Cavalry.

    26 field batteries.

    6 regiments of Garrison Artillery (including 13 heavy batteries).

    5 companies of Engineers.

    106 battalions of Infantry.

The peace strength of the " Permanent " Militia was 3000 of all ranks: the non-Permanent mustered 60,000. During the war there was enlisted a grand

APPENDIX

total of 628,964 men, of whom 399,807 were sent to France. Apart from Cavalry and other units the Canadian Corps had four divisions; the 5th Division was a draft-producing organisation.

Australia, with a population in 1911 of 4,478,068, had in that year and on Kitchener's recommendation, introduced a Defence Scheme based upon Compulsory Service, which, however, applied mainly to the training of cadets. There were in 1914, 2669 men " Permanent Force," and 31,282 " non-Permanent," besides 49,564 members of rifle clubs and 88,708 senior cadets undergoing training under the Defence Act.

During the war Australia raised 412,953 men, of whom 331,781 served in France and other theatres of the war.

New Zealand had a population in 1911 of 1,008,468, and had at the same time introduced a Defence Scheme similar to that of Australia. Her peace establishments provided for a force of 30,000 partially trained troops. During the war she raised 128,505 men, of whom 117,175 served in the New Zealand Expeditionary Force.

The Union of South Africa, with a white population of 1,276,242, raised 136,070 men, who served mostly against German colonies.

Other colonies raised 134,837 officers and men.

Canada, Australia and New Zealand, with a population, all told, of 12,693,179, raised between them 1,170,442 men.

Australia and New Zealand, with a joint population of 5,476,536, raised 541,458 and were successful in keeping as many units afoot as the Dominion of Canada, which had a population of 7,206,643. Canada, however, played a greater economic part in the war; men being needed for munitions factories.

British India, with a population of 243,933,178,

APPENDIX

maintained in peace, apart from British troops, a native army with:

> 40 regiments of Cavalry.
> 12 mountain batteries.
> 19 companies of Sappers and Miners.
> 140 battalions of Infantry.

The establishment was 2751 officers and 161,085 of other ranks, with 35,700 Reservists.

There was a Volunteer Force made up of Europeans and Eurasians, with an establishment of 1524 officers and 37,382 of other ranks and 3093 Reservists. These, organised into units of Cavalry, Artillery, Engineers and Artillery, besides Infantry, provided during the war a valuable reservoir for officers and drafts for newly raised formations.

There were also the Imperial Service troops, 20,000 strong, raised and maintained by native princes under supervision of British officers. These did admirable work during the war. All told, India raised 1,440,437 men.

In the United Kingdom herself, from a population of 39,000,000, 2,257,521 joined up in the fourteen months from August 1914 to September 1915; 2,632,682 were enlisted prior to the Conscription Acts, and 2,338,360 subsequent to these, a total of 4,971,042 men. The total for the Empire was 7,130,280 white troops; plus native, 8,654,467.

The figures quoted, amazing though they be, illuminate the difficulties of an Imperial concentration. The outbreak of the war found us with half our Regular Army, and this, the *best* half, scattered abroad in India or in overseas garrisons. Time was needed to bring them home and replace them by second-line troops, and when by a miracle of improvisation five new Regular divisions had been

APPENDIX

formed, the failure to provide mobilisation stores on an adequate scale in peace, led to precious months being wasted. It was never possible for the British Empire to collect even one-half of the magnificent Canadian and Australasian troops together for a decisive stroke at the decisive moment in the decisive theatre of the war. The contingents came dribbling in, full of patriotism and full of fight, the flower of a magnificent manhood, but lacking in training for a European war.

Thanks to the efforts of the Committee of Imperial Defence, a certain general approximation in organisation and equipment had been achieved all over the Empire. Canadian, Australian and New Zealand battalions, brigades and divisions accepted the British establishments. Moreover, the Dominion Forces had been trained under the auspices of Regular staff-officers, carefully chosen not alone for professional attainments, but for personal qualities. These men had done wonderful work. But the Dominion Forces were only sketchily trained in time of peace; their Governments were no more inclined to "militarism" than the Government at home; and if it was in Australia and New Zealand that the warnings of military professional advisers were more readily heeded than elsewhere, this must be attributed to the Eastern Peril at the very doors of the Commonwealth and Dominion.

Generally speaking, the young democratic Governments shared in the popular view of a war which would be quickly over, and it was the prestige and counsels of Kitchener which induced them drastically to revise their original proposals.

The Dominion Forces were thus just as much "Kitchener Armies" as the New troops raised direct in the United Kingdom—and a very fine contribution they were, too.

www.ingramcontent.com/pod-product-compliance
Lightning Source LLC
Chambersburg PA
CBHW032124160426
43197CB00008B/510